THREE LOST WORLDS

"In 1967, I left the Wichita, Kansas, of my youth, and a series of long, glacially slow swerves carried me into places that don't exist anymore," writes Jim Gilkeson. Inhabitants of these places are spiritual seekers, energy healers, and gifted artists. His fascinating journey takes him to San Francisco, Germany, The Netherlands, Scotland, Denmark, and Harbin Hot Springs in Northern California. Gilkeson tells his story with humor as he suggests ways people are attracted to groups, what these hidden worlds are like, and what limits their sustainability. He documents these "lost worlds" and retrieves much wisdom for us, his readers, to savor."

~Denise Low,
author of *The Turtle's Beating Heart:
One Family's Story of Lenape Survival*

"*Three Lost Worlds* surprised me! I really couldn't put it down. A delightful read, both humorous and serious, Jim's intriguing life journey and his struggles with identity and purpose make *Three Lost Worlds* intimate as well as universally recognizable. At times, it brought a tear to my eyes. I loved it and highly recommend it!"

~Mary Kamiński,The Netherlands

"I really think this book should be a best seller. It's not just a biography, but a lived-in perspective on the creative, cultural ferment of the 70s. *Three Lost Worlds* is like visiting an amusement park of the mind, filled with vignettes of a time both poignantly familiar and deliciously different."

~Diana Lonsdale Haynes,
former director of the Auburn School of Health & Wellness

"*Three Lost Worlds* is a story that no one would believe except for those of us who were there. Evocative and compelling, Jim invites the reader into a virtual reality of his life that proves that "All who wander are not lost." Read this if you want to know how we can reincarnate, as many times as needed, within the life we currently hold."

~Lia Findley Jennings,
Managing Director, Harbin Hot Springs

"Thanks for this reminder about the lessons and the journeys to places we could never have known about if we had just followed what was put before us. Beautifully written!"

~Lisa Upledger, DC, CST-D, FIAMA

"My, my, the things that come to mind reading Jim Gilkeson's memoir *Three Lost Worlds*—from Herman Hesse's *Siddhartha* to Dr. Seuss's *Oh, the Places You'll Go!* A summer "walkabout" in Europe leaves him craving a life of deeper commitment, personal discipline, meditation, and spiritual enlightenment and begins a journey into the "three worlds" that make up his adult life. Gilkeson's memoir is an odyssey, entertaining and instructive, a life among mystics, healers, and life-artists, the most authentic and honest of stories, told with flair and a twinkle in the eye."

~Rick Mitchell,
former Gallery Director, Lawrence Arts Center,
former professor of Art and Journalism, Rutgers University

"Jim's airtight prose brings his experiences into razor-sharp focus, . . . tears and wry humor between the words. He finds himself in situations that are both God-smacked and completely comical at the same time. I find myself right there with him. (And thanks, Jim, for reminding me of the "Breatharians," who only eat for taste!)"

~Inika Spence-Whaley,
Aquatic Bodyworker and Instructor,
Harbin resident from 1996-2015

"Reading a great story is like getting a skilled energy healing session: you know something is changing in you, though you don't quite know what. It just feels right. *Three Lost Worlds* is one such story, an adventure cast across time, following a traveler between realms, a student of spiritual modalities, and a deep listener into the twists and turns of life. With his cinematic depictions of the many forks in the pathways of his life, we go along willingly, into the great questions of *What would I do? How would I handle myself?* And the ever important: *Where have I traveled?* A luscious read!"

~Jay Golden, storytelling coach and author of *Retellable*

THREE LOST WORLDS

A MEMOIR OF LIFE AMONG MYSTICS, HEALERS, AND LIFE-ARTISTS

THREE LOST WORLDS

A Memoir of Life Among
Mystics, Healers, and Life-Artists

Jim Gilkeson

Mammoth Publications
Healdsburg, CA

MAMMOTH
PUBLICATIONS

Published by
Mammoth Publications
610 Alta Vista Dr.
Healdsburg, California 95448

Cover design by Aimee Eldridge
Cover image by Diane Tegtmeier
Author photo by Diane Tegtmeier

ISBN: 978-1-939301-62-8

1. Autobiography. 2. Spiritual Communities. 3. Personal Growth.
4. Alternative Healing.

Manufactured in the U.S.A.

This memoir is dedicated with love to the special friends and fellow travelers in these pages and to what has moved us all from behind the scenes.

CONTENTS

Part IV: The Life-Artists

Coda: Wildfire Country

FOREWORD

"You ask: what is the meaning or purpose of life? I can only answer with another question: do you think we are wise enough to read God's mind?"

~Freeman Dyson, physicist

Somewhere, there's a literary rule that warns: if you're writing a foreword for one author's book, you shouldn't begin it by talking about another's. But bear with me. My reason for doing so will be revealed in a moment.

In her book *Maps to Ecstasy,* Gabrielle Roth offers an anecdote about the first leg of her spiritual journey. In her preteens, growing up in the city, most of her friends were boys. Being a bit of a tomboy herself, she was always trying to prove she could do anything they could do. One day they challenged her to jump from a certain rooftop. They all claimed they'd done it many times. Not to be outdone by her male counterparts, she climbed to the peak of the designated roof. And jumped! Obviously, she survived to tell the story, with no apparent damage. But that was not the point of her story. Nor was it to prove her courage. Rather, in her summing up she tells us, "In the space between the roof and the ground, I found God."

Gabrielle's story suggests something about the nature of the spiritual journey which kept popping into my mind while reading Jim's book. Often the most fruitful of these journeys are as foolhardy as jumping off a roof. And our greatest insights come in the space between the roof and the ground.

Such adventures in literature are often called the Fool's Journey. This is not because we're deficient in some way. It's more because we set off on them not knowing what we are seeking. We may find promising paths and enlightening teachers along the way. We may even experience breakthroughs that give us piercing glimpses of God and the meaning of life. But if we continue, and we arrive home again, we do so with the treasure of knowing that what we were seeking cannot be known in the usual ways of, say, learning how to operate a computer or how to drive a nail. This doesn't mean we have failed. If we live to share what we've learned, our stories will reveal what we experienced in the space between the proverbial rooftop and the ground. And those are the stories that change our lives.

There's something essentially comic about our spiritual journeys, however sincere, committed, and even profound they may be. We are entertained, and even enlightened, not so much by the conceits of our victories as by the courage to look beyond our human limitations and blunders. The philosopher Henri Bergson talks about how, by their very nature, our finite brains are not up to the job of enlightenment. We try to understand the spiritual, which is infinite, using the finite tools of our brains. When you think about it, that's a little like dissecting a corpse to find the spirit of life. The Fool's Journey is rather a mind-bender, but maybe the ultimate path to enlightenment.

Jim tells about his childhood efforts to understand his Sunday school teachings, deducing that, "God is Buffalo Bob working marionette strings." For those too young to remember, Buffalo Bob was the host of the early TV kid show, *It's Howdy Doody Time*. Howdy Doody, the star of the show, was an apple-cheeked marionette with comically big ears, huge freckles, and a squeaky voice.

Jim's childhood efforts to understand the spiritual mysteries through puppetry and the magic of TV, may have hit closer to the mark than one might think. We're constantly trying to understand what we don't know by comparing it to what we do. And in doing so, we are destined to miss the mark, never to learn anything we don't already know.

Three Lost Worlds is wonderfully entertaining, even zany, irreverent, and wise. But it's also a a profound reflection of one man's spiritual quest, which offers us a compassionate mirror to find ourselves. I loved hanging out in this world with him for the few hours it took me to read his book. As fun as it is, I also found its serious, thoughtful, and prayerful side. That's its most valuable takeaway. And you'll hardly know you are learning. Jim's book is like a spiritual GPS—or at least the beam of a flashlight—guiding our own Fool's Journey. If you decide to come along, you may very well discover your own private Buffalo Bob pulling your strings, and learn to appreciate the wisdom of the freckled, apple-cheeked puppet who stares back at you in the mirror.

Who is the Fool who sets out on such journeys? What is it that drives us? Instead of being motivated by the usual restrictions and bonds of societal expectations, the classically defined Fool characteristically seeks wisdom and transcendence beyond the safety of social norms. The treasure we bring home is wrapped in the realization that what we've been seeking can be experienced but never known. In the words of the poet William Blake, "The fool who persists in this folly will become wise."

Read this book for the fun of it. When you do, you'll maybe agree that life is, as the ancient bard once said, *a tale told by an idiot*—or in this case, a Fool—full of sound, fury, and a few chuckles, signifying something we can't quite put our finger on.

~Hal Zina Bennett,
7/13/2022

"Pay attention, that's all," Eliza said. *"Notice things. Connect what you've noticed. Connect it into a picture. Think of how the picture might be changed; and act to change it. Some of your acts may turn out to have been foolish, but others will reward you in surprising ways; and in the meantime, simply by being active instead of passive, you have a kind of immunity that's hard to explain."*

~Eliza, a character in The Confusion,
by Neal Stephenson

"Never turn down an adventure without a good reason . . ."
~Rebecca Solnit,
author of The Faraway Nearby

"People are made of stories. Our memories are not the impartial accumulation of every second we've lived; they're the narrative that we assembled out of selected moments."

~Ted Chiang,
author of Exhalation

LOST WORLDS, INVISIBLE CITIES

In 1967, I left the Wichita, Kansas, of my youth, and a series of long, glacially slow swerves carried me into places that don't exist anymore. To tell of those places is to tell of lost worlds—three in particular, not counting the lost world of childhood, all connected by the same underground root system. These worlds continue to echo in me: meeting mystics in my twenties, healers in my thirties, and artists in my sixties. In each of my lost worlds, I met, loved, and lived with a curious conglomeration of persons, some saints, some spiritual monsters, but mostly strangers in a strange land who, like me in my haphazard way, were caught up in the protracted spiritual walkabout of a generation.

This memoir is a collection of tales that involve my years under vows in a spiritual order, learning energy healing with teachers in Northern Europe, and living in a "clothing-optional" community of gifted life-artists in Northern California. I believe these hidden subcultures, and others like them, have made an unrecognized contribution to the broader story of social and spiritual exploration in this country and world. They have played an enormous role in the path I have been on in this life and the qualities that have grown within me—some by my own conscious work, some by the dark of the moon—that I now can share with the world. The person I have become could not have happened any other way.

Each of these scenes has become a place in my heart. Behind my eyes, their telling is a rediscovery of invisible cities where I have lived. When I revisit these periods of my life with special attention to what has moved me through the various stations of my life, they surprise me by turning into mystery. The strands of my life have braided themselves together into something unnamable.

Ashland, Oregon, 2022

PART I
THE WICHITA VORTEX
(1949 - 1969)

"The myth is the public domain and the dream is the private myth. If your private myth, your dream, happens to coincide with that of the society, you are in good accord with your group. If it doesn't, you've got a long adventure in the dark forest ahead of you."

~Joseph Campbell

1.

ACORNS AND CRAZY BONES

I can't help but wonder about what I brought with me into this life. Of all the theories I've run into about how a person comes to be the way he or she is, I've grown a particular fondness for James Hillman's "Acorn Theory." It says that an oak tree is an oak tree right from its acorn beginnings, and probably has intimations of being an oak tree from the get-go. Hillman's theory gets attacked right and left, of course, by those who think it sounds too deterministic, but I don't care. It's not that I knew from an early age that I would grow to be such and such, but I look back on my growing up and wonder at all the things rattling around inside me like acorns in a hollow gourd, things that were not products of my upbringing, things that didn't exist, to my knowledge, in the environment around me. *How did they get there?*

I look back at my childhood, and I may as well be a tree looking inward at its earliest rings. Everything is built around these first years, and it's all still there. I look into baby pictures and see a bumptious, bowling ball-headed baby with gleaming eyes, an imperious little power-being in diapers with fat little arms who needs to be propped up for the photo by the invisible hand of his mother. The same big head gets stuck under the backyard chainlink fence when I try to wiggle myself free on one of my early unsuccessful escape attempts. I see a child seeded with odd acorns, germs, kernels, and spores that send time-release signals out into the universe, and then wait decades for a solar flare in another galaxy to start them growing.

At some point, I start having an inner life. This comes with experiences all my own, my own private inner narratives, and consequences. I learn, to my great dismay, that I am not the only center of the universe. I throw loud, endless fits when my will is not done by those around me. When the distinction of being declared the "leader" of a firefly hunt is granted to some other child at a midsummer birthday party, I fly off the handle and make life so miserable for one and all that I have to be removed from action. At some single-digit age, I convince myself that I am strong beyond my years and attack my YMCA judo instructor out of the blue in the middle of his demonstration of *o soto gari*. I manage to get him in a headlock until he slams me to the floor. I'm not invited back. There are more pain-in-the-ass episodes until,

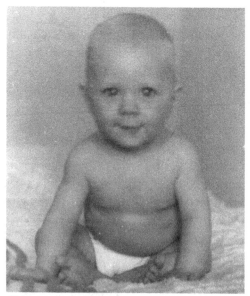

1950: Me and my big head.

somewhere in early childhood, I go from being the Child Emperor of All Creation to an introverted Charlie Brown character with a lingering sense of not fitting in.

As a child, long before reading *1984,* I pretend that I am the only free thinker in a totalitarian world, and therefore need to hide my true thoughts behind a scrim of conformity. I'm told by astrologers that my Scorpio Moon gives me a hankering for secret worlds and a certain flair for covert, subterranean activity, as well as intensity. Mix all that with other aspects in my chart that flirt with the hidden side, and this cocktail of forces amounts to an astro-psychological crazy bone—to the chagrin of those who occasionally attempt to improve me.

My Chief Enabler

My Scorpio Moon crazy bone sets me up for other tendencies, among them, pyromania. This involves elaborate late-night rituals with packs of matches from my parents' cigarette drawer. As a hormonally driven fourteen-year-old, I ritually burn my under-bed collection of skin magazines in what I call a "Grand Fire of Catharsis." *Where did that come from?* Did I, in another life, live in Renaissance Florence in the days of Savonarola's Bonfire of the Vanities, ritual burnings of objects thought to be "occasions of sin"? I also have a compulsion for spitting and a knack for staying in the blind spot of people around me. I gravitate to things about which people in my immediate environment are ignorant. My specialties are secret languages and outlandish theories of how the world is put together.

I don't lack for imagination. My chief enabler in that department, whether she knows it or not, is my mother. Since she died of cancer when I was twelve, any picture I paint of her is a partly imaginary mosaic of little boy memories and mental snapshots. As a child, I have no way of understanding that she, too, is a bundle of contradictions—par for the course when you're part Irish—part hawk, part closet bohemian, entertaining,

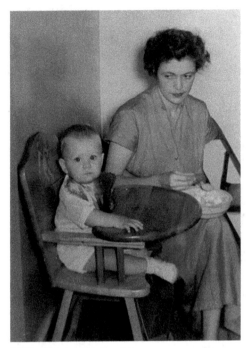

1951: With my chief enabler.

terrifying and, at moments, furiously funny.

If anyone gets me as a child, she does. She is the center of my emotional universe, and I read the world in the constant mirror of her reactions. When my mind snags on an idea, it instantly makes a beeline for the nearest available absurdity. I tell her with Burning Bush certainty that the reason veins bulge from the arms of the muscled-up boys in the neighborhood is that each person has only a limited allotment of skin, and when you get muscular, it pushes the veins out. I tell her about a kind of acid that is so strong that it eats itself, leaving nothing but air, and warn her to not get any of that on her. I tell her about two musclemen who die when they pick each other up at the same time. They rise so high in the air that the fall kills them when they stop lifting. I know I'm on the right track when she cracks up laughing.

Words are bright yellow butterflies flapping through my little wordsmith mind, and when I find a new one, I'm more than happy to make up a meaning. She notices this streak in me and calls me a "sesquipedalian"—literally, a person who speaks with sixty-foot words. The fact that she even knows that word says that she is one, too.

My mother knows things off the standard cultural radar of Wichita in the 1950s. When I find her sitting in a full lotus, she answers my curiosity by wrapping my supple six-year-old's legs around my neck. When I ask her why she is sitting that way, she tells me that this is how yogis pray.

Music is a part of my mother's private Bohemia, and it becomes part of my own secret life, too. I spend hours with my ear pressed into the speaker of our record player, listening to the jazz and Broadway musicals in her collection. The music is a wild animal, so I keep the volume low, afraid to let the sound escape into the house. I'm unsure if it's truly alright to like something so edgy. I'm scandalized by my mom's secret crush on Nat King Cole, and I wonder what my father would think if he found out. When she asks if I would like to have piano lessons from a man who she describes as a "Black, blind jazz musician" who could teach me to play by ear, I turn down the offer. It's too far outside my comfort zone. Still, when the "Winston tastes good . . . like a 'BOP!-BOP!' cigarette should!" jingle comes on TV, I am amazed at the double-time strings of sixteenth notes flying out of the trumpets. "How do they play so fast?" I ask. Without hesitation, she says, "Oh, they're all on dope."

I experiment with actions and their repercussions by registering the shades of my volatile mom's reactions. Outrage and spankings result from hitting the neighbor girl in the head with an ice ball instead of a snowball. There's more retribution for indoor spitting and for the time when I find a real, honest-to-God .22 caliber bullet and throw it down on the street to get it to explode. The slug zings right past my dirty little face and sends my mother into hysterics. Then there is inexplicable laughter when I get busted for holding my pet turtle up to the neighbor girl's skinny white belly, whereupon the turtle sticks out its old wrinkly head and bites off a chunk.

My mother and I go on a "date" (her word) to see *Gone With the Wind.* She tells me she is seeing it for the tenth time. *Why so many times?* "I go there to emote," she tells me. On the screen, Scarlett O'Hara stands, limned by the smoke and orange firelight of her ravaged plantation, swearing on a fistful of Tara's dirt that she will never go hungry again. Years later, I realize my mother went to movies to emote and grab hold of her own fistful of resolve during the last two years of her life.

2.

EARLY RELIGION

Thankfully, my parents give me the gift of benign neglect most of the time. My father has work, and my mother has no problem with letting me and my brother spend every minute of non-school time outdoors. In summer, when we come home for dinner, filthy from rolling in the dirt with the dog, she makes us strip down behind the house to our dirty underpants and hoses us down like muddy elephants in a zoo.

I am still in my preteen bubble of latency in the early sixties. At ten, my hormones haven't yet turned any sexual corners. Girls are hardly on my radar, but my mother feels obliged to get a head start on what she knows is coming. She knows from having brothers how disgusting boys can be.

My idea of protecting our house is to blow up ant colonies in the front yard. I pack a thick glass medicine bottle with gunpowder scrimped from firecrackers and crimped tight with toilet paper. I miscalculate on the fuse, however, and when the bomb goes off, it blows a hole in the yard and shoots glass shrapnel into my knee. This is the kind of thing that fits my mom's Big Reaction template, which I avoid by walking the six blocks to the Wichita Clinic, blood streaming down my leg, to take care of it myself. The doctor sponges me off with alcohol-soaked gauze, applies a clean bandage, and sends me home. In time, the skin heals over until pieces of glass begin to emerge, glistening obsidian-black, out of my knee. Doctors are no help for the serious stuff, as I've discovered, so I lock myself up in the bathroom with rubbing alcohol, tweezers, and a fingernail clipper. The surgery goes well. One by one, I lay out several jagged quarter-inch cubes, tiny trophies of bloody glass, on the edge of the bathtub, when the agitated knock comes.

"I know what you're doing in there!"

"You do?"

"Of course I know what you're doing, so stop it right now!"

I don't catch on to the anxieties generated in parents by teen music. Elvis, Carl Perkins, Buddy Holly, and the Big Bopper are all still alive. So is the widespread fear that rock 'n' roll is going to send children into sexual frenzies that my mother's own generation remembers with guilt and nostalgia from the era of wine, women, and song. For all of her knowledge of bohemian ways, my mother exhibits very conventional fears when it comes to me growing up too fast. She needn't have worried. My secret energies—and with my Scorpio-lunar crazy bone, I have plenty of them—are not yet focused on glimpses of luscious female skin in magazines or romantic fantasies depicted in the insipid songs of popular radio. As a ten-year-old I have other fish to fry.

At St. James Episcopal Church, the adults have the good sense to sequester us children in Sunday School where it's marshmallows and cartoon pictures of Jesus walking on water. God is Buffalo Bob working the marionette strings. Episcopal liturgy, for all its stately beauty, is not for children. And still, when I am finally allowed into the dark wood-and-sandstone church, my imagination simmers in the sounds of communal prayers in King James English. The church calendar is peppered with words that sound like short poems, or long names of serious girls I would like to meet: Septuagesima, Sexagesima, Quinquagesima. Better yet, the priest's name is Father Flye.

There's covert activity at night. If you were to hold your ear against my bedroom door and listen closely, you would hear me leading my invisible congregation in my rendition of the beautiful, archaic convolutions of Episcopal group confession. I've latched onto this relic of High Church English, and it features nightly in my services under the covers. Together with my congregation, we acknowledge and bewail our manifold sins and wickednesses, which we from time to time most grievously have committed, by thought, word, and deed, against God's Divine Majesty, provoking most justly His wrath and indignation against us . . . I follow the bewailment by administering the Body and Blood of Christ. I reach out to bless each head. *May the Body of Christ give you strength. May the Blood of Christ keep you to life everlasting. Amen.*

My invisible congregation comes every night. Several times a week, I baptize them and give them Last Rites (I have never seen Last Rites administered, but I know they exist). After Com-

1939, Wichita, KS. My dad.

munion, you can see a pointed shape like a short tent pole poking up and down under the covers, moving this way, then that, my fingers making the sign of the cross as I give the final benediction. After that, my congregation goes home, each into his own land, relieved of sin. I look back and wonder, not for the first time, *where does this early affinity with religion come from?* On three separate occasions, psychics have told me I have had numerous past lives as a monk.

After doing religion for a while, I go into another mode. I settle in with my transistor radio and trawl for signals from the big world, hungry for whatever comes bouncing along out of the ionosphere. I know that if the sounds I am funneling into my ear at this hour were to escape into the house, the whole operation will be detected and summarily shut down by the forces of repression sleeping down the hall. So I curl up on my side with my tiny transistor, antenna extended, sandwiched between my head and my pillow to muffle the sound.

XERF, one of the famous Border Blasters, is there, waiting for me, just over the Texas border in Mexico. I press my pillow tighter, lest even one decibel escape and give me away as Wolf Man Jack plays B.B. King and tries to sell me boxes of baby chickens and autographed photos of Jesus. I know that if I hang in there long enough, I will get to what I'm waiting for: Brother Al Wyrick, a radio preacher, who invites me to place one hand on the radio and one hand on the "afflicted place," and pray with him the Prayer of Faith—Brother Al *knows* the Power will come right through the radio—upon which he speaks in The Unknown Tongue: *"Hilamo Sha-TA!"*

All this on a school night! It's my introduction to energy healing.

In sixth grade, my best friend and I, both sesquipedalian collectors of big words and ideas, lie on our backs in his sloping backyard. Under the night sky, we "contemplate." *Does God see us here on the hill? Do the rocks record sounds from a million years ago, like in the episode about the paperweight we saw on* Science Fiction Theater? *Are there flying saucers hiding on the other side of the moon like in the movie* The Mysterians? *If a human "does it" with a dog* (we only have vague ideas of what "doing it" entails), *will the baby be part person and part dog? Are we going to die when the commies drop an A-bomb on Wichita?*

I become a closet "nonconformist." At first, it's a word I latch onto without knowing what it is exactly. It's something bad, I'm sure. Another friend's father is a member of the John Birch Society, and he drinks, which means he pounds his fist on the table and rails against minorities and the commies any time his frontal lobe is disinhibited. He says nonconformists are people who don't believe "what we Americans all believe," and they're just as bad as the commies and need to be rounded up. *And then what?* I have no idea what I believe. On TV, Superman flies through space holding an American flag, so America is the best country, and the only reason people are commies is that they just don't know any better. Everybody knows that. But when people go on a big emotional binge about it, like my friend's father, I am outside of their bubble. I'm not able to believe anything so much that I would want to *kill* someone over it. It means I don't believe what everybody else believes, but I don't tell anyone.

Hospital visits are increasing for my mom. No one is spelling anything out for my brother and me, so we take each new development at face value. By then, she has started turning slightly orange and spending the day in her bathrobe with her Chesterfields and coffee. When she comes home from the hospital with her chest painted with iodine marks, she tells us it's a target to help the doctor aim the radiation. *Cobalt? Kryptonite? Aim at what?*

In mid-October of 1962, I get a summons to come home from my friend's house. An unusual number of cars are lined up on our street in front of our house. I'm met at the door by Aunt Susan and my dad who says, "We lost Mommy today." I know

33

what that means, but I ponder as I stand there whether they have been looking for her and just can't find her. In a dream that night, my mother appears, driving up in a top-down jalopy with a purple sausage for a steering wheel. She kisses me goodbye— maybe I kiss her back—then she drives away.

My mother dies shortly before my thirteenth birthday. My universe is bewildered and goes without a center for a long, long time. Years later as an adult, I unearth a copy of a letter she sent to President John F. Kennedy in the early 1960s. In it, she announces that she is " . . . an old reactionary, deep-dish, hunting-case Republican by tradition, blood and conviction," [but] she is "still able to think for herself." She goes on to tell JFK that she approves of the job he is doing so far (though she didn't vote for him), that she has a mind to run for the Kansas State Senate (at the moment, she has less than two years to live), and that she hopes we will be able to "get them [the commies] before they get us." I think to myself, *yep, that's her all right!*

3.

INTIMATIONS OF ANOTHER WORLD

My big breakthrough in high school is foreign language. There, I find some territory of my own. I belong to that enclave of high schoolers who are slightly invisible, and German is catnip for me, a secret language, an Unknown Tongue, known only to me and other kids nerdy enough to get into it. At first, all we know how to say is *"Wie geht's?"* and *"Es tut mir Leid,"* but later it scratches my sesquipedalian itch to learn monstrously long, glued-together German words with very specific meanings, like *Fussbodenschleifmaschinenverleih* (floor grinder rental service) and words with no equivalent in English like *Tafelschoko-ladensollbruchstelle* (the place in a bar of chocolate where it's supposed to break when you bend it). With German, we get our Nerd's Revenge, chattering away in our crypto-language right under the noses of the unwashed. At the time, it never occurs to me that there is an actual country (Germany) where everybody conducts their daily lives in the Unknown Tongue, and for whom there is nothing exotic about it at all.

The world of adults turns suspect. In my junior year of high school, I'm confronted with a booklet with names and photos of girls and boys my age. I'm supposed to select a date from among these daughters of "old Wichita families." Years later, I learn that the organizers include my future step-mother, Sue Mulloy Gilkeson, and her buddy Mary Koch, mamma of the famous billionaire brothers Charles and David Koch. I'm quick to smell the rat of social engineering in this ploy, but totally inert when it comes to figuring out what to do about it. The immediate problem for me is that I have almost no experience with dating and no girlfriend.

I take a magnifying glass to each of the photos and land on Paula. Her qualifying assets are these: she's pretty and she goes to another high school, which means we don't know each other. We sniff each other out at halftime at a neutral football game and find each other to be sufficiently unloathsome to proceed. Fact is, I'm semi-smitten by her. She is blonde with high cheek bones. She's watchful with a laid-back demeanor. What's more, she seems to have something approaching a sense of humor about the forced date ordeal. We weather the dance evening and end up afterward talking until two in the morning in her backyard, a terribly adult thing, along with other small firsts like drinking coffee in order to stay awake. After Paula loans me some money, I take a taxi home. The crowning glory of all this new worldliness is talking freely to another person for the first time in my life, an initiation into the joys of actual conversation that isn't pegged to some social role.

New Food, Expanding World

A family in our neighborhood owns a small grocery store. Two of their sons commandeer a tiny building on the same corner for an outlandish business idea. It starts as a wee hole-in-the-wall, but in the fullness of time it will be carefully scooped up, intact, and gently placed on a giant flatbed trailer. Traffic will be rerouted as the tiny house is carried in solemn procession with a police escort, like a dignitary in a state funeral, to its final resting place in front of the School of Business at Wichita State University. This is the original Pizza Hut.

This is our first taste of pizza in those parts, and it enlarges my food world by several magnitudes. You enter a room with three or four tables with red and white checkered tablecloths and order though a literal hole in the wall. By and by, one or the other of our neighbor's sons emerges from the kitchen and serves you a pizza pretty much identical to what you would get today.

In 1965, the novelty of this new food is overwhelming. Not only does it transcend fish sticks and creamed chipped beef on toast, Pizza Hut becomes a portal to unknown worlds. One Saturday trip to this new food, I walk in to find one of the teachers from my high school at a corner table, absorbed in a book. In front of her on the checkered tablecloth is a half-eaten pizza flanked by a cigarette smoldering in an ashtray next to a glass of beer. She doesn't look up. East High is a big school and since I am not in any of her classes, she wouldn't necessarily know me. But I know who she is, though she looks different in pants and a man's shirt. When she raises her head in my direction I catch a wry look of vague recognition through the blue of her smoke. For a moment, I can't take my eyes away from where she sits, Brillcremed and butch, beautiful in a way I've never seen before. She takes a long pensive drag on her cigarette and something in the way she lets the smoke escape in my general direction tells me there is more to this world, this Wichita, than meets the eye.

Elsewhere in the same city, actual Beats are in Wichita coffee houses, applauding poets and folk singers by rapping their knuckles on cigarette-stained tabletops. A handful of "magic locals," like Michael McClure and Charles Plymell, make their way into San Francisco poetry circles, bringing lore from the "Wichita Vortex," a mystical force field that keeps drawing Wichita natives back into itself. Bob Dylan's "Subterranean Homesick Blues" is so beyond the reach of local cultural gatekeepers that it gets played on Wichita radio stations as a novelty song. Meanwhile, Allen Ginsberg, a lonely man traveling on a Guggenheim fellowship, is reading his *Wichita Vortex Sutra* in front of Wichita State University. By the end of my senior year

37

of high school, there is definitely something in the current, and I find myself among people for whom the goal of life is to get out of Wichita.

My brother Bruce and his wife Cecilia.

4.

WALKABOUT: LEAVING THE WICHITA VORTEX

January 2019
I have a dream. In it, I am walking with my younger brother
Bruce. We come to a river and find boats on the bank. I wrestle
one into the water and climb in. The boat is made of metal and
partly submerged. The current takes me away, leaving Bruce still
on the bank. I wake with a sense of sadness and longing.

Bruce and I loiter over coffee at Starbucks. An hour before
I have to leave for the airport, an honesty sets in between us.
Bruce tells of the many cues he took from me as we grew up. I
was heedless that I was being watched and emulated. He tells
of a time after high school when the river took me away, leav-
ing him high and dry. It was a parting of the ways. I am the one
who left.

In 1967, I start at the University of Kansas, a confused,
straight seventeen-year-old dressed like a golf pro. All around
me are angry bikers and guys with long hair. Vietnam is
revving the motors of protest, but nothing outside my personal
bubble is real to me. In my first year at KU, I enroll in Air
Force Reserve Officer Training Corps. Why? Because I think
it would be fun to learn to fly an airplane. There is an entrance
exam, of course—they don't let just any high school graduate
take military science classes. On the way to the test room, I
am handed a sheet with instructions to go to the campus quar-

termaster and pick up my uniform. *My what?!* I deliberately flunk the exam.

I study German and Italian. Foreign languages are tendrils reaching into worlds beyond the Midwest. After my sophomore year, I hitchhike through Europe for two months, a common enough junket for White, middle-class university students. It's my first real walkabout, my first time on my own. I hitchhike up and down the continent without the slightest clue of what I'm doing. Cluelessness breeds unforced errors, and the errors bend tiny angles in my trajectory. In the process, I discover within me a magnetic attraction for little one-off events, fringe-dwellers, and other people's tempest-in-a-teacup dramas. In Europe, my crazy bone wakes up and sits bolt upright, broadcasting invitations to unconscious forces.

I careen from place to place like a character in a certain kind of French comedy in which the clueless hero bumbles through busy streets, head in the stratosphere, oblivious to swerving cars that absolutely have to hit him, but don't. Then come the muggers and the hookers and the swindlers to separate him from his money and finish him off. But, like Peter Sellers in *Being There,* he muddles through intact, passing through the chaos like a linseed through the alimentary tract of a camel. God takes care of fools.

In less than sixty days in the era of *Europe on $5 a Day,* a time punctuated by short-lived love affairs, smoking hashish for the first time, hanging out in Copenhagen with an East Indian pick-up artist who ends up marrying the woman he targets, and an uncomfortable brush with European nobility, I manage to string together an unlikely collection of one-offs. I get thrown, bodily, off a moving train just outside of Ravenna, Italy. In the Dolomites, I hitch a ride with a journalist who, after driving for hours in utter silence, knocks back a couple of *grappas* at a rest stop while he tells me, tears streaming down his face, that I, and I alone, am all that stands between him and the suicidal abyss into which he is about to throw himself. I become the lead character in a tiny situation comedy in East Berlin that could easily have landed me in jail for currency violation. Thinking I'm checking in at a youth hostel in Stuttgart, I end up living a week for free at the Johannes Falk Haus, a halfway house for young punks who have recently been released from prison. I travel for a spell in Italy with a German couple making their way around Europe by shoplifting. I become their half-witting accomplice by engaging shopkeepers in the front of their stores with my charming hands-and-feet Italian while they are in the back of the store stuffing their *Tragetaschen* with bread, cheese, and wine. In an inadvertent switcheroo while hitchhiking together, they end up with my passport. Once I arrive in Rome, I get down to my last cent, only to be taken in and fed for several days by Marxist students at the university. At the very moment I'm seated at an outdoor café, spending my last *lira* on *spumoni* and beer with tears streaming down my face, the city goes nuts. Before my eyes, television sets are carried out into the plaza, trailing yards of extension cord, and all attention is focused on the American moon landing. When it's found out I'm American, I am treated to drinks and food until I can hardly walk.

It's 1969 and, underneath it all, I nurse an awareness of a larger world and, cliché though it may be, I feel I'm being carried along by something bigger than me. I have located a source of energy for my life, and I chafe at the idea that this two-month jaunt has only been a prelude to settling down. If anything, my resolve to someday live in Europe is only stronger. Circling over JFK on my return to the States, now heavy with a nineteen-year-old's gravitas, I look down on what appears to be a miles-long serpent slithering along. Fascinated, I follow this stream of traffic winding northward from the city. A feeling rises in me that everything is going to be different from now on. My Uncle Paul, a lawyer for TWA in New York, meets me at JFK. I ask if that was typical rush hour traffic I've seen from the air.

No, " he says. "They're all headed up to some kind of music festival upstate in Woodstock." I think nothing much of it, but from the time I land back in 1969 America, I am on another path, sleepwalking into a precarious, fluid moment of history.

PART II
THE MYSTICS
(1971 - 1983)

"I think there are enough spiritual people in the United States that it would surprise even America."
~*Murshid Samuel Lewis*

5.

A TINY CONVENTICLE OF LIGHT

Paia, Hawaii, March 2015
Waiting for my partner Diane, who has ducked into Mana Gro-
cery Store, I take a short drive down B. Street. Immediately, my
eye is drawn to a man carrying a full-size crucifixion-grade
white cross along the crowded sidewalk. The horizontal beam is
slung over his shoulder and "JESUS" is stenciled in black let-
ters where the two beams intersect. A sixty-something, wind-
beaten, silver-haired Hawaiian in an open white shirt, the man
waves joyfully as I drive past him.

He's enjoying the lift that comes from getting a peculiar
kind of attention. It's a heady thing, after all, to step out like that,
out of the world of consensus about what normal people do.
Think about it: a man feels a calling—does anyone carry a cross
down the street without feeling called to do that?—and follows
it. Suddenly, for a moment, he is free of the mass mind and its
way of insisting that we all act alike. Having jettisoned that bur-
den, he looks upon the gawkers with compassion and joy. He has
braved being thought crazy, passed through the membrane that
surrounds normal behavior, and now he rests in the ecstatic zone
that lies beyond. It's a powerful place to be.

I did that. No, I didn't carry crosses down busy streets, but
I did frequently step through the above-mentioned membrane.
Every day, in fact, when I was a robe-wearing brother in a spir-
itual order. I know firsthand what it is like to be held in that par-

ticular arm's length wonderment we reserve for those whose ac-tions are incomprehensible, for those who manifestly occupy a different world.

There was a time in the mid-1960s when three old men were rip-ping around San Francisco and Golden Gate Park, influencing young people in strange ways. Between them—Earl Blighton, also known as Father Paul: a former electrical engineer, healer, and Rosicrucian mystic; Murshid Samuel Lewis of the West Coast Sufis; and Joe Miller of the San Francisco Theosophical Society— they had a sizable following among the local hippies and bohemian types. This was a time when there were countless murmurations filling the spiritual air of America. Even in my small world of Lawrence and Wichita, Kansas, I had encounters with disciples of Swami Muktananda, Yogi Bhajan, Meher Baba, Maharaji, Maharishi Mahesh Yogi, followers of Stephen Gaskin as they made their way from San Francisco to "The Farm" in Tennessee, Bubba Free John, the Ananda Marga Yoga Society, the Self-Realization Fellowship, Sufis, numerous Jesus groups, Christian sects and movements. In those days, temple bells were constantly ringing. The Road to Damascus was choked with traffic. Among these movements was the Holy Or-der of MANS. I will simply call it "the Order,"[1] since that is what everyone else called it.

The Order was a semi-monastic co-educational spiritual or-der, founded in 1968 in San Francisco by this same Father Paul. His friend, Sufi Samuel Lewis, became the Order's first Direc-tor of Spiritual Education. While Father Paul was still alive, the Order represented a confluence of Science of Mind á la Ernest Holmes (with echoes of New Thought philosophy that my grandmother would have recognized), Rosicrucian and Theo-sophic-style mystical Christianity, all with a splash of UFO re-

---

[1] Not to be confused or conflated with other organizations or the televi-sion series called "The Order."

search, West Coast Sufism, Kriya Yoga, and Haight-Ashbury culture dabbed behind the ears. Father Paul and his mystic friends were part of an avalanche of provocative, charismatic innovators tumbling into the culture of the West Coast at the same time as the founding of the Esalen Institute and the rise of the Human Potential Movement. Together, they found a ready audience of experimental and independent-minded young people who were itching for new varieties of spiritual experience.

Father Paul was an industrial-strength triple-Aires mystic, trance medium, and healer. He had revelations and visions and followers. By the one and only time I met him personally, he was the central figure of the Order. Stories abound and accounts vary, but from what I understand, Father Paul had a rift with the "Ancient and Mystical Order Rosae Crucis," the Rosicrucians, where he was both a high initiate and a burr under their saddle. He founded the Science of Man Church and, according to one story, the Rosicrucians ran him and his church out of town for wanting to teach their secret material to the public. In 1963, the Science of Man Church burned down. Out of the wreckage of that time came visions of a new order based on what he called "sacramental initiation" and the Christian Mysteries, without the straitjackets and muddy galoshes of the past 2000 years of Christian history.

I occasionally run into former Order members, and their stories run the gamut. Many went along with the Order's swerve from esoteric school to Christian Orthodoxy, found a spiritual home there, and stayed put. Some went out and founded their own knock-off of the Order. Others knocked off a bottle of Jack Daniels a day. Some still rage about the emotional scuff marks they sustained in the Order. Others became academics, artists, healers, and spiritual practitioners of various kinds. It's all in a day's work for movements that come along as spiritual storms, phenomena, forces of nature, at turns merciful and merciless.

My own history in the Order began a few years after its official charter as a non-profit religious and educational organization in San Francisco during the West Coast consciousness boom of the 1960s. I arrived in late 1974, just after the death of Father Paul. By then, the early history of the Order was wrapped in layers of mystery, and he had already acquired mythic status.

The Order had obvious resonances with Catholic teaching orders, a Franciscan joy and simplicity mingled with Jesuit-feeling rigor and militance. All the trappings of traditional orders were intact: vows, regular fasting and prayer, and communal life. Members wore clerical garb and performed charitable service. The Order's Raphael House, an emergency shelter founded in San Francisco in 1971, is still alive and thriving, receiving numerous prestigious awards through the years for community service.

But there was also something else in the atmosphere, something right out of a Bob Dylan song. *There's something going on here, but you don't know what it is, do you . . .?* The Order, as anyone in it would tell you, was also a mystery school, a secret society like the Rosicrucians and the Freemasons, and not quite of this earth. And everyone associated with the Order has their own telling of the Order's origins and what it was like to live in it.

The Order, when I first joined, was set up like a hermetic lodge with a hierarchy and an initiatory ladder. The outer trappings were identifiably Christian: we deliberately cultivated the image of clergy, wore clerical collars and ebony crosses in public and robes and vestments in our services and ceremonies. The teachings were a blend of Christian Mysteries, esoteric reading of Scripture, selected strands of various mystery traditions, and channeled teachings through Father Paul, who was believed by many in the Order to be the present-day incarnation of a very well-known figure in Biblical and Christian history.

I can talk now with some equanimity about aspects of life in the Order, how we lived, worked, and prayed and how, at one time, for me, the spiritual life of the Order was invested with extraordinary power. Other aspects are more elusive. It wouldn't mean anything to most people if I said I was a member of such and such a degree in a Christocentric school of spiritual initiation. It might sound like I was a Mason, like my grandfather, with his ceremonial sword with the entire history of the Masonic Order engraved on its hilt and blade. Still, long after my departure from the Order, I came to recognize that despite its unique character—clearly congruent with the experimental mind expansion movement of the 1960s and 1970s—its deeper roots placed it in context with the Western Hermetic tradition, dating back to the Crusades and the Knights Templar, and further back to the Grail mysteries. The Order was a mixture of traditions, what Umberto Eco called "a tiny conventicle of light and faith."

The "C-Word"

I am occasionally asked what it was like to have lived in a "cult," and I'm always taken aback by the question. The cult question is a bit of a hairball. It tends to come from those who remember the murder of Sharon Tate by followers of Charles Manson in the late 1970s, and sensational stories of young people being kidnapped, brainwashed, and sexually abused by self-anointed prophets, culminating in the Jonestown mass suicides. It's a valid question, but I resist the cult label when it comes to the Order.[2] I resist because the term tends to get applied to any group that organizes around a charismatic individual who has the ability to influence a large number of people, making no distinction among the followers of Jesus, St. Francis, Susan B. Anthony, Elvis Presley, Jim Jones, or Donald Trump. When I finally en-

---

[2] For a look at the inside of an infamous cult, I recommend Lauren Hough's *Leaving Isn't the Hardest Thing*, Random House, 2021. The order I was in certainly had cultish features—the same could be said about traditional Roman Catholic orders. Compared to what Hough depicts about growing up in the Children of God, however, the Order was relatively benign.

tered the Order, I committed freely to its vision and the demands of the community. The Order contributed significantly to my spiritual formation, and I, in my way, contributed to the Order's evolution.

Father Paul was definitely charismatic and had a huge influence on his disciples. Difficult to fit into a single category, the Order was a kind of platypus for researchers of New Religious Movements (NRMs) who have valiantly tried to trace its improbable arc, shapeshifting over the course of twenty years from an eclectic Western esoteric school of initiation to an Orthodox Christian order. This wild ride contrasts with the majority of such groups that just fizzle and die after the charismatic founder is gone.

I came into the Order when it was going through its spasms of change after Father Paul's death. I did not find myself in a "Father Paul cult" among peers and teachers who were slavishly keeping his memory alive. While I benefited from what Father Paul had set in motion, I was never his direct, personal student. What I found in the Order was my personal dose of monastic formation in a community where that was possible, as well as access to a body of universal teachings that enabled me to form my own understanding of spiritual process. The Order was the rabbit hole I fell into in my early twenties.

6.
ONE WHITE HAIR

My approach to the Order is anything but a straight line. While my contemporaries finish their education and sift into family and professional lives, I set out on a prolonged series of switchbacks. In 1971, as I approach the end of my senior year at the University of Kansas, I have no complete education, no skills, no art, and no idea who I am. I'm not even a good hippie. No matter how stoned I get, I just can't buy into "the revolution" that's supposed to happen tomorrow or next week, when the governments, the fat cats, and the pigs are all going down. I have slept through Vietnam with student deferments. With a high draft lottery number, I have no brushes at all with the draft board. For me, "the revolution" is what is happening in my mind and heart, and in my convoluted theories about life that twist and gyrate, as David Feherty put it, "like an octopus falling out of a tree."

My various cover stories soon begin to come undone, especially the one about being a student. I attend many a lecture at KU looking down a long tube of lysergic acid- or psilocybin-induced tunnel vision. When I get "dismissed for poor scholarship" and eventually bounce back to Wichita to face the music, I'm a sullen twenty-one-year-old hiding behind a peach-fuzz mustache, slouching in a chair with a beer and a cigarette. I shrug off my dad's massive and justified disappointment.

Other days, I'm working on being a magic man. I've read my Huxley, Burroughs, Castañeda, and Kesey. My crazy bone imagination has given me a fairly loose commitment to the time-space continuum to begin with, and by the time mind-altering secret substances and a few quasi-spiritual practices enter my life to further loosen the screws, I'm pretty sure I can turn into a sunbeam without too much trouble.

Shortly before my exit from KU, I'm on my weekly power-foray into inner space when a traveling salesman offers me a wad of what I think is cocaine. It isn't. Whatever it is, it's a bad combination. Instead of paroxysms of bliss and manic sensuality, I spiral into inner hells and wander around Lawrence, zigzagging the empty late night streets shouting existential questions at houses and passing cars. I find my way to the house of the only friends who will grok my situation. From somewhere, they supply me with a dose of Thorazine and a bed to lie on while my mind turns to butterscotch pudding. Next day, I buy a bouquet of flowers at Dillons, a local grocery, and write a check for $35 to be initiated into Transcendental Meditation. The check bounces, but my spiffy new mantra works anyway. Under its influence, I drop like a pebble into a deep state like nothing I have known before. I hardly realize it at the time, but I'm turning a corner.

Overnight I find myself among meditators who, like me, have been druggies just a few months before, people who say things like "Heavy Kali Yuga, man!" to let you know how profound everything is now, and how they are totally on board with the whole Vedantic thing and can now think in terms of 26,000-year cycles. A friend sends $3.33 to the Lama Foundation in New Mexico and in a few weeks receives a pizza box with a 33 1/3 LP of Hindu chants, photos of East Indian gurus, and the spiral-bound text of what later becomes Baba Ram Dass's book *Be Here Now.* With this as our guidebook, we do yoga asanas, meditate, and talk a good game when it comes to enlightenment.

It would be easy to look back on that time and write it off as nothing more than the feckless wanna-be spirituality of drug-addled dilettantes. But reading Ram Dass implants the idea in me that there is such a thing as a spiritual path that transcends religion, and that I am in some way on it. This leads to reading Yogananda's *Autobiography of a Yogi,* and Yogananda leads to more meditation and an upsurge of spiritual ferment in me. I read the Christian mystics, who lead me to Thomas Merton, and to an order of mystics which I end up joining. This takes me to Europe, and eventually to a woman and a teacher who lead me into healing work.

But before all that, it leads me to a Wichita bar where a guy named C. Major is on stage, flatpicking a jangling Martin guitar, just tearing up a lead on "Muleskinner Blues." I'm there with a Japanese-American woman I have met. Call her Aiko. She's compact and energetic, and I can't take my eyes off a single snow white hair threaded through her comet of black follicles.

7.

MEETING THE ORDER

By the time I migrate from Lawrence back to Wichita, I have sworn off psychedelics and cannabis and tobacco, earnestly striving to turn my abstinences into better meditation. Without the ballast of pretending to be a university student, I put myself into being a full-time magic man. I believe I can fly, and, if the circumstances are right, perhaps raise the dead and dissolve into white light. I eat brown rice with gomasio, and I can talk a blue streak about planes of consciousness, especially if there's a woman I want to impress. I make the rounds of the yoga and *kirtan* groups with their shaved heads, their Hindu names, and little drums and chimes, but find no resonance with them. The Bible-thumping Jesus people on the street around the university are likewise not my tribe. I'm a meditator, a would-be ascetic, as God-struck as any of them, but when I look at these spiritual groups, I feel no kinship. I just see a bunch of sheep and feel allergic to their mindless uniformity.

In 1971 there are not many women with Japanese heritage in Wichita, so Aiko stands out. We collide in a strange hit-and-run fling that could only have been orchestrated by my (and maybe Aiko's) spiritual crazy bone. She's from California. She's exotic. How she has gotten to Wichita in the first place and ended up working for the city (the police department, no less) is her story to tell. When she wants to, she can talk planes of consciousness like no Wichita girl I've ever met, and when we go to hear live music at the bar, she slides her hand up my thigh like no Wichita girl I've ever met. One day, out of the blue, Aiko says to me, "Jim, there's someone I think you ought to meet."

I realize I've run into this outfit before. Sometimes you would see them walking in pairs downtown. Intense men in tobacco brown robes with hoods and blue cords, or black Roman Catholic clerical garb. They are all pipe smokers with resonant voices that vibrate your solar plexus. Something about them is uncanny and familiar to me, as if we were distant cousins who know each other from long ago. I feel the jingle of some shared spiritual DNA, and I think to myself, *I've run into a secret esoteric brotherhood of some sort,* except that they can't be all *that* secret if I'm running into them in Wichita, Kansas. And they all seem to know Aiko.

Soon, despite myself, I'm attending public classes at the house they call the "Abbey," which gives me regular exposure to the terrifying Abbot, who seems to be channeling esoteric spiritual masters and Vaudeville comedians at the same time. He's intense, entertaining, and a master of benevolent manipulation, dropping his voice and drawing you to his bosom one moment, then slamming you up against the wall the next.

The encounters unnerve me. I'm magnetized and repelled at the same time. *Is this outfit really,* as they keep saying, *an extension of the Great White Brotherhood?* (To be clear for twenty-first century readers, this is not a reference to a white supremacist organization, but rather a slighty archaic name given to certain orders of ascended spiritual masters—in some circles also called the "Great White Fraternity"—an esoteric brotherhood, believed to guide human affairs from behind the scenes.)

The Abbot and the brothers are constantly referring to the Light and to a massive shift taking place in the world at large, part of a larger cycle of rising vibrational frequency as we enter the New Age. It's a stock Order teaching that puts a name to something I feel every time I enter the Abbey. The Order people and the Abbey itself seem to vibrate differently, as if a moist finger is sliding around the rim of a giant crystal goblet, setting the whole place to humming, just below the threshold of hearing. When I'm near one of them or in their house, I can feel my body trying to match vibratory levels with them. One of the disconcerting sensations I come to associate with this is what I call "freeze foot," as if one of my feet has become rooted to the floor, unable to come along when the other one wants to take a step. Other times, I feel like I'm breathing a different kind of oxygen, or like a diver coming up to the surface too quickly, or like a house about to explode in a tornado, as if my insides are under sudden pressure.

This is clearly a Christian order of some kind. That much I understand, although nothing about it reminds me of church Christianity or the Jesus people out on the street, despite Sunday services and Communion, which these Order people take very seriously. I don't recall hearing the words "Second Coming of Christ," or "Apocalypse." Still, the implication is there in their teachings that things in the world are about to change in a monumental, global way. In public classes, they teach that Heaven and Earth are in the process of merging, and that the brothers and sisters of the Order have a role in facilitating this epic transformation. All this crystallizes my perception that this rising vibration thing is happening to me, in my own body and energies. From there, it's an easy step for me to see that the same thing will be happening in the world at large.

8.

BAGHDAD BY THE BAY

I'm on the edge of something uncontainable. The very existence of the Order draws an invisible line before me: take one step over that line with both feet and I penetrate a veil between worlds. Every day, I approach and avoid that line in a state of deadly fascination.

At the end of a family trip to my step-brother's wedding in Los Angeles, I take a detour on my way back to Wichita. Aiko has filled my ear with miraculous stories about Father Paul, the Order's founder, and suggests that I ought to meet him. By now, I know that Aiko, at some time in the past, has been a sister in this Order, although now obviously not any more, since she is operating as a free radical in the beer bars of Wichita. *A talent scout for the Order?* The thought occurs to me, but by now I feel impelled for reasons of my own to take the Greyhound from L.A. to San Francisco to see if I can drop in on Father Paul and see what a real magic man looks like.

Like the Abbey in Wichita, the Order's headquarters in San Francisco holds public classes on Tuesday evenings, so I attend one. The front room of the Victorian house has bay windows looking out on Duboce Park. It is crammed full, people sitting on the floor and huddled together on sofas, all raptly following the teaching delivered by a crisp, intense man in black clerical garb. Afterward, I ask him if I could meet Father Paul, just for a minute. The Order brother gives me a look—*are you sure you know what you're asking for?*—then smiles and tells me to come back on Saturday for the monthly meeting of the "Esoteric Council." I feel like I'm being politely brushed off. Then he asks where I'm from and suddenly it's a horse of a different color. "Wichita!" he exclaims, "in the Land of Ahhhs!" (Apparently, this was an Order gag before it became a Kansas marketing jingle.) Yes, he was stationed there at the Abbey when he was in the men's suborder. He tells me how much he loves the terrifying Abbot and then asks if I have a place to stay that night. I tell him I don't, and he asks one of the class attendees if he could put me up. "Sure, no problem!" Signs and miracles!

Next morning I'm awakened at six after a night in a sleeping bag on the floor of a drafty Victorian house in the Haight. My hosts are in a hurry, so I need to get dressed and out the door with them, or else we'll be late for breakfast. We strike out on foot in the cold, foggy air, climbing the city's vertical streets up and down to churches and rescue missions that serve free breakfasts. It's not enough to hit just one. We need to eat enough to keep up our strength so we can make it to *all* the places while they are serving: Salvation Army for pancakes and coffee and St. Vincent DePaul for eggs and sausage, with a couple of stops in between. That's how we spend the next three mornings. Afternoons, I walk the city and make my way to Golden Gate Park where I meet a pod of people dressed vaguely like elves who invite me into their nest hidden in a tangle of cypress trees. Later they show me the three known portals—right there in Golden Gate Park!—to Middle Earth. Welcome to "Baghdad by the Bay!"

Thus educated, I make my way to the Order house on Saturday morning. I'm led upstairs to a room. In it are seated six or eight men and women in robes and clerical garb, all a trifle amused that someone would want to just "drop in" on Father Paul and say "hi!" Behind a desk sits a man, littler than I expected. His head is bald on top and somewhat flat, with a fringe of white hair. He's wearing gold-rimmed glasses and all I can see is a doughnut of light around his face. He reaches out of the light and shakes my hand. I stammer a few words about wanting to say hello from Aiko.

"Aiko?" He says, as if this was the last name he expected to hear. "She's a good girl." The crinkle of mirth in his voice ripples through the room. I also mention the terrifying Abbot, and Father Paul allows as how he's a good boy, too. More mirth. Then he thanks me for coming all the way from Kansas to deliver their greetings and instructs one of the seated priests to take me downstairs and make sure I get a cup of coffee on my way out. Before I turn to go, he extends his hand again and locks in on my eyes.

"Join us. Let's get some work done."

Do I fly or take the bus back to Wichita? I don't even remember. Whichever way, the curse is upon me. I get back to Wichita, a rabbit on the run. Being around these Order people is exhilarating, but the conflict I feel makes me crazy. The next time I see Aiko, I walk up to her, root through her thick black hair, find the gleaming white one, and yank it out. Then I leave Wichita and take a job doing hard labor.

9.

FREDONIA HERMIT

A month later, I'm living on the edge of Fredonia, Kansas. I'm a do-it-yourself hermit living in a run-down shack on the grounds of the Excelsior Clay Products brick plant, a supplier for my family's building materials business. Hard physical labor by day, solitude, and candlelit meditation by night—all of it suits my ascetic needs. I'm a grilled-cheese vegetarian, accompanied only by *The Autobiography of a Yogi* and the esoteric Christian teachings of the Order.

Brickyard work provides all kinds of opportunities for going into a trance. Everyday loading accidents leave piles of rubble and unstacked brick scattered around the open yard. Gangs of us form short relay lines to stack and rebundle the remains. Bricks from a pile of rubble are flung, two at a time, in a kind of two-handed softball pitch in my direction. I catch them (or not), turn, and toss them to the next guy. The rhythmic sway-and-turn of this is hypnotic. When I turn back again, two more bricks are already in the air heading in the general direction of my face. I don't remember anyone wearing gloves.

At one end of the brick plant property stands a small shale mountain. A giant mechanical scraper travels back and forth across its fractured face, shaving off chunks of shale which are fed into a pug mill, ground to dust, and mixed with water and binding agents. The resulting blue-gray glop is mixed to the right consistency and excreted in a continuous slab which passes on a conveyor belt through an infernal revolving guillotine of piano wires that slices it into individual bricks. These "green" bricks dance out on another conveyor belt to be off-loaded and hauled on carts into kilns sprinkled throughout the brickyard like giant, medieval beehives. Each brick has two holes cut out of its middle to reduce weight and give you something to grab onto.

The Fredonia brickyard is near a railroad junction with a real hobo jungle. Most mornings, a handful of crusty John Steinbeck characters sign up at the brick plant office for a day of work, and the next day they're gone. These travelers make up half of the conveyor belt crew each morning.

The hoboes are a flinty bunch, eager to tell me where they've been. One tells me in some detail how to make Sterno camp stove fuel drinkable by filtering it lengthwise through a loaf of Wonder Bread. "Serves in a pinch, Jim, an' it don't even mess up your vision all that much." The same guy has the amazing ability—maybe it comes from drinking Sterno correctly—to fall asleep while working on the conveyor belt. He grabs a couple of the fat "green" bricks and sways with his arms dangling back and forth like a pendulum between the conveyor belt and the drying cart and falls asleep. He even snores, but never lets go of the bricks, until the foreman comes and whacks him awake.

Every evening a Mennonite man with a Captain Ahab beard rides up on a horse. He is the night "fireman," who tends the kilns. His job is to climb on top of the giant beehives every hour and thrust a metal rod down through a hole in the top to measure how much the bricks have shrunk in the firing process. When we arrive in the morning, we find this fireman, a diabetic, lying on his back under the shower eating chocolate bars to get his sugar back up before mounting his horse for the ride home.

The dust and heat turn my throat into a wasteland. All the old timers chew tobacco to create a phlegm barrier at the back of their throats as a guard against ingesting too much shale dust. On a break, I head for the water cooler. I tip the yellow plastic cooler toward me and fill my cone-shaped paper cup. As I'm lifting it to my lips, a dry hand covered with shale dust stops my arm. "Don't do that, Jim. Don't *drink* it. Do this." He takes the cup from my hand, shows me a spot on my wrists, and tells me to pour the cold water there. I try it and feel my whole body cool down. My hobo intro to acupuncture meridians.

The monotony of the conveyor belt that puts the hoboes to sleep has a different effect on me. The back and forth endless repetition opens a hatch in my psyche. One morning, I find myself talking with Brother T. of the Order. I don't know what we talk about, but his vivid astral form is standing right beside me as I off-load unfired bricks onto the drying cart. Then he's gone, leaving no particular message except his visit itself, which adds to my awareness of the very thin veil between the worlds.

10.

DUENDE AND ASTRAL VISITORS

I get used to keeping to myself and wearing myself out with work. I am an amateur ascetic, albeit one who is taking his asceticism seriously, pumped full of scenes of bi-locating yogis and ascended masters and saints from my readings. At the time, I think all this is original, but I'm following an inner tradition. I look now at the film *Into the Wild* and see an extreme portrait of the young man I was in my early twenties. He lives for intensity, driven out of the familiar world into his own wilderness by the same radical desire for white-hot purity and the *duende* of absorption in the eternal moment. He penetrates all false nicety and tolerates no compromise. He's ready to be an arrow fired into the sun. How he does it matters not: he's a saint meditating on a bed of nails, a soldier, suicide bomber, drug addict, street savage, survivalist, starvation artist. He looks neither right nor left, eyes wide open staring at the sun as the dross of his old life burns away. He desires initiation at the hands of the highest and most ruthless gods, leaving no residue of the boy. I'm in a ferment in my own gathering storm.

By and by, my hermit time passes and I find myself in Wichita again, living with my step-brother John, going to public Order classes, and bouncing around at night with the woman next door. I buy a used Gibson Hummingbird guitar and hang out with a bluegrass band called The World's

Largest Prairie Dog. I'm as muscled up as I've ever been, lean and intense.

I work by day in a sandwich shop, but my psychic hatch is still wide open. In my mind, I'm a quiet prophet in Babylon witnessing the change of an age as I wrangle the meat slicer and swab the floors. It's my front row seat at the emergence of a new world, a new order rising up behind my eyes. I can no longer walk down the street in downtown Wichita without seeing it as a fading, transitory world, a failed experiment. In meditations, I have visions of dust balls and locusts, the whole human enterprise coming undone. This occupies me day and night. Then I fall in love.

I don't know what it is about Barbara that has taken me, but I'm head over heels with her, whether or not she is with me. She's tall, funny, and astute. We roll around for hours on the floor and make out. I take her to hear the World's Largest Prairie Dog and to the Order house. I introduce her to the terrifying Abbot as if I'm asking him for permission to just be a normal guy. She draws goofy pictures, and I play my Hummingbird for her. It's a sweet time and my heart is open.

One night, I dream I'm being touched by something high-voltage. My body expands bigger than the room, bigger than the house, while my heart tries to explode out of my chest. I'm wide awake. I'm dying. I'm freaking out and screaming for Jesus to rescue me. When I eventually calm down, I remember the terrifying Abbot teaching about being "worked on from the other side" at night. *What is that? Is that really a thing?* I remember him teaching about "night work" by beings on the other side. *Angels? Ascended masters? People who had gotten so holy that their vibrational levels skyrocket them into the astral worlds so they're free to walk through walls and travel around at liberty on the inner planes and work with humanity from behind the scenes?* All this seems to be in play.

The Abbot went on to say that when you get to the point where you are able to work on others—I recall no mention of asking whether these others *want* to be worked on—you have to learn the ropes. It's one thing to send them Light and blessings. That's standard operating procedure for spiritual nighttime work. But don't *touch* them. It's more or less like this: since you are at such a high level of vibration in your astral form, it's *verboten* to touch the physical body of someone. It is too much of a vibrational mismatch, and you can damage the other person. As I lie there buzzing from my nighttime experience, I click though all the ramifications of this injunction. *Have I just been the victim of some kind of spiritual malpractice? Were the Order people, the terrifying Abbot, Father Paul, or someone from the Great White Brotherhood sitting around working on me from the other side? Did one of them touch me from the other side and nearly explode me with energy and kill me?*

I can't think of anyone else to ask about it, so I go to the Order house. The Abbot isn't there, so I have an audience with one of the brothers.

"It looks like your heart *chakra* got opened. You'll be okay."

Whew!

11.

WHAT JESUS TELLS THE ABBOT ABOUT ME

I'm split. I do and I don't want to be worked on and have my heart *chakra* opened. I also know I don't want to be shocked and scared like that ever again. I continue with classes, and after one of them the Abbot takes me aside. I follow him upstairs into a part of the Abbey marked Off Limits to outside people. We enter a room with double bunks and little prayer shrines, a dormitory for the monks.

"This is where the brothers sleep, Jim," says the Abbot.

"It's really okay for me to be in here?"

He looks at me with an expression I would come to know well. *This should be intuitively obvious to even the most casual observer.* "If the Abbot says you can come in here, then you can come in here."

We return to his office. *Why is he showing me the brothers' sleeping quarters?* The Abbot fastens his dark eyes on me and says, "I had a meditation about you, Jim. In it, Jesus told me you belong in the Order." I'm stunned and just stare at him.

"If you don't believe me," he goes on, "all you need to do is go into meditation yourself and ask Jesus about it. I'm sure he'll tell you the same thing he told me."

Easier said than done. Easier done than *really* done. I'm content, enthralled even, with my own intensity and my life as an amateur mystic. But the idea of actually going into the Order, tying myself to vows and wearing a robe, submitting to discipline, especially one that isn't of my own design, is a bridge too far. But here is the Abbot himself telling me I've been drafted by no less a being than Jesus to be in the Order. I don't have a solid enough sense of myself to tell him that this is *my* decision and no one else's. Whoever these people are, they're serious about what they're doing, and they don't mind letting me know that having been drafted by Jesus, my petty personal concerns are irrelevant.

Massive ambivalence. I've spent more than a year with my nose against the window of a dedicated spiritual life, and I carry my young man's tendency to see the whole thing in absolute terms, as long as it doesn't mean any radical sacrifice. And then there's Barbara.

My cards have been called, so I opt for melodrama: Here I am, So In Love, but I need to answer the Call of The Great Mysteries and Service to God (we Mystics put all the Truly Transcendent Stuff in Caps). In my mind, I cast myself as the young would-be monk about to disappear forever behind the cloister wall, heroically exiting from the world to sacrifice himself on the Altar of his Great Calling. I say my tearful goodbyes to my girlfriend and my Wichita family, who are baffled about what I'm up to, and board a train to Chicago where I will enter the Order's novice class. Goodbye world!

I last three days.

12.

NASHVILLE TO NASHVILLE

Chicago kicks my ass. It's my first time in a big city, a real one. The Order house has big city types, the kind that wear hats and trench coats and closed, no-bullshit city faces when you first meet them. For us newbies, it's up at four a.m. for Communion and meditation and breakfast. Then we cook breakfast for the vowed brothers before they go out to jobs in the city. The rest of the day, we clean the house and stay busy and silent.

Technically, I'm not even a novice because I haven't yet taken novice vows. The ones who have just taken vows spend three days in the chapel, semi-fasting on raw fruits and vegetables. The Order takes these cleansings seriously, and that's what the fruits and vegetables are about for people who have freshly come into the Order from "outside."

There is also the matter of learning to keep your feet on the ground and not get spaced out in the high vibration. It's a common issue in a spiritual pressure cooker like the Order, part of a kind of inter-dimensional shock that happens when your body goes up in vibration quickly, and "freeze foot"—getting rooted to the floor when one foot forgets how to walk—is the least of it. The vibrational difference between the Abbey and other places was already considerable, but, for me, the Chicago house is off the scale. I'm completely out of my element. The Order people do their grounding through hard work, solid food (meat), and tobacco, which shocks me, amateur ascetic that I am. All of it serves to highlight the real train wreck within me, namely the fact that I'm split within myself about being there at all. I'm faking it. My ideals of becoming an illuminated being are not helping.

After three days, I go to the director of the Chicago Order house—as with the Abbot, the Order only seems to install terrifying guys in these positions—and tell him I'm seriously uncomfortable and want to leave. With no hesitation, he punches a button on the intercom, calls the novice master into his office, and tells him to show me the door. On my way out, he says, "I couldn't care less about your comfort. You have no inkling what's going on here." Over and out.

The Benedictines of Three Rivers

I hit the street hard. Radical Spirituality is not turning out to be anything like I thought it would. After a couple of days with a cousin who lives in the city—he has no clue about the turmoil I'm in—I'm on the train back to Wichita, back to square one. But I can't even do that. I get off the train in Lawrence and wander around in a paranoid fog. I can't go back to Wichita, to Barbara and life as it was before. Wichita has an invisible dome over it, inaccessible for people like me who have flunked the Order test after making such a big deal out of answering my Calling.

I find the KU campus Episcopal house and talk with the priest, who seems to have a clue about the state I'm in. Two days later, I'm on a bus to an Anglican Benedictine monastery, St. Gregory's, in Three Rivers, Michigan. I'm going for a retreat to get myself sorted out enough to at least know my next move.

Compared to the Order in Chicago, the Anglican Benedictines of St. Gregory's are an easygoing bunch. I work alongside the monks, landscaping and planting. We follow the eleven-hundred-year-old rhythmic cycle of the Rule of St. Benedict, *ora et labora,* pray and work. Several times a day, a bell rings. We drop whatever we're doing and file into the chapel. The monks pull cassocks over their work clothes, and we kneel, sit, stand at prayer. In the refectory at meals, one monk reads aloud from *Two Years Before the Mast* by Richard Dana. There's no talk. The other monks just eat.

One morning, on the way to *labora*, I discover a squirrel clinging to the outside of the dormitory with its claws tangled up in the mesh of a window screen. As a kindly would-be monk and servant of God, I pull on my thick leather work gloves and race outside to the rescue. I have never placed my hands on a live wild animal before, and it's a shock to feel the coiled energy in its muscles. Especially its jaws. For my act of kindness, the little sonofabitch bites me.

Aside from the squirrel encounter, I have meditation time in nature and no pressure to be anything. The monks comment that they admire my fervor, which perplexes me. My failure to take to the Order immediately haunts me. Every day, I meet with the Benedictine guest master, who tells me I am experiencing "metanoia." I take the word to mean "metaphysical paranoia," which perfectly describes my state. He assigns me readings from *The Dark Night of the Soul* by St. John of the Cross and sends me to the monastery library to check out *The Seven Storey Mountain* by Thomas Merton, which I gulp down in a week. In Merton's confused and joyous story of becoming a Trappist monk, I find someone who seems to get me. I learn of his untimely death in Bangkok in 1968, and he becomes a mystery man in my mind.

Two weeks after arriving at St. Gregory's and reading Merton's autobiography, I've caught my breath, but I'm still running from the Order, and not about to settle in with a bunch of old Benedictines. One of the monks drives me to Highway 131, where I stick out my thumb with no idea of where I'm headed. I have forty dollars in my pocket.

Later that day, in the flat land south of Indianapolis, I'm standing on the on-ramp of Highway 65. A sign catches my eye. It points west and says "NASHVILLE 17 MILES." *No way! Where am I?* I know I'm disoriented, but not *that* disoriented. I get a ride from a couple of guys my own age. They're coming from the direction the sign is pointed. I ask where they're coming from and they say, "Nashville."

"Which one?"

"Indiana."

"How far you going?" I ask.

"Nashville."

"Which one?"

"Tennessee."

13.

27 Cents an Hour

In 1972, I know exactly one person in Nashville. When I arrive unannounced and knock on her apartment door, I can only hope she knows who I am. It's somehow okay for me to crash on her couch. She goes about her own business by day, and I take to hanging out in the Student Union at Peabody Teachers' College, drinking endless coffee, and thinking the thoughts of a spiritual refugee while my forty dollars run out. A job notice points me to a house renovation crew in need of more hands, so off I go to pound nails for a couple of bucks an hour.

An encounter with the house owner's Down Syndrome son, which includes tickling him without mercy until he pees, proves to be a game changer. The boy's father gets wind of this, and the next day calls me aside. He's heard that the two of us have had ourselves a good old time, and it started him thinking about something. I'm new to Southern speech and haven't sorted out the "y'alls" and "all o' y'all's," and I don't know where this is headed. After a couple of conversational gambits, he asks if I'd like a job working with "non-ambulatory a-dults." I have to ask him just what exactly a non-ambulatory a-dult is. The next day I find myself in an interview with one, a quadriplegic woman named Judy. She has cerebral palsy and also happens to be the Chairwoman of the Board of something called New Home, a group home for handicapped adults. Her speech impediment is so strong, it takes me two hours before I'm able to understand her without three or four repetitions. My tenacity impresses her, and she invites me to apply for an open position as a house parent at New Home.

There are no other applicants, and I get the job. My brief is to assist a live-in married couple in running the house for six adults with varying degrees of developmental disability. As a state-funded program, we have access to volunteers from the nearby teachers college, idealistic Special Education majors who use New Home as their internship. Our residents see to it that they either take immediately to the work of feeding, wiping, and wrangling unwieldy bodies in and out of wheelchairs, bathrooms, and beds, or have sudden changes of heart about their majors.

Part of New Home's mission is to get our folks out into public. In restaurants, on several occasions, to the amazement of other diners, I perform improvised Heimlich maneuvers to dislodge mis-swallowed food from our residents' gullets and make sure they don't bite their tongues while they thrash on the floor during seizures. I lean hard on the New Home slush fund for huge tips for the restaurant waitstaff.

Our wheelchair brigade is a regular sight at the Grand Ol' Opry in the years before Ryman Auditorium is declared a fire trap and the Opry is moved to a theme park. We go to church picnics where preachers routinely pray over our folks and declare how up in Heaven, where every tear will be dried and every hurt healed, these very Children of God, these residents of New Home, will truly find a new home where they will run and skip and play.

I calculate my hourly income for being on duty twenty-four hours a day, seven days a week at $0.27/hr. I have no training for any of what I do there, but I have a room to myself, three meals a day, and a houseful of people in wheelchairs who think I'm wonderful. I tell myself I've found my calling. For a spiritual refugee, this is more than enough compensation.

14.

MUSIC AND LIGHT

In parts of Nashville there is a church on every corner. Every off-shoot of every splinter group of every reformed, reorganized branch on the tree of American Christianity has an outpost in Music City. There, I find tongue speaking, holy rolling, laying on of hands, swooning in the Spirit, hallelujah shouting, and, in the hills outside of the city, I hear there's snake handling. And you're never far from a breathless preacher itching to take you down to the Cumberland River for your baptism by total immersion. There, in Nashville, Tennessee, I do something I wouldn't have dreamed of doing even a couple years before: I get baptized.

For this, I don't go down to the river with any of the Nashville preachers. I'm still spiritually radioactive, with more than a little metanoia coursing through me, largely due to my aborted attempt to join the Order in Chicago. Within two weeks of my arrival in Nashville, I run right into brothers of the Order on the street. Soon after that encounter, I get baptized by them and am given the name Joshua.

So it happens that I begin using a different name in Nashville, a spiritual alias I end up using for more than a decade, despite not liking it. Given the circumstances, I don't feel I can give it back and ask for a new one. It is explained to me that a spiritual name, given at a moment of initiation, comes with a certain power and specificity, even if you don't happen to like the sound of it. I never get comfortable with the shushing, susurrating sounds, not to mention the open-ended vowels at the end of the name "Joshua." It's too foreign to my ear, and holds Sunday school associations with the Joshua who "fit the battle of Jericho." I'm told I'll to grow into the spiritual gifts the name carries, namely the ability to make walls come a-tumblin' down. So I start using it. The Hounds of Heaven are still on my trail, and I figure getting a different name would throw them off the scent. And it works for a while. There are people in my life who have never known me by any other name.

At New Home, a pattern of sorts sets in. Evenings, I put volunteers to work with the residents, requisition the yellow Toyota station wagon, and decamp to the Exit Inn or the Old Time Pickin' Parlor to hear live music. It's 1972 and Nashville downtown music institutions along Broad Street are still intact. Tootsie's Orchid Lounge, Ernest Tubb's Record Shop, and Linebaugh's Cafeteria are still open, not to mention the Grand Ol' Opry, still at Ryman Auditorium. Country music star Porter Wagner's shortcut to Music Row takes his limousine right by New Home most mornings, and we look up from our work and wave to him. For the price of a drink at the Exit Inn, I hear Muddy Waters two nights in a row, Mose Allison, Larry Coryell, John Hartford, Leon Redbone, Norman Blake, Vassar Clements, and a host of up-and-coming solo acts, all good. It's Music City after all.

Other evenings, I go to the Order house for classes. By then, I'm bringing New Home residents with me to Sunday services. This is well outside the Bible-believing Baptist world they are accustomed to, but they don't care. They soak up the attention and high energy of the Order brothers.

A new priest, Reverend B., has arrived. As with the characters at the Abbey in Wichita and the pressure cooker Order house in Chicago, an intensity radiates from him like radio signals from a broadcast tower. *Where do these people come from?*

He seems to be made of different substances than other humans, titanium or something. Soon, Reverend B. is showing up in my meditations and dreams. All very benign and benevolent and I begin to feel his astral presence riding on my shoulder while I go about my day. He seems to single me out and always has some little instruction or tip for me.

Things intensify. By now, I am the director of New Home's "respite program," designed to give residents of the main Tennessee state institution the experience of a more home-like setting. One weekend, a respite guest proves to be a problem child. On the first night of his stay, I lie in my bed, suddenly aware that this young man is up and roaming around downstairs in the house. In a split second, I'm downstairs confronting him, telling him to get the hell back in his bed. In another split second, I'm back in my bed hearing him hightail it back to his room. The weird thing is, I never leave my bed. I remember Brother T.'s impromptu astral visit to me when I worked at the brick plant.

Reverend B. puts me on raw fruits and vegetables for five days and tells me to drink eight glasses of water a day. I pee a lot and feel myself getting lighter and lighter while a powerful current buzzes through my body. After Sunday services, he asks me to drop by that evening. He is uncharacteristically vague about it, but I don't need to know why. He is my spiritual teacher, and I trust him. At the Order house that evening, the brothers are out on street mission, so it's just Reverend B. and me. Without any preamble, he leads me into the sanctuary and tells me to enter. This is new for me. I've only ever seen the priest and the brothers enter that zone. The ritual triangle of candles is lit. He has me kneel down. When he places his hands on the crown of my head and calls down the Light, I slowly open and become a column of Light joining Heaven and Earth. Then the ritual is over. He explains to me that this is a gift, and that the Light is now sealed in my body.

On my way out of the house, he says, "Don't let anyone touch you for three days."

I spill like a mountain stream into the next week, utterly still inside, emotionally neutral. Something is different, but I have no words, just a lingering image of being washed inside with cool water. Years later, I read Sufi verse with the image of a clear crystal pitcher of clear water suspended in a pool of the same clear water, and I think, *that's what it was like to have the Light sealed in my body.*

There is so much I don't know about the Order. These people are magic. They astrally project, and when I spend time with them, so do I. They put me through changes with a sideways look. If they are not part of some kind of intergalactic conspiracy of angelic beings, then they sure are doing a good impression of one. Their presence in Nashville is uncanny, and I imagine them to be the tip of a vast spiritual iceberg.

Within three weeks, Reverend B. and the brothers are gone with no goodbyes, replaced by three specimens of Order life that I haven't encountered before: Order women, the female counterparts of the intense, pipe-smoking men.

15.

NOT GETTING MARRIED TWICE

New Home becomes my life for two years, my practice pad for letting the Light come through me into the world. After the gut-dread I have been carrying since leaving Wichita, things are fitting together for a change. The Light I am taking on in my meditations and spiritual practices and my growing association with the Order all feed into the work with my charges at New Home.

I've found a satisfying niche. I live in Music City, and life is good. For once, my contradictions aren't getting in my way. That said, my ambivalence about joining the Order never fully relaxes; I can't get away from a niggling undercurrent: *why aren't you in the Order?* New Home is a breather, a respite, but the Hounds of Heaven are not done with me by a long shot.

I write to Barbara. In a new spin of my emotional wheel, I figure now that since we were never "together" in any formal sense, we therefore hadn't "broken up" when I left for Chicago in order to not join the Order. I don't know what we are, so I invite her to visit me in my little world. I fly her to Nashville, one-way, and get all frisky, trying to show her what a great, spiritual life a person can live on twenty-seven cents an hour. She is sweetly amused by my little kingdom and sets out to educate me on making proper hospital edges on sheets when I make the residents' beds. I'm smitten all over again and ask her to marry me.

The proposal is not met with rapture, or much of anything. Barbara, it turns out, hasn't been idle since I left Wichita and went largely missing. She's gone through a few changes of her own.

"I can't," she says. "I'm going into the Order."

With the failure of my grand marriage proposal scheme, all I can afford to do is put Barbara on a bus back to Wichita. Understandably, she's pissed at having to endure a day and a night on the Greyhound. Depressed but rebounding, I throw myself into being a magic man as hard as I can, which includes working by day and finding available women by night. In the evening, some of us huddle around the television to follow the news that President Nixon has resigned. It feels like the world has taken a crazy turn. To make matters worse, one of the New Home residents, Marcella, develops a crush on me.

Not good. Marcella is tiny. She weighs about seventy-five pounds. Most of her days are spent perched in a child-size wheelchair where she throws adult-size tantrums when she doesn't get what she wants. Her legs are rigid, and her hands and arms writhe almost non-stop in slow-motion athetoid corkscrews. This never stops, not even in her sleep.

I flash back to my first interview with the New Home Board, several months before my twenty-third birthday. My emotional immaturity and utter lack of professional experience are on full display. Board members do their best to spell out what I would be getting into with Marcella. Imagine a cerebrally palsied woman in her forties, they tell me, quadriplegic, living with a massive speech impediment in an impossible, corkscrewed body. In her whole life, she has never taken a single step, never eaten a single bite unassisted, or had a conversation without extreme effort. Since leaving home when her mother could no longer take care of her, she has only ever been touched custodially. She has never had a lover and knows she never will. Imagine this same person with an alert mind and full mental capacities and a tempestuous Irish emotional life, none of which are numbed out by barbiturates or Thorazine like the others around her.

One of the Board members leans out over the table and looks me in the eye. She is a large, serious woman with the sleeves of her white blouse rolled up to her elbows. "Josh, we only got us a little tiny budget from the state, so there gonna be plenty o' times when there ain't gonna be a female house parent to take care o' Marcella." She pauses to let the implications soak in. "Which is gonna put you on th' spot. You're a mighty nice young man, but this is where you're gonna have to get tough. With all that totin' an' puttin' her on th' bedpan an' gettin' her dressed an' all that . . . jus' think about it, Josh . . . whatcha gonna do when Marcella goes an' falls in love with you?"

Marcella's telepathic gifts are razor sharp. Her antennae are all the way out all the time. It takes her no time at all to figure out that this tall Barbara woman who came and left after a few days has turned me down on something important. Marcella also knows that since Barbara's departure I've been seeing other women and have an active nightlife, in spite of being technically "on duty" 24/7.

Mornings, I creep out of my upstairs bedroom as unobtrusively as I can. But every morning, the second my toe hits the bottom step, a strangled voice howls from Marcella's bedroom at the end of the hall. This morning is no different.

"Aauaaaa!! I eed a edddpaaa!!" "Joshua, I need a bedpan!" I put on my work hat and enter her bedroom. Her little button eyes are fastened on mine as I peel back her blanket and sheet, lift her nightie, roll her away from me while I wedge the bedpan under her hips, and then roll her back on top.

"Hank You! Ohhhh! I almoss expohdd!"

"I'm glad you didn't explode, Marcella. You sleep OK?"

"I deem a-ou you!"

"You what?" By now, I've become a pretty good interpreter of her speech. Actually, I know what she is saying, and I'm stalling for time.

"I deem a-ou you!" *Oh, shit.*

"What did you dream, Marcella?"

"You an' m-me, we get m-maaa-weed!"

I can't say I haven't been warned.

When I tell Marcella that we are not going to get married, she goes apoplectic. All I have to do is walk into the room for her to cut loose with a torrent of Anglo-Saxon expletives, unmistakable despite her speech impediment, shake her clenched fists until she starts hyperventilating, and turns blue. She threatens to get me fired for sleeping with women in my room at New Home. I'm unprepared for any of this, and when she doesn't let up, I know New Home is over for me.

The Nashville Order sisters are kind but unyielding. Whatever I try to talk about with them, the unspoken signal from them is always, *why aren't you in the Order?*

16.

DESERT PASSAGE

What exactly is it about me that makes people like the terrifying Abbot and the Nashville Order people think I'm supposed to be one of them? Do I have an invisible sign around my neck that says I'm earmarked for the Order? Do I emit some kind of renunciate pheromone? Did I sign some kind of agreement to join the Order before I came into this life? I'm busy around the clock with questions like these.

I'm being patiently herded toward something, haunted by New Testament images of being slowly reeled in by a giant fisherman until the fish finally submits. (Other days, it's tractor beams from a spaceship.) I live with the all-or-nothing idea that I must literally leave it all behind, reinforced by New Testament rhetoric about who is and isn't worthy of the Kingdom of Heaven.

I'm painfully aware of my approach-avoidance with the Order: my dramatic exit from Wichita, only to bolt from the Order in Chicago, followed by my landing in Nashville and my fledgling career serving the handicapped. *Isn't that good enough?* I don't want to leave the world. It's much better to keep hovering around these mystics at a safe distance, then settle down somewhere as a spiritual guy with a wife and children. But then I run right into the Order again, and Reverend B. puts me into a Light experience that changes me. And then there's the debacle with Marcella which sends a jolt through my vision of staying with New Home. The message is "you can't stay here."

In the winter of 1974, I exit from Music City, stage left. I take the southern route, silently descending the ladder of westbound interstates: Highway 40 away from Nashville, 30 from Little Rock, dropping to 20 in Dallas, and Highway 10 in El Paso, each step a descent into a desert passage, surreal with ghosts and memory. I cry and shake and lapse into road-hypnotized stillness. Once, I park by the side of the road and walk into the trackless desert until I can't see my car anymore. My orientation spins and, for a moment, I freak out. After that, I sleep in my car and keep to the rest areas and gas stations. In San Clemente I sell my car to my step-brother for one dollar and realize I am now un-plugging from the world I have lived in. I arrive in San Francisco on a Greyhound, a fugitive finally turning himself in to the Order authorities.

17.

SAN FRANCISCO

January 1975

The N Judah streetcar winds its way from Ocean Beach through the Sunset District on its way to the Embarcadero. It clanks though a short tunnel, and I get out and walk the length of Duboce Park, a small patch of green that tilts toward Steiner Street. At the end of the park, a husky man in a rumpled purple windbreaker stands frozen with his arms outstretched in front of him, a storybook sorcerer emitting rays of malice through his fingertips at a Victorian house across the street from him. It is a cool January morning and Duboce Park, just up from the Mission district, is empty except for a scattering of morning joggers. The man reaches above his head, gathers more psychic lighting, and hurls it with a karate shout, "AAAHKGH!" at the house, fingers fibrillating with energy, then continues, again and again.

I watch this spectacle as I cross Steiner Street, heading for the Order's headquarters, the house this man is cursing to hell. I arrive in time for the monthly meeting of the Esoteric Council, when the Order's priests and teachers meet to confer on matters of importance to the Order. This includes appearances by candidates for ordination and people like me from "the outside" who come to apply for entrance into the Order.

After a brief meeting with the Esoteric Council, I am accepted into the Order's novitiate. Later that day, my suitcase is added to the collection in the attic, and my hair gets cut down to nothing. The brother who does the shearing is upbeat. He pauses midway and switches off his clippers, leaving me half-scalped as he goes to the window and looks out into Duboce Park. I'm lucky, he tells me. Not everybody who wants to come into the Order gets in. This morning, a scary man came and met with the Council. He was turned down, and apparently didn't take it well. The next morning, I'm taken to the chapel, where I start three days of silence, raw fruits and vegetables, and a review of my life. I have just turned twenty-five.

The entrance to the chapel is behind the house. Shoes line the walls of the vestibule to the Order's inner sanctum, a rarified space of meditation, prayer, and initiation. There, I begin three days of seclusion and introspection. At twenty-five I lack the reflective inwardness for a deeply felt life review. *What is there to review?* While I do understand that I'm being given a period to make the passage from my old life to this new one, I'm still on a magic man mission to transcend my body and become a Light Being who knows all kinds of esoteric things. In me, there is nothing resembling a religious or emotional conversion taking place. I tell myself that this time in the chapel is about cleansing toxins from my system so that I can withstand the high vibrations on the way to self-realization. I have the vague idea that if enough bad stuff can be eliminated, only the Light at my core will remain.

Order people come and go, periodically bringing me food, but otherwise they leave me to myself. For all they all know, I am just another guy from the Tenderloin in for a few days of respite from the street, and the Esoteric Council is giving me a chance to straighten out. I fast. I sleep on the floor. I break the silence when I crunch on my raw carrots and celery. I kneel and pray to be totally and immediately cleansed of all impurities (a typical style of prayer among naïve novices who then get their prayers answered in the form of nasty sore throats and colds). I wear myself out with the effort of attempted self-illumination.

85

I also chew on information I have gleaned since arriving at 20 Steiner. For one, I learn that Father Paul, the Order's founder, has recently died. For another, I hear that no permanent Director General has yet been named, so the interim leadership is being passed among the Master Teachers, each serving a one-year term. I'm still in my three-day seclusion in the chapel when I hear a thunderous Sunday sermon by the new Interim Director, Master R., the same terrifying priest who showed me the door in Chicago.

Days blur. I emerge from the dimly lit chapel and my semi-fast to find myself among strangers, the diversity of spiritual types and temperaments the Order attracts. My novice class is a menagerie of black sheep and odd ducks, no two alike. One early Order friendship begins here with an Englishwoman whose twin daughters would years later be born in an Order house in which we both live. A novice from Arkansas conjures up a distant, bygone world with his odd locutions and Ozark accent each time he opens his mouth. I have a memorable encounter with a tall, gaunt fellow from New Jersey. He has an amazing amount of black hair on his arms and legs, which I observe firsthand when I mistakenly walk into an unlocked bathroom stall and find him squatting like a gargoyle, naked, with both feet on the front of the toilet seat. Looking up at me from his perch, he calmly treats me to his elaborate theories on posture and healthy bowel movements.

Not everyone stays, and this eases some of my guilt feelings about having bolted after three days from the novitiate in Chicago. I get a nose for who will head for the door. First, there are those with a Haight-Ashbury "once a freak, always a freak" vibe about them. For them, the lifestyle is too austere. Then there are the star children whose feet never touch the ground. The Order's rather heavy diet doesn't suit them. And then there are the older men with weathered faces and Navy anchor tattoos on their forearms, looking displaced in their novice uniforms, who never manage to eradicate the dust and exhaust of years on the street. While straightening up the novice quarters, I find a loaded pistol under the pillow of one of the older guys, who doesn't last long in confinement. Twice on morning runs, the only time we ever leave the house, a couple of my classmates keep running straight ahead when the class takes a turn. They are never seen again.

I stay this time, along with fifteen or so intrepid souls who don't take off. What we all have in common is the Order, and everybody has stories to tell about how they first encountered the Order and eventually joined. We all know our place in the pecking order as probationers during our novitiate. It's widely understood as a time when we can expect to be tested and pushed around. We bond. This group becomes the core of my first-year class.

18.

WHAT THE TERRIFYING ABBOT DOES WITH THE ABBEY

One morning, three weeks into my novitiate, I'm engrossed in the details of sweeping the sidewalk in front of the house. I've had an Order-style energy surge and extended my efforts into the street and around parked cars when I'm summoned to the office of Master P. This happens to be one of the Teachers I'm not terrified of. He asks what I did before I came to the Order, and I say I'd worked with handicapped people in Tennessee. He gestures toward the world at large and allows as how there are a lot of spiritually handicapped people out there. Am I ready to go into service? I ask if I could finish sweeping the street first. He smiles. "Sure," he says, "take your time. The bus leaves in an hour."

My whole novice class lands in Fort Worth, Texas, F.O.B., fresh off the bus, from San Francisco. There, we join the rest of our first-year class, and I have my first taste of the ritual of getting an outside job in the Order. Pray, set an intention, and then go out and take the first job you find. That's the instruction. My first job has me clearing a block of trash. Folks in the neighborhood have never seen a White man work so hard. Some ask if I'm planning to plant crops. Then, as soon as I settle into a daily schedule and learn the bus routes, we are shipped wholesale to Wichita.

It's one of the whirlwind reshufflings that flavor up life in the Order—one of God's little jokes because I'm *from* Wichita!

I'm right back where I started. The white Victorian house with its high-ceilinged rooms is still the Abbey of the men's celibate suborder, but this time, the entire place is in a stir of intense activity. Orders have come down from on high that the suborder is to be relocated to Detroit and replaced in Wichita by my first-year class. As a result, our greenhorn batch of Order newbies is temporarily co-housed with the most monastic branch of the Order. We are greeted like long-lost family members by the terrifying Abbot.

The suborder brothers go about their day in the Abbey, silent and focused, as if they are all sharing the same inside joke. When the terrifying Abbot enters the room, they bounce to their feet as if they have springs on the bottoms of their spit-shined shoes. Instructions come with crisp formality and simple imperative sentences. Replies are "Yes, Father! No, Father!" Standard protocol in a hierarchical, almost military world. I see the humor crinkling the terrifying Abbot's eyes and the love that flows between him and the brothers, but I'm too nervous, too new to be part of it. Friday evenings come, and the Abbot sits down with the whole house to watch *Kung Fu* on television.

    I learn that, before the Order, the terrifying Abbot made his living as a stand-up comedian. He is a master at cutting short small talk with a withering glare, but his talent for comedic timing is uncanny, and it has rubbed off on the brothers. In the locker room world of spiritual men, celibacy jokes abound, with frequent references to erections and wet dreams. Once, as one of the brothers is blessing an evening meal, the feral yowl of a cat in heat pierces the air from just outside the window. Without missing a prayerful beat, the brother asks God, " . . . and please tell that horny cat she really needs to take 'the Vow.'"

    A brother tells me with a wink and nod that there are those who work and those who *pray* for those who work. Almost immediately, I begin to feel the Holy Spirit moving me to prayer and meditation when there is housework to be done. One day, after my regular chores, I'm hiding out in the chapel when the terrifying Abbot slips in. From the invisibility of my dark corner, I watch him proceed into the sanctuary, light the ritual triangle of candles, kneel, and do something very specific-looking. Whatever it is, it takes him all of five minutes. Then he douses the candles and leaves. Later that day, I screw up my courage and ask him what he was doing there in the chapel.

I've startled him. Instantly, he pivots and staples me with dark eyes that gleam like polished coffee beans, set off by his tobacco-colored robe. He seems to be focusing on my left eye, peering deep into my brain, and he is so abruptly present that the air catches in my lungs. Then he gives me a smile and one of his looks, reserved for the spiritually deeply clueless.

"I was putting the Abbey in my pocket," the Abbot says, as if this were intuitively obvious to even the most casual observer. He sees my double-take and lets go with a terrifying Abbot belly laugh, which lets me off the hook. I resume breathing.

"Did you actually think that the Abbey was this *house*?" I had never considered that the Abbey *wasn't* this house.

"The Abbey," he says, as if he were explaining shoe-tying to someone whose self-help skills are not entirely in place, "is a seat of spiritual transmission that has been entrusted to me. All I did was uninstall it from here and put it in my pocket so I can reinstall it when we get to Detroit." Then he turns and leaves me wondering exactly where I have landed. *What kind of outfit is this, where grown people talk seriously about putting an abbey in their pocket?*

19.

BODY PARTS AND LIGHT

I get a job as a transportation orderly at St. Francis Hospital, the same hospital where I was born. My daily rounds take me into every corner of a massive organism in constant motion. Patients need to be driven to dialysis, wheeled to the radio isotope lab, or delivered for minor surgery, then returned to their rooms. Once, I wheel a patient to a part of the hospital I have never seen before. There, I am asked to put on scrubs and a surgical mask and watch as a specialist uses what looks to me like a household hand drill to bore a hole in the side of "my" patient's head and drain a full cup of fluid into a beaker.

I hustle around the back halls of the hospital carrying wire baskets of green-labeled white paper sacks bearing tubes of blood, urine, and fecal samples on their way to laboratories. I schlep operation room waste, glass vials, plastic syringes, wound dressings, and stained bedding, still moist with body fluids, all double-wrapped in thick plastic bags, to the double-burning incinerator. As the soiled materials are thoroughly burned, the smoke is collected in a separate chamber where it, too, is incinerated. Above the chimney on this specialized crematorium, only the shimmer of hot air.

St. Francis was founded in 1889 by an order of Catholic nuns. Church teachings infuse the hospital's daily practices. One day, I am summoned to the morgue where two long wooden boxes of organs and amputated limbs are pulled from the freezer and loaded onto the bed of a pickup truck. I'm told that Catholic doctrine prohibits the incineration of whole body parts. These I drive to a cemetery where I watch the grave digger excavate a casket and dig new space in the ground beneath. There, these organs are given a burial so that they can be reunited with their respective bodies come Resurrection Day.

The Wichita, Kansas, where I grew up is out there somewhere, a short bus ride away. But here, in the tiny world between the Order house and my hospital job, classes, spiritual practices, and bumping around in the whirlwind of Order activity, I live someplace utterly different than my home town. I've been a haphazard but earnest spiritual student for a good five years now, and I've had glimpses of spiritual growth. But always they are accompanied by voices telling me I've just been imagining the whole thing. At St. Francis Hospital this begins to change.

The hospital is an ideal setting for learning to handle the energies moving through me. Daily group prayer and meditations, not to mention daily life in the Order, have raised my vibration. It's not so apparent inside the Order house—I have gradually gotten used to it—but stepping into the hospital is a different proposition. The contrast is striking. Walking down the halls of the wards pushing a wheelchair, I'm suddenly hyperaware of my own energy field. I feel energy being sucked like wind through me into the rooms of patients whose own energy fields are depleted and hungrily drawing on whatever is available for their healing. It takes me a while to not feel like I'm being pulled bodily into the rooms instead of relaxing and letting it come through me. St. Francis Hospital in Wichita is where I first know without doubt that I carry the Light.

In Spring of 1975, the men of the suborder finally make their exit in two Dodge stretch-vans. They are a brown-robed army traveling light with one suitcase each, while the Abbot carries the Abbey with him in his pocket. The priests in charge of the Fort

Worth house have accompanied us to Wichita, but they turn out to be on their way elsewhere, too. Information is given only on a need-to-know basis, and we learn that our class will be handed off to our First-Year School teachers, who will be arriving any day. Judging from the few words that filter through to me, we're in for something different.

20.

WHAT YOU CAN DO WITH THE RULES

Not for the first time this week, I find myself in a dumpster. With scores of dusty cardboard boxes to flatten and compress into the smallest possible space, it's easiest to just climb in there with them, armed with work gloves, a box cutter, and twine, and slowly assemble dozens of brown papery ingots. By and by, the blocks become my floor, then steps, and finally I'm standing high enough to jump out of the dumpster and land on the ground with a paratrooper's roll.

I'm being watched. I wave shyly to a woman who has appeared silently at the screened back door. Her black hair is pulled back into a severe bun that accentuates her thin face and the exophthalmic bulge of her green eyes. She is dressed in black Roman Catholic garb, modified into a trim jumper with a white clerical collar and an ebony cross suspended from a navy blue ribbon. Blue vapor extends through the screen as she draws pensively on a white Meerschaum pipe. A tiny child hugs her leg.

Reverend R. and her husband, Reverend J., are both from the South Side of Chicago, and they turn out to be a hoot. In no time, they and their growing family—two preteens and a toddler—colonize the house. My classmates and I find ourselves with a pair of interesting, oddball spiritual parents. Together with a life-vowed brother and sister who cook and run the house, they oversee the First-Year School, a period of training and immersion in Order life designed to prepare our class for life vows.

With time, the people of the Order, its teachings, and grand mission to help usher in the New Age become less foreign to me. I'm no longer totally immobilized by the high vibration, and I figure it's something you get used to, like living at high elevation in the mountains. Still, it never once occurs to me that I could learn to enjoy myself here.

In my spiritual early-adolescent state, I yearn for immutable rules to follow. I have concocted the idea that the daily routines of the Order are a sacrosanct method for enlightenment, all dictated from above, down to the way the dishes are dried and the particular brand of matzo used for Communion. I am scandalized when Reverend J. says in a sermon that the Spirit doesn't do well with rules. This relatively relaxed attitude asks me to loosen my death grip on what I think spirituality is about.

One evening, I enter the dining room and find a woman with white hair braided around her head in conversation with Reverend J. On the back of her blue hand-stitched tunic, it reads "25,000 Miles for Peace." The letters on the front spell "Peace Pilgrim." Reverend J. introduces her as an old friend of Father Paul, who gave her an open invitation to stay as long as she needs at any Order house in the world. After dinner, she tells her story. Years before, she had a spiritual awakening and started walking. If someone gives her a ride or offers shelter or food, she accepts, but never asks for it. She can stay with us as long as she likes, but she is there for only a night. Her task in this life is to keep walking back and forth across America until there is world peace. I am astounded that there could be such a person.

The house is in constant tumult. Compared to the Abbey, with its ironclad daily protocols, relieved by terrifying Abbot-inspired slapstick, the First-Year School is the opposite. Our two priests are parents of three precocious, high-energy children and, therefore, masters at rolling with whatever happens. They unapologetically throw curves and break up routines, lest anyone get complacent or think they can predict what's going to happen next. *Hold no thought, hold no concept.*

We read *The Practice of the Presence of God* by a seventeenth-century French monk named Brother Lawrence: "I have abandoned all particular forms of devotion, all prayer techniques. My only prayer practice is attention. I carry on a habitual, silent, and secret conversation with God that fills me with overwhelming joy." I routinely come home from my job at the hospital to find the whole first-year class down on the floor, silently scrubbing the carpet with toothbrushes, or standing on ladders, armed with putty knives, as they scrape chipped paint off the outside of the old Victorian house. Other days, everyone is carrying furniture and bedding, switching the men's and women's sleeping quarters in order to "rotate the yin and yang polarities" of the house.

One evening, I'm called into the office. *What have I done wrong?* Reverend R. sits me down and asks me how I'm doing. I hear myself saying things I think she wants to hear. Reverend J. opens a drawer and produces a bottle of Drambuie, fills a shot glass and slides it my way. He pours a glass for each of them and refills mine. The sweet brown liqueur warms me inside, but I accept the gesture from this big-hearted man with difficulty. They are reaching out, and I'm exasperated with myself for being hopelessly uptight. I hold my breath, near tears, and want to escape.

"Where were you before you came in the Order, Joshua?"

"Nashville."

"Nashville, no kidding! Who was stationed there?" The Order is a small world with an active grapevine for tracking who is where. I name the priest who put me through the Light experience while I was working at New Home.

"No kidding! So they sent him to Nashville! Now there's a strange guy. What'd you make of B.?" *The informality of first names only.*

My throat relaxes with the Drambuie. "He was intense, but I really liked him. But then he and the brothers were gone all of a sudden."

When I tell them about Reverend B.'s replacement, Reverend R. cracks up. "Oh my God! You got C.! What a tight-assed bitch!" They both crack up at the look on my face.

Reverend R. leans toward me with a conspiratorial smile. "Listen, Joshua, here's why I asked you to come in. We have to stay here this evening, and I wonder if you could run an errand for me. There's a cigarette machine at the gas station down the street. Would you go and get me a pack of Luckies?" She presses a quarter into my palm and holds it there a moment. "No filters, OK?"

It's a clandestine mission. In the Order, no one is *required* to smoke, but nearly everybody does—tobacco is an essential grounding agent in the Order, as is the meat consumed at many a meal. But an Order-wide regulation says pipes only.

It's another double-take moment for me, and Reverend R.'s laugh is high and sweet. Then she grabs my shoulders and shakes me. "Lighten up, Joshua! You're trying to be so good, but I wonder what you're really like on the inside. You can be yourself here, you know. I just can't stand smoking this stinking pipe all the time!"

21.

STONES IN A BAG

After getting gently "worked over" by Revs. J. and R., I begin to thaw out and become more at ease with the paradoxes of this life of rules and rule-breaking. As first-year students, we get used to constant change. The high vibration and divine presence infusing the house and the experience of living through massive amounts of inner experience in a single day make for a hothouse quality. We are told that, in terms of spiritual growth, a day in the Order is like a year "on the outside" (Ordertalk for the world outside the Order). The Order is an esoteric school, but our education is more about changes inside ourselves than accumulating hidden knowledge. The teachings we all think we are there for are but a sideshow to the internal changes we see reflected in each other's faces. Our bodies change in surprising ways: sudden weight loss or gain, even changes in shoe size, are not unusual. Upheavals come and go like cloud shadows on a windswept hillside.

Years later, I listen with big ears to a Leonard Cohen interview with Terry Gross as he describes his time from 1996 to 1999 as a monk at the Mt. Baldy Zen Center. He could easily be talking about life in the Order. Regardless of the forms it takes, monastic life amounts to a system for overthrowing the strong egos of hyper-idealistic twenty-two-year olds. It makes use of a young person's ability to abandon all for the sake of a burning ideal.

The Order shares a tradition common to all kinds of monastic orders, whether New Age or going back to early shamanic initiatory societies. You enter an arrangement like that in order to shed what you think makes up your identity, so that you and your fellow travelers can be transported, in Thomas Merton's words, "beyond the brim of the enamel world." In a setting like this, the person you believe yourself to be gets knocked off rather systematically.

Joining the Order throws me into a conundrum: despite a lifelong aversion to herd mentality, clubs, societies, cliques, fraternities, regimentation, military, school spirit, command performance family functions, and the like, I up and join an order in which individuality is not part of the program, in spite of Reverend R. telling me I can be myself. It only starts with different clothes, no hair, my changed name. I shed the social role, such as it is, that I've played up to now. I look around at others in the Order and see that everyone has shed many skins. Money, education, and former status in the world count for nothing. No one cares that you were once a great bass player or a badass biker or the hard-working respite director in a home for handicapped adults. We deliberately become marginal persons as far as the world is concerned, stones in a bag, rubbing up against a bunch of other stones in the same bag until we polish each other clean. That's the ideal, the monastic project.

As a novice and first-year student, I sleep in a room with triple bunks with eleven others. I wake at two a.m. to the sounds of a brother crashing into my dreams while performing blind T'ai Chi moves in the dark. My inner body vibrates with the visceral snoring music of another brother's deviated septum. In meditation, I slowly learn to live in a more infinite space within myself, reduce my internal reactivity, become less determined by external conditions. Despite the Order's New Age gloss, we are seeking to renew an age-old experience of enlightenment that monastics have sought for millennia. Even with the relatively easy-going life in the Wichita First-Year School, the foundation of Order life is conformity to a rule, daily subordination of our personal druthers, tastes, preferences, vanities, self-images, and illusions. It's a pattern of living that is ruinous if we insist on thinking we are hot shit. An order is something you enter in order to find out that you're not hot shit.

At five in the morning, the house steward wanders through the men's quarters singing "Morning Has Broken," a Celtic hymn made popular by Cat Stevens. Otherwise, the house is still as we rise like a silent army, dress, and snap our beds into shape. We make our way from our quarters to the bathroom and file into the chapel where we join the whole house on our knees for Communion. Housework fills the days for an army of sweepers and dishwashers who relentlessly scrub and dust behind and under every object. No corner of the house escapes a dose of militant, loving scrutiny.

My inner vocabulary lacks a word for the state I'm in, strangely devoid of personal memories and experiences that attach to just me. I have glimpses of being a cell in a vast body, a synapse in the "hive mind" of the Order where other, bigger things are taking place through the clatter of dishes and groceries. Classes and meditations fill the evenings and, despite my resistance, I sense a slow turning in me. I am glad I'm there.

Household tasks keep my hands busy while my inner world turns. Insights drop on me at odd times. On a coffee table in the living room, a copy of *Letters of the Scattered Brotherhood,* a quiet spiritual classic from the 1940s. The title plays in my mind and I have an intuition about the Order. *Together now in this present form, but only for a time and a season.* When I finally plop into my bed at night, so much has happened in me that I fall asleep immediately at the end of each year-long day.

My years in the Order, especially First-Year School, turn into my most concentrated time of immersion in the esoteric traditions that honeycomb history. This includes exposure to the Kaballah, Tarot, and astrology, alongside Buddhist, Hindu, and Western hermetic teachings. Required eclectic readings include the Catholic mystics, Dietrich Bonhoeffer, and Marie Corelli. I read Thomas Merton, Joseph Campbell, Samuel Lewis and cultivate a mystic's appreciation for allegories of spiritual processes in literature and science. In that spirit, I devour the books of Ursula K. Le Guin and Tolkien. For one of my book reports, I create a large pictorial chart illustrating Michael Faraday's *Chemical History of a Candle.*

Everything takes place in an atmosphere of reverence and spiritual discipline. We live a blend of Christian piety, a wry sense of New Age hipness, and a felt sense of kinship with every yogi that ever rolled his eyes back, every dervish that ever twirled around the sun, every hermit and anchorite that ever fasted and self-mortified, every nun that ever flew, and every shaman that ever clambered into the fourth world through the open door at the top of his head. Moreover, we believe ourselves to be anointed members of a spiritual elite. Despite my skittishness about joining the Order, once I get over my hang-up about the rules, I drink this all in. It's a full dose.

Looking back on this time, nearly five decades ago, I see this spiritual formation as a gift.

Is it real? Jazz pianist Les McCann would ask back, "Compared to what?" A better question would be: *Does it have a real effect?* It does. For a time and a season, the Order galvanizes my spiritual life. I am magnetized by its power and certainty. The Order reflects the mood of the time and the spiritual search that has broken out in earnest in most of the people I know. It's "millennial" in the traditional sense of a sincere belief that we are living through the change of an age.

22.

VOWS

In 1976, at the end of my time in Wichita, my classmates and I take life vows. The night before the vows ceremony, from evening prayers until morning Communion, we attempt the most complete examination of our lives that we can muster. Our knees and lower legs go numb from kneeling all night. We have taken root like trees in the darkened chapel, arms and hands outstretched like branches and leaves, hungrily gathering in every available photon of spiritual Light. This is our graduation, the culmination of eighteen months spent as novices and first-year students. We're all scared.

It's a curious, atavistic thing to do, considering my conceit when I first entered the Order that I would turn into one of God's Sunbeams, and that would be that. Most of us are in our twenties, true-believing New Agers, all interested in fast-track spiritual growth, and here we are, taking vows that harken back to the earliest human attempts to break away from the mass mind of their societies, align with the spiritual forces that undergird all of life, and allow themselves to be infused with Light. It's a radical, monastic version of "Turn On, Tune In, Drop Out."

One by one, we take vows of poverty, humility, service, and obedience, the latter being a monastic way of maintaining a military-style chain of command, and a clear hierarchy, presumably all the way up to God. The vows follow the ancient rationale of freeing the monk to pay attention to spiritual practice without the distractions of family or the marketplace. (Since there is marriage in the Order—somewhere down the line, we're told—the traditional vow of celibacy gets traded in for a vow of purity.) By now, we have had training and a period of living with training wheels versions of the vows we will be living under when we enter the main body of the Order as full members.

Even in a maverick, semi-monastic outfit like the Order, where vows look a bit different from those of traditional orders in the Catholic, Hindu, or Buddhist worlds, it's not hard to spot age-old monastic ideas about how these vows shape a person's worldview and inner life. Far from just being a set of vague agreements to stick around, act meek, take orders, and keep our genitalia to ourselves, these vows are part of the method behind the madness of joining a spiritual order. They act as agents of change in our psyche, bumpers that keep us on track, grinders that whittle away at our conditioning, time-release teachings that unfold as we attempt to live them, attitudes and tools for spiritual growth, and channels for the life force running through us.

The vow of poverty, for example, is a standard monastic vow: no personal money or property. I'm oddly relieved to land on my feet in a world of fewer personal things. On paper, it's a requirement laid on by the IRS so orders can claim certain exemptions as non-profit religious organizations. For the monk, however, the vow of poverty not only chips away at bedrock assumptions in the capitalist psyche, it is also a portal to the mystery of having access to more by owning less.

When I enter the Order in San Francisco, my dented but functional blue-green Samsonite suitcase is stowed in an attic. There, it joins the eternal ebb and flow of suitcases circulating through the world of the Order, and it ends up seeing more of the world than it would have if it had remained exclusively mine. Need a suitcase? Go up to the attic and pick one for *this* trip, but ditch the idea that it's *yours*. What's mine? Seven pairs of socks, seven sets of underwear with my name stitched into them, two sets of clerical garb and a robe, one set of work clothes, a pair of dress shoes, a pair of work shoes, my personal toiletries, a bible, and the book I am currently reading.

We're not begging-bowl monks by any stretch of the imagination. When I work a job out in the community, as a lot of Order members do, I turn over my pay as a one hundred percent donation to the Order. Living expenses, medical needs, and, in some circumstances, education are covered by the Order. Every Saturday, I get an allowance of five dollars so I can go to a movie or buy a pouch of Sail pipe tobacco. It's a mode of living, "holding all things in common," straight out of the New Testament depictions of the earliest Christian communities. With a vow of poverty in this semi-monastic community, I learn to see how money buys distance from the street, and I appreciate how far I am from it.

23.

MEN IN ROBES

"What if you get an erection?" Nobody laughs. It's a serious question, full of grave implications for all of us. The terrifying Abbot—the one who put the Abbey in his pocket in Wichita and reinstalled it in Detroit back when I was a first-year student—has been impressing upon us newly vowed brothers the surpassing grace bestowed on us to be wearing the sanctified robes of the spiritual renunciate, while also dispensing practical advice on robe management. It's the first time I have opened my mouth since arriving at the Detroit Abbey after taking vows. The Abbot takes a good look at me, and I get ready to fry.

Except for married Order members, the next step after life vows is to enter either the men's or women's celibate suborder for at least a year. This is the most traditional taste of monastic life the Order has to offer. The men's suborder wears tobacco-brown robes, vaguely Franciscan, vaguely Jedi Knight. It's a way different proposition from the black Romanesque clerical garb worn by the main body of the Order. In black clerical garb you can still find yourself in some remote sector of the Western Male Dress Code. You can still adopt a certain debonaire Oskar-Werner-as-Father-Teillard-de-Chardin-in-*The-Shoes-of-the-Fisherman* suave dreaminess. But robes are another deal altogether. Robes set a man apart lickety-split, and boy, you had better be ready. First, there is the cross-dressing thing that our homophobic culture frets about. Then, as soon as the cross-dressing piece falls away, you're left with the curiosity of people who will cross the street just to ask what the hell you're supposed to be. When you haven't figured that out for yourself, which I haven't, it makes for strange encounters.

"Robe training" in the celibate suborder is no joke. Robes accentuate the way I move my body and teach me empathy for women who get stared at by men. I learn a new sensory experience in robes that both inhibit and accentuate every move I make and hobble me when I take long steps. Even with long pants on underneath, thick polyester and wool robes electrify the hair on my legs in winter, and thin cotton robes—no long pants underneath—make me feel naked in summer. I learn to pick up my robe slightly when I walk up and down stairs, first one foot and then the other, so I won't catch my toe in the hem and trip and fall and really look foolish, even if I don't break my neck. The robe is held together by knotted cords, tied around my waist with loops hanging down to knee level. Robes have to be gathered and tucked into this cord if I want to run or play basketball. Cords also need to be under control at all moments to keep them from lassoing doorknobs and the arms of chairs and bringing all forward movement to an abrupt and violent stop. On a trip cross-country by Greyhound bus, I get to watch the un-handsome spectacle of a fellow newly-minted brother who, in his diuretic urgency to get off the bus at one of the scheduled potty stops, snags a seat arm with his looped cord. He jerks to an immediate halt as both his black-shoed feet leave the floor. He lands, spread-eagled on his back on the center aisle with his robe hiked up, revealing his mostly clean white Fruit of the Looms with his spiritual name stitched into them.

The year is 1976. Twenty-first century sexual sensibilities are not in evidence in male monastic robe training at the Abbey. In the classroom, we are all newly-vowed brothers, and I'm simply asking the question that is on everyone's mind. Try crossing a street wearing a thin robe in front of cars while they wait at a traffic light. Feel the cringe that steals through your body as drivers watch your ass move. You'll see what I mean. Try it when a strong headwind makes the fabric cling to your body like Saran Wrap. Now consider the anxiety of robe-wearing men when it comes to erections.

"Finally!" the Abbot lifts his eyes to Heaven. "Thank you, Brother Joshua! You might not be aware of it, son, but you've popped the only relevant question of the morning." He lets me bask in the glory of being a good little question-asker, then turns to address his captive audience.

"The rest of you keep asking questions about the 'esoteric significance' of The Robe. You ought to go get your heads examined! 'Will bullets bounce off my chest now that I'm wearing The Robe?' 'Would it be a good idea to be buried in The Robe?' 'Will the White Light infusing The Robe illuminate my path to the other side?' Great damned questions coming from you 'spiritual' gentlemen. You're all lying your heads off because each and every one of you is hornier than a TWO-PECKERED BILLYGOAT!"

We crack up, relieved. The terrifying Abbot is a gas when he gets going.

"Here's the thing, gentlemen, and I use the term very advisedly . . . you don't realize it now, but in the not too distant future you're all going to be *out there*." He sticks out his hitch-hiking thumb. "Out in stations all over the country. Some of you might even get sent out of the country. And guess what? A number of you are going to be counseling people who come to the Order house. And some of those people . . . get ready, brothers . . . are going to be *women*. And believe me, gentlemen, a woman can tune in to a horny priest or brother in nothing flat, and that is going scare the pants off some of you. Probably literally!

"You can laugh now, but in a year's time, I want you to count up how many times women have made it clear to you that you could have them as lovers. You think I'm kidding? Why,

107

there are women who are going to find you guys *exotic*. Don't ask me why. There are women who make a hobby out of getting priests in bed with them. They can't stomach the fact that you could love God more than you love them.

"Brother Joshua, bless the top of your pointed little head! The first answer to your question is this: If you get an erection, EVERYBODY'S GOING TO SEE IT! Second answer is: Whatever you do, keep it in your pants!"

Oakland, 1976

My first assignment after the Detroit Abbey is the Order outpost in Oakland, California. It's just across the Bay from San Francisco and Order headquarters, but we are expressly forbidden by the terrifying Abbot to come into that city. I live in rooms behind a small storefront just off Foothill Boulevard with two Order brothers. As everywhere, our main mission is to keep the patterns of the Order. Communion in the morning, work a job, walk the street in pairs in the evening, hold Sunday services for the public, and teach classes twice a week. All of these conventions are related, right down to the preference for leather soles on our shoes instead of rubber, to the spiritual transmission of which we are part.

The Oakland Order station is where I learn the fine art of preparing and teaching a class to an empty room. Nobody comes to our little storefront. Still, we set up a blackboard on a stand, arrange chairs in a semi-circle, give an opening prayer, and hold forth on matters of esoteric significance. We of the Order are part of a spiritual transmission that is not picky about who the recipients are—Saint Anthony preached the Gospel to the fish in the Marecchia River, after all—and we don't mind teaching any invisible beings that happen to be present. I get animated, physically and verbally, and jump with no problem over the surface absurdity of playing to an empty room. It's catnip for me.

One Tuesday evening, I'm all set up to teach New Age esoteric Christian things to throngs of discarnate beings. Tonight's lesson is from the Book of Acts about the high vibration events that start happening to Jesus's followers after the Resurrection, featuring the moment when Jesus appears to Saul of Tarsus and knocks him off his horse on the Road to Damascus. I tell the tale of my own out-of-body visit from an Order brother when I worked in a brick plant and other astral projection experiences I have had. I imply that many of us will be experiencing such things with the whole world's rising frequencies as the New Age progresses.

I'm about to launch into stories of mystics who can walk through walls and end with a reading from an Order favorite, *The Ways of the Lonely Ones* by Manley Palmer Hall, when a middle-aged man steps, hat in hand, through the front door of our storefront. He has the recently-shot-from-a-cannon look of an old Oakland street guy. He's respectful and quiet and stays through the entire class about the astral projections of the followers of Jesus. Rudy is one of our first regulars at Sunday services and classes.

One day, a man stops by to tell us that Rudy is in a hospital detox unit and having a hard time. Maybe we could go and see him. After dinner that evening, all three of us catch the bus to Highland Hospital where we are escorted by an elderly volunteer down miles of corridors and covered passages that stitch together the scores of buildings that make up the hospital complex. Eventually, we reach an annex that contains the Detox Unit. Rudy's room is at the end of a hall made dingy by the collective miasma of men going through DTs. But we are carriers of the Light, and we have a heart for those who have hit bottom. This is our wheelhouse.

At nine o'clock, visiting hours are over, and we take leave of Rudy. Instead of retracing our steps to the front entrance of the hospital, we decide to leave through the exit at the end of Rudy's hall. Once outside,we find ourselves in a walled courtyard, a genteel reminder of Oakland's Spanish architectural past, overlooking the traffic streaming down 14th Avenue. Further reconnaissance reveals that we are locked out of the hospital. No amount of knocking and "hello!"-ing manages to catch the attention of a nurse or volunteer. Because of the indestructibility conferred on us by our holy robes and the brimming confidence that comes with them, we improvise a breakout from the Detox Unit. It's a cool, starry Bay Area evening when, to the amazement of twenty or thirty drivers waiting for the light to turn green, three medieval figures in brown robes appear atop the Spanish wall of the Detox Unit and leap in unison to the sidewalk ten feet below, brown robes ballooning. They parachute at first, but then all hems head northward, revealing six pasty white legs and three sets of Order-issue undies, as they plummet to the street below.

Salt Lake City, 1977
It's a hot, wind-blown day on the streets of Salt Lake City, extra wide due to a vision had by Brigham Young. In accordance with Young's dream, water runs along gutters to keep the streets clean. It's morning rush hour. At a major intersection, four lanes of cars wait out a red light. The Mormon eyes of the drivers are fastened on a brown-robed figure making his way across, into the heavy wind that presses his robe against his body, revealing the details of his bones and flesh. That brown-robed figure is me. The Abbot's words about robes and hard-ons come flooding back to me. Thankfully, for once, I don't have one.

24.

ABBOT APPEARANCE

By the time I get to Salt Lake City in 1977, I have begun to like the relatively autonomous life of small Order stations. There is something about staying under the radar (in as much as you can actually do that in a brown robe in a city full of Mormons), keeping the Order's patterns, and plugging away with my spiritual practices that appeals to me. The Order is not about proselytizing or trying to covert anyone, and this suits me fine. The overriding belief is that we are carrying something special, a spiritual transmission that has an influence in the world and on the people around us just by showing up and being there. Each of us has gone through considerable changes in the process of becoming members of the Order, and people go through changes when they get around us.

I have never forgotten my early encounters with the terrifying, intense Abbot in Wichita, and the unsettling business about putting the Abbey in his pocket. Ever since that moment, not to mention the earlier episode when Jesus told him I was supposed to be in the Order, he has remained a potent figure in my psyche. I go through changes just sitting in the same room with him! Now, here I am in the suborder, under his direct command, and he's always there in the background, telescoping into my awareness at odd moments. As a result, it's not a complete surprise when I arrive home one day from my lumberyard job, open the door to the bedroom of the Order house, and find the terrifying Abbot himself standing there, beaming at me. Instantly, I'm riveted to the floor.

With no preamble, he says, "Brother Joshua, I've come to let you know about some changes. I'm getting 'kicked upstairs.' I've been promoted to Master Teacher, which means I will no longer be your Abbot."

I mumble something incoherent, but my powers of speech are disconnected. Then, he vanishes. Not with a poof of smoke or a crack of stage thunder or anything like that—he's just not there anymore. Suddenly, I can talk again, but my mind is a blank. The next day, three letters arrive, one for each of us brothers of the Salt Lake City Order station. It announces the promotion of the Abbot to Master Teacher and the appointment of the new temporary Abbot of the suborder, which turns out to be the Teacher who had me unceremoniously escorted out of the Chicago house on my first run at the Order.

In a postscript, I'm informed that I am being reassigned.

25.

Northwest Passage

Boise, Idaho, 1977

Relocation. I get off the Greyhound in Boise and spend the night at the apartment of a priest of the Order. I'm traveling solo for the first time as a brother, momentarily free from the strictures of Order life. Reverend H. is obviously not interested in the protocols of Order hierarchy. He greets me in jeans and a flannel shirt. We eat baked beans and salad and wash it down with a shared can of beer. That evening, we see *Close Encounters of the Third Kind.* We talk until midnight about Light Beings arriving in spaceships and how that's all right around the corner as we approach the Change of the Age. It's a moment of camaraderie I haven't experienced before in the Order. I let go to the feeling that I am part of something big and cosmic, all set off by a Steven Spielberg film and a momentary whiff of friendship and equal footing with another person. The next morning, I get back on the bus, and I'm off to my new assignment in Portland, Oregon.

Portland proves to be a full dose. By this time, I have middling status as a vowed brother in the men's suborder, and I become the steward for not one but two houses, one of them a First-Year School, in the northwest quadrant of the city. In no time, I'm in way over my head. I need to be more organized than I've ever been, focused and ahead of the curve in all matters. As steward,

I am also the purchaser, so I need to learn the city pronto. But I get lost every time I venture out on shopping runs, which throws my schedule off. There's a pesky off-ramp I never figure out, and I keep ending up across the Columbia River into Vancouver, Washington, while others are waiting for me back at the house.

Besides being the steward, I'm also the cook. Three meals a day for twenty-five active adults in the Portland First-Year School. I don't know what I'm doing. Right off the bat, I singe all the hair off my head and face when the giant gas oven blows. I dive into *The Tassajara Cookbook* and *Diet for a Small Planet* with all its nifty ways to coax more protein out of specific food combinations, but my arithmetic fails me when recipes have to be multiplied by twelve. To make things worse, I'm still figuring out the difference between tsp. and Tbsp. I also learn too late that there is a difference between baker's yeast and brewer's yeast. I heap tons of the former into a recipe that calls for the latter. While the brothers and sisters are praying over their meal, I'm down on my knees in the kitchen, praying for their lives as I imagine their abdomens inflating and exploding.

Every day hits me with debacles like this, small and mostly non-life-threatening. I'm at the rock bottom of every single learning curve, and I get the message that I'm not good at anything. Two evenings a week, I have to teach classes to the first-year students and pretend to know what I'm talking about.

The Portland house runs me ragged, and I don't wear it well. The Order operates at the intersection of the Peter Principle (promotion until you reach your level of incompetence) and an ethos that thrusts you into difficult situations so you can overcome your limitations. By this time, it is all too obvious that I'm incompetent to manage two houses, but Order logic demands that I stay on as cook and steward. To compound matters, for my failings, I get relentlessly dressed down by the priest in charge. The Order's hierarchy is, in my mind, still monolithic. I am bruised but unenlightened by his constant criticism, and I take way more of this than is good for me. I know nothing of the therapeutic benefits of telling a bully to fuck off and suffer the humiliation of allowing myself to be pushed around.

Instead, I turn mute. My throat *chakra* implodes so badly that it sticks out the back of my neck, and my inner contradictions about even being in the Order rear their heads. My whole project as a holy man is unraveling on me. I feel like a bag of shit all the time, and I stay that way as winter melts into spring, and finally summer, when bags of shit really begin to smell.

Relief of sorts comes in a couple of unexpected ways. Up to this point, I haven't met anyone in the Order who is willing to get in the face of the priests and teachers. Life in the Order is so geared toward self-abnegation and setting aside your own will that it breeds sheep. It's time to meet a goat.

Evenings in the Portland house, when the kitchen is put to sleep and the first-year students are busy with their studies, my time on non-teaching nights is my own for a couple of hours. I walk around the block to a neighborhood movie house that plays genre films. Currently, they have two "festivals" running, switching off between Marx Brothers and classic Samurai films. An inveterate fencesitter, I decide to go to both.

Animal Crackers is a revelation and shows me something about the state I'm in. I'm so pent up that I completely lose it in the theater. I laugh until I'm sobbing. I watch the extras cracking up in the backgrounds of scenes where the Marx Brothers go off script and stay there. When I learn that the film was released in 1930, an insight drops into me. This insanely stupid, funny film came along in the thick of the Depression, following the stock market crash of '29. It was tailor-made medicine for a freaked-out nation. And now, *Animal Crackers* drops into the thick of my own depression. I become a Marx Brothers addict. They save my soul in a way that all the Order discipline doesn't.

The "Samurai Festival" is actually an Akira Kurosawa festival. The Japanese master and his versatile, feral collaborator, Toshiro Mifune, wind me around their fingers and manage to scratch a different itch. The Marx Brothers help me laugh and unpent, but Kurosawa and Mifune deliver a medicine I can't name.

It's a different audience for the Samurai films. One evening, as the house lights come up, I spot Brother John sitting by himself. Like me, John is a brother in the suborder, but he has taken a different path to the Portland house. He has a gig with a charitable non-profit in the city and is seldom seen at the house.

We talk. Kurosawa. Cabbages and kings. The Order. We go for beer, and I loosen. Together, we chip in and buy the Order house a paperback copy of *Shogun*. John proceeds to "chop" and cleverly bind the fat book into three volumes, a way of sharing the read with others, starting with the two of us. I watch with big eyes. John keeps a motor scooter hidden in the bushes around the corner from the Order house. I'm thrilled by his clandestine possession and the freedom of joyriding all over Portland. On a high summer evening we are a pair of brown-robed figures on an old Vespa with chipped maroon paint, nearly getting whooshed to our deaths by semis off the Fremont Bridge, hoods flying, high above the Willamette River.

One day, I overhear him in a shouting match with the boorish priest in charge. My ears immediately pick up on the fact that Brother John is addressing this "superior" by just his first name and, whatever they are on about, he isn't backing down. John's voice jumps into my ear: "Let's get something straight, my friend: I work in conjunction with you, not *for* you." Equal footing again. More medicine.

Somewhere deep inside me, an embedded rusty screw begins a slow quarter turn. I'm twenty-nine in the summer of 1978 when an official letter arrives for me. The return address on the envelope bears the fiery cross nestled in the circle, square, and triangle of the Order's logo. It's from Order Headquarters in San Francisco.

26.

ORDAINED . . . INTO WHAT?

The letter from Order Headquarters is proof that God's mercy is infinite. I read it a second time before the full content sinks in. I'm being sprung from the odium of stewarding the Portland houses and transferred to the Order house in Cologne, Germany. Except for speaking university-level German, a fact buried somewhere in my file at Headquarters, I have done nothing to request this reassignment. It's a dream come true. Things move fast and, for once, I'm not dragging my feet. In less than a month, I'm back at Order Headquarters in San Francisco and find myself in a rare world between the worlds as I await deployment.

After my year as a poor schlemiel in Portland, I am suddenly full of optimism about my calling. The Order's Headquarters in San Francisco is arguably the busiest of all Order houses and, for once, as I wait to be transferred, I have nothing to do. Eventually, the gods of housework details catch on, and I am assigned the job of night guard, which means I sit on the front stoop of the Order house and talk with street folks who wander into Duboce Park from the Tenderloin at three in the morning. Several nights of this put me in a strange sleep pattern. One morning, while the house is bustling all around me, I dream that a small hand-printed billboard is dangling in front of my face. On it are words in clear print: "GO REQUEST ORDINATION."

The idea of asking for what amounts to a promotion, just before I am to head out for Germany, is absurd. I'm no star in the Order, and my time in Portland was anything but distinguished. Besides, going from being a simple brother to an ordained minister or priest would mean taking on more responsibilities than I'm ready for. I turn on my side to make the billboard go away.

When it doesn't go away, I take my dream to the next meeting of the Esoteric Council, the ones whose unerring judgment decides such things as who gets ordained. They hear my tale and send me out of the room so they can deliberate the strange request. I'm so nervous about my uncharacteristic, audacious move, I walk a valley in the common room, drink left-over breakfast coffee, and pee five times. I'm sure they're going to tell me to apply to be in the ministerial ordination class like everybody else, either that or turn me down flat.

When I'm called back into the council chamber, the Director informs me that I will be ordained in two weeks and that my transition to the Cologne Order house will be my training. In a mystical outfit like the Order, pronouncements like this coming from on high are always fraught with portent. The strong implication is that *things would be happening to me* between San Francisco and Cologne that will amount to a fast-track ministerial training. I tell myself to expect the unexpected.

The Order's Ford van shuttles a number of brothers and sisters to the Forestville retreat center. It's a relaxed rural setting near Santa Rosa where Order members can swim and hike in the Sonoma County hills and get a respite from their lives in a spiritual pressure cooker. All except for me. I am sent directly to the chapel to prepare for ordination: three days of seclusion, again with instructions to make a thorough review of my life.

For two endless days, my body fidgets, and my mind spins. I can't settle or meditate or sleep. I'm back in the seclusion of my first entry into the Order, this time due to a dream and this crazy bone business of asking to be ordained.

At the peak of my agitation, Master I. looks in on me. She is tall and silent with a wreath of auburn braids around her freckled face. Up to this point in my Order life, she has always been in the background. I have never even heard her speak. She invites me into a side chapel and stands behind me as I sit in the sanctuary. I feel her hand on my back, light fingertips on a single vertebra of my mid-spine. Her touch is comforting, but also highly specific, as if it could only be this spot on this vertebra. All by itself, my breathing changes and I fall into a spacious stillness. An inner veil drops. I lose my bearings and, in a sudden crescendo, I feel myself expanding and contracting from this very point on my spine. I enter a place deep in my body where I hid my twelve year-old's premonitions about my mother's impending death. Master I.'s touch has located a tiny nexus of body and memory, not more than a few cubic millimeters in terms of flesh-volume, locked away and numbed out for years, that went without an anesthetic through the operation of losing her. Grief swells out of me, wet and hot, as I mourn the loss of my mother and the fracture of my childhood. I mourn the sacrifice of my young adulthood on the altar of my spiritual ideals. I mourn how utterly out of step I am with my era and my time of life.

The night after I'm ordained, I continue to keep vigil in the chapel. My senses are sharp, my nerve endings extended in all directions. In the darkness, the whir of an insect invades my ears, accompanied by a perfume I can't identify. I fan the air to keep the little buzzer away from my face, but he's elusive. Turning on the light reveals nothing, so I turn it off. Soon, I'm Brailling my way along the dark halls of the sleeping house, following the buzz and the perfume. The chapel is at the far end of one long wing of the sprawling ranch house. At the far end of the opposite wing is the kitchen where the buzz and the scent are leading me. The high pitched drone turns out to be the refrigerator as it cycles. I open the door and there before my eyes is the perfume source, an apple wrapped up in a Baggie.

1978, Forestville, CA: Just after my ordination.

The open refrigerator is a sudden island of light. When it closes, I am once again blind. I retrace my steps down the black tunnel of the hall. Instead of returning to the dark chapel, I find the back door and step, dazed, out of the ranch house into the luxuriant late summer night. I stand at the door, immobile, and the world falls silent. The smell of baked mineral earth enters my nostrils and the cricket choir starts again. Over me, new stars wheel the enormous indigo sky.

Outdoors under that sky, I'm calm, as if I've finally found a container large enough for my charged aura. The small swimming pool beckons. I stash my clothes under a heavy tarp and slip in. Cool water strokes my body with no obstructions. My skin shouts relief. I close my eyes and float on my back, far from anyplace I have ever been before, my anxieties replaced for the moment by night, stars, water, peace.

By and by, daybreak, and I can hear the first rustlings of activity in the house. I don't want to get caught naked in the pool. My Wichita upbringing flits in and out. I remember the atmosphere of taboo around our bodies and other things we didn't talk about, the way mouths would tighten and voices would dip when speaking words like "bathroom" and "bowel movement." In the heavenly pool water, I'm unashamed, but I have no idea how the newly-ordained are supposed to act. I slip out and hide under the tarp where my clothes are stowed and hear a couple of brothers walk by on their way to do maintenance on the retreat grounds. Invisible, I am deliciously, sensually hidden under the tarp, a secret stowaway animal, ordained into the feeling, absent for my whole life, and more so in my spiritual life, of my own body.

27.

Learning To Savor The World

In late August of 1978, I fly out of San Francisco, the first leg of a journey that will ultimately take me to Germany. In the meantime, I am allowed a short vacation between Order assignments. For two weeks of relative freedom I bounce around the map, visiting family members, two of whom I see for what turns out to be the last time. During the whole trip, I'm still reeling from the effects of my recent experiences. I have fits of manic laughter, busting emotional buttons every time I turn around. I am suddenly too big for my own body.

But for her name on the door, I wouldn't have recognized the skin and bones resting uncomfortably in a fetal curl in the hospital bed as my grandmother. The bed's side rails are up to prevent escapes, but she is barely conscious, and I have to identify myself three times. Smells of dead skin and urine compete with Lysol.

She tries to focus, but the effort is a lot for her. "John-Pat-Jim-Bruce (her patented method of getting grandson names right) . . . You're Jim," she finally declares in a voice that is mostly air.

"Yes, I'm Jim."

She points an unsteady, arthritic finger at something across the room. "Go to the closet. There's a box. Bring it."

In the box, right on top, a creased black and white photo

of a horse suspended in mid-air over a white picket barrier. On its back, gripping tight handfuls of reins and black mane behind the horse's head, a young girl in jodhpurs and white long-sleeved shirt, dark vest, and white riding cloche. Her skinny butt is a foot off the saddle, and she's crouched low, halfway up the horse's neck, with a look of feral concentration that would frighten Greta Thunberg. My mother, at thirteen. For my grandmother, this is the child who died.

"I want you to have this," she says, then turns her face back to the wall.

My mother at thirteen.

I go south to visit my step-sister and borrow her car, following the white rabbit of an urge. Denizens of a roadside stop tell me to drive on Highway 1 to a place two miles south of Marine World and look for a break in the metal guardrail along the ocean side of the road. Sure enough, when I climb down the perilous embankment to ocean level, I discover a "free beach" with scores of naked people enjoying the sun and surf. Later, I visit my aunt and uncle in their golf cart community in Sun City, Arizona. At night, all I have to do is slide open the glass door of my bedroom, creep out, deposit my clothes on the patio, and go sprinting among the greens and sand traps. My skin tingles in the dry desert air with the sounds of javelinas and night birds all around me.

I arrive at the Order community in Cologne as a closet nudist.

My early acculturation in Germany coincides with the first broadcasts of the American TV series *Holocaust,* now dubbed into German. This triggers waves of denialist backlash and threats of firebombs to television stations. Less than a year later, the denial turns to grudging acceptance and self-flagellation as scores of Holocaust articles and books by German authors appear. A television series airs, *Blut und Eisen, Blood and Iron,* even more damning than its American counterpart, as Germany begins to face its past.

I learn my new world through the veil of a new language and my own cultural prism. In my eagerness, I venture out into this two-thousand-year-old former Roman colony and accost strangers on the bus to ask their help with some point of German vocabulary or grammar, only to find that Cologne speaks a French-kissed dialect of German, *Kölsch,* leftover from the time of Napoleon's occupation of the city. On forays into the countryside around Cologne, I find rural folk with epicanthic eye folds, genetic reminders of the Mongol hordes that long ago made it this far west, which gives substance to ancestral fears, quite alive in modern Germans, of being overrun by invaders and immigrants from the East. I myself manage to slip the category of "invader." As an American, even one in some kind of strange order, neither Roman Catholic nor Protestant, but one who is trying so desperately to learn their language, I am a "good foreigner."

This is my first Saturn Return, that point in a person's life around twenty-eight years of age when astrologers predict a tendency for everything to take a turn all at once. I'm still absorbing the changes in my world. In less than six weeks, I've been plucked out of my abysmal life as hapless steward at the Portland houses, taken seriously by the Order's Esoteric Council after a morning vision, thrown into the spin cycle of a fast-track ordination and promotion into the middle ranks of the Order's hierarchy, and sent to what may as well be another planet. I discover the beauty and upliftment of administering the sacraments, invoking a Higher Power, and feeling a new degree of spiritual transmission come through me. All the while, I'm also silently chewing on whatever it was that happened to me under the poolside tarp the night after I was ordained.

It's fast. It's heady, a full dose, but I'm into the grand adventure of it, eager to stretch myself over cultural and personal lines. My command of German grows like crabgrass in all directions as I sink into my surroundings. Over time, all of us in the Cologne house catch on that the Order's bushy-tailed New Age go-getter style doesn't blend well with a culture that is old and cynical, and yet mature and clear-eyed in the ways of the world and the kind of spirituality it takes to live in it. Our provincial sense of American exceptionalism wanes, along with our smug sense of mission as a spiritual elite, here to show the locals a thing or two about higher consciousness.

It turns out that we have way more to learn from Germany than Germany has to learn from us. Every day is a winding path as we take the bus to jobs and plod home, exhausted and amazed. Evenings, we sit around the dinner table with gobsmacked tales of how things are just *different* here in Europe. Peanut butter, we're outraged to learn, is unobtainable, except at a health food store where it must be special-ordered. We lay in a five liter supply of this staple of the Order diet. Typically, it's the little things that deliver the message we are in a new world.

My own friction point is the work I find in the city. Thanks to an Order connection, I translate news stories for the British Forces Broadcasting Service and for *Deutsche Welle,* the German-language equivalent of the Voice of America. But even with all my Order training to be a vehicle for the Light and a catalyst for change, I have no grand sense of mission. I'm a stranger in a strange land, a jumble of worldly and spiritual identities. I have no "higher purpose" in mind other than discovery. In Cologne, I decide, like E. B. White, that instead of trying to save the world, it's often better to just savor it.

One evening, all members of our growing household sally forth to dine in a Greek restaurant, where my palate loses its virginity to a dish of prawns braised in a garlic-feta sauce. That night, an impending late summer thunderstorm electrifies the atmosphere. I awaken in a state of agitation. Silently, I open the back door right next to the bedrooms of sleepers and slip out into the walled garden. Beatles lyrics come to me: "Stepping outside, she is free . . . " Lightning cracks white, followed a second later by deafening thunder. If any of my holy Order brothers or sisters were peeking out their window at that moment, they would be mortified, or amused, see my newly ordained naked body running in circles around the giant chestnut tree, photo-negative in the light show, jumping and pirouetting like a lunatic in the downpour.

1979: Order members in Cologne, Germany

28.

The Accidental Teacher (Take 1)

The lofty stated mission of the Order is to "guide all of mankind and the churches to Union with the Divine Self of God within, the Divine Spark." It's quite a load to guide all of mankind to anything, especially a teaching with so many capitalized words. We have loads of this sort of rhetoric on our tongues by the time we are vowed and ordained Order members. Fortunately, it's also a school of initiation. This means that, in addition to having a lot of rarified language in our heads, all of us have been put through experiences with Light and carry a strong belief in our ability to be a channel for something big and wonderful to come through us when we mingle with the world. When it comes to outside jobs, the Order's ethos is clear: take any job you are offered, knowing you'll be covered by the invisible host of guides and angels that are watching over you. Your real job is to get out among regular people and carry the Light.

The German Labor Office sees it differently. In Germany, jobs fit together like the teeth of a gear wheel with the training available in the educational and vocational system. It's a country in which everything is "normed." That means, for example, that every Made in Germany sheet of paper will fit into every Made in Germany envelope, provided you fold it correctly. And every one of those envelopes will fit precisely into the inside pocket of every Made in Germany men's dress jacket. And on and on. International standards for paper size based on the German DIN system (*Deutsche Indus-*

trienorm) are used in many parts of the world.

One result of all this norming is a Germanic form of relaxation that sets in when everything fits together with everything else. The obvious fly in the ointment appears when things *don't* jibe: a single delayed train can leave day-long domino effects rumbling up and down the country. With the centuries of wars and upheavals wound into the DNA of their collective memory, many of the older Germans I meet seem to know all too well what chaos is like and therefore thrive on predictability. For this reason, German employers are filled with suspicion when a job applicant applies for a position outside the narrow confines of his or her specific training. The idea that the skills of a person trained to stuff pork sausages might transfer to stuffing *beef* sausages without massive retraining is a stretch for some job counselors at the Office of Labor. Experience is good, I'm told after my stint as a translator dries up, but apparently I have *too much* of it, having a number of jobs on my resume, which makes me hard to fit into the system.

The Labor Office places me in a job counting tires and fan belts in a Goodyear warehouse right down the street from the Order house. Ostensibly, I'm only there to help out as temporary labor. At the same time, I'm given to understand that this position is mine for as long as I want it. I don't understand what's going on. There are winks and nods—*who's going to know?*—and the duck-face shrugs Germans use when getting around rules and regulations. This is all coming at me in *Kölsch,* the local dialect, which I'm struggling to understand. Little by little, I piece the story together. The employee I'm filling in for has gone into the hospital for an operation, and the wrong organ has been removed. He's expected to die soon. In spite of everything being normed, shit happens, even in Germany. I *think* that's what they're telling me. *Would they pull my leg about something like that, me, a gullible foreigner?*

After three weeks of dust and tractor tires, I'm met at the warehouse door by a red-haired man. He's wearing my smock. My predecessor has risen from his deathbed and is now rubbing his ruddy thick-fingered hands together, obviously eager to get back to his V-belts and steel-belted radials. It doesn't seem to bother him one bit that the wrong organ has been removed. It's none of my business, of course, but I ask him about it. His Kölsch German is totally incomprehensible to me, but his dismissive gestures are unmistakable: *a real man doesn't let a thing like that get him down.*

I'm laid off now, free to find other employment, so the next morning I make a phone call to a small private language school. The phone rings and rings with a slight echo, as if the signal has had to bounce off satellites through eight or nine time zones to reach a phone on the other side of the world. The receiver is finally snatched from its cradle with a "chinggg!" and a rapid-fire last name. I ask if the school needs an English teacher. Instead of asking me about my qualifications, the voice at the other end of the world says to come right away, and to please hurry. I sense the desperation in the man's voice, and I'm on the next bus downtown.

At the street entrance, I ring the school's bell. The door unlatches immediately with a hard metallic snap that reverberates through the stairwell. I climb two dark flights and poke my head through the open door of a second-floor office filled with blazing orange plastic furniture. A head topped with limp rings of auburn hair darts out of a classroom to see who has come in. My eyes blink involuntarily to make sure they are seeing correctly. The man is the spit and image of Gene Wilder in *Willy Wonka & the Chocolate Factory.* He dashes through the room in a fit of manic fury, busier than the proverbial one-armed paper hanger, as he straightens and restraightens the orange furniture and fusses with papers and multi-colored pens with plastic flowers on their ends. Before I can introduce myself, he stops abruptly, and groans in the direction of the ceiling. I have arrived at a moment of crisis.

"You're the one who called?" His words are fired at me like bee-bees. I tell him I am.

"And you're sure you really speak English?" I assure him I do. He checks his wristwatch, closes his eyes and slaps his forehead with the flat of his hand, *"Ach du Je!"* End of interview.

The next thing I know, I'm being dragged through the street to the nearest taxi stand. We jump in a cab, and for the next thirty minutes we plow through stop-and-go city traffic while he regales me with his predicament, all the while thanking me profusely for saving his ass. Only three days ago, he says, his entire staff mutinied. They took off with the school's cash drawer and the Rolodex with all the school's client contacts. Willy Wonka wants me to know that he regards each and every one of them as insufferable *Gesindel* and ungrateful *Mistmenschen,* and that—mark his words—he intends to sue. They've left him holding the bag on contracts that he has to fulfill, now without any teachers. *Ach du Je!* And so it comes to pass that, at noon that day, I am introduced as the new English Teacher at the *Gesellschaft für Reaktorsicherheit,* the Nuclear Safety Commission. What could go wrong?

I'm a natural. I've been speaking English all my life, after all, and I've had a few years of college German, which ought to count for something. Not only that, I also discover that I am possessed of a certain God-given *je ne sais quoi* when it comes to teaching languages. For the next two years, I teach English to the nuclear safety experts. Interspersed with business English, I tell them Kansas and Wichita stories. In the process, I become a little ambassador for the Sunflower State and the Air Capital of the World. I tell them about Satchel Page and the big airplane that crashed in a neighborhood in North Wichita. I tell them about cowboys *im wilden Westen* and treat them to the incomprehensible story of how a landing strip for crop dusters in rural Kansas became the Fredonia International Airport for one week. I show them how to speak just like they do in Kansas by gently biting down on the insides of their cheeks and talking without opening their mouths. I tell whoppers about "wheat surfing" across the "amber waves of grain" and about the giant tornado that took a chunk out

130

of the Kansas State Capitol building in Topeka in 1966. I learn to stretch out as a storyteller, help these nuclear reactor experts relax, improve their secondary vocabulary, and make up a lot of irrelevant hogwash. It seems to work out, as long as it's in correct English and entertaining.

When Willy Wonka tries to hire me out as an interpreter at a trade fair for the perfume industry, I rebel. There, I learn the hard way that real professional interpreters are a subspecies of human unto themselves. They are mutants, and they're not cheap to hire. It only starts with needing a near-native command of both the source and target languages, as well as serious knowledge of the vocabulary and idioms of the subject matter. True simultaneous interpreting requires going into an altered state of consciousness, a specialized trance, in order to toggle freely between language worlds.

As an interpreter, I'm found to be an imposter in short order by the *parfumieres* at the conference who politely tell me to take a seat. I'm embarrassed, but I stick around long enough to jump over my own shadow, eat their sandwiches, and drink their Gewürztraminer. There, I get to watch a genuine specimen of the of the German◇English interpreter subspecies at work. To me, it's poetry in motion to watch such an agile-minded true citizen of the world.

I quit at Willy Wonka's Orange Plastic Language Factory for putting me in that miserable position and promptly find another job I'm not qualified for, this time teaching German to *Gastarbeiter* kids in Düsseldorf. But what the hell? The Light is with me, so it's okay.

Change in the Air

I'm enjoying my life. A world-bridger at heart, I relish having one foot in my identity as a New Age holy man and one in the immigrant scene of Cologne and Düsseldorf as a teacher of Turkish youngsters. I live in a polyglot house where everybody nurses a similar sense of adventure about what they are doing. For an Order house, it's very live-and-let-live, as the cosmic ideals of the Order, so much in the foreground in the States, take a back seat to the everyday tasks of communal living. Simple Order patterns of daily Communion and nightly study and prayer are a safe haven for me as I explore my ex-pat world in Cologne. On paid vacations from work, I travel with my brother to Yugoslavia and to Rome with my father and step-mother. For a time and a season, I'm in my element.

The European Order houses in Madrid, Bordeaux, Amsterdam, and Cologne are somewhat isolated from the main body of the Order in these pre-Internet years. Snail mail takes its sweet time, and international phone calls are only for urgent communiques. Still, the Order is an organism with its own telepathic network. Like redwoods joined by underground root systems and webs of fungal mycelia, we sense significant changes percolating through the forest of our community. Some have to do with events in the world at large and some with ticking time bombs baked into the culture of the Order. And yet, when I arrive in Cologne in 1978, the transformation that the Order is about to go through, like the transformation of Gregor Samsa in Franz Kafka's *Metamorphosis,* who wakes one morning to find he has become a beetle, is unforeseen by most of us.

1980, Düsseldorf: With one of my classes of Turkish teenagers.

29.

WHEN THE END OF THE WORLD DOESN'T COME

"Do not expect too much from the end of the world."
~Stanislaw Jerzy Lec

In the Order, we have plugged into something different from the world we have known, something big, living, and electric that enables us to stride around the city in Roman Catholic clerical garb and spread Light. We can look you in the eye and say with conviction that the Veil between Heaven and Earth is getting so thin that it's only a matter of a few years until the New Age will be upon us in full. In our way, we are like those Puritans who believed the Apocalypse was set to arrive in 1666. I also liken it to the "Great Disappointment" of the Millerites, the American Christian sect whose leader calculated that the Second Coming of Christ would happen in 1843. Miller's followers took to wearing their white Ascension Robes and waiting on hills and rooftops to be lifted up in glory into Heaven while crowds mocked them from the streets. At the time I entered the Order, this meant sometime around 1976. It's now November of 1978, and we haven't ascended.

Two months after I am assigned to the Cologne house, over nine hundred people at the Jonestown People's Temple in Guyana drink cyanide-laced Kool-Aid in a mass suicide. Overnight, the world is on edge about cults. In response, the Order's newly installed Director General, Father A., immediately

133

begins a campaign to align the Order and its public image with mainstream Christianity. He publishes erudite articles in the Order's glossy publication, *Epiphany,* to establish the Order's theological bona fides, taking great pains to distinguish between a sect (which the Order is, according to the Director) and a cult (which it isn't). In the early 1980s, he has a pivotal encounter with an Orthodox priest, himself something of a renegade. Father A. begins to steer the Order in the direction of Orthodox Christianity, which strikes a number of us, myself included, as bizarre. But not everyone, obviously. In the years that follow, a significant number of Order members disavow the "heresy" of the Order's esoteric roots and become Orthodox monastics, while the rest disperse. The faint sound I think I hear during that period is Father Paul turning over in his grave.

After Jonestown, the message comes through from the Director General about how mainstream and unesoteric we're now supposed to be, not members of some nasty cult. Keep the fact that you believe in reincarnation and the interdimensional transmission of the Light of Christ through the Anointed Vehicle of your consecrated body under your hat. Just get out there and mingle with regular people and serve. Be it and do it, rather than talk about it. Fair enough. In Cologne, most of us are ex-pats, and we have each carved out our little niches in the community. We keep up the Order patterns and lifestyle, and we carry on.

As these changes are getting going, two wheels of life are turning in the Order as a whole and in the Cologne house in particular. One is turning too slowly, and one too fast. The first wheel is this: when the New Heaven and New Earth fail to fully manifest in the late 1970s, and I haven't been translated into another dimension, the allure of Order life begins to ebb. I'm not alone in this. The Order's early promise of fast-track spiritual transcendence seems to not be coming true. We already have the robes, and our own vibrational levels have certainly gone up over the years in the Order, but the world at large is taking longer.

Meanwhile, another wheel is turning, a biological one.

Whether we admit it or not, a number of us Anointed Vehicles of the Light are starting to squeak and shimmy and blow little gaskets. I'm starting to get squirrelly in ways that go beyond my turn as a secret nudist. I have bounced around the map with the Order, having been reassigned eight times in four years, and questions are seeping up from the sub-basements of my mind about what the hell I'm doing. I'm no longer a twenty-two-year-old brickyard hermit gorging on meditation and spiritual teachings. I'm no longer running from my putative calling to the Order (I couldn't lick it so I joined it), but no longer the picture of the obedient Order brother, no longer automatically willing to act out the patterns of an ideal spiritual community.

At the time of my ordination and transfer to Germany, I reach the end of my tenure in the celibate men's suborder. The vow of celibacy has been unexpectedly liberating, allowing me to focus on my spiritual growth. But two years of that is enough, and I feel the difference as soon as I put on the garb of the main body of the Order. And every time I turn around, I whack the crazy bone of my Scorpio Moon, which is trying to tell me that something is missing from my life.

30.

THE ORDER MATING GAME

As the median age of Order members edges into the mid-thirties, a bio-switch flips. Overnight, it's mating season in the Order. Libido and longing are sleeping in bed next to us, sitting at the dinner table, meditating and praying in the chapel right alongside us. For all its resonance with traditional Christian monasticism with its cloisterish trappings, suggesting a celibate, single lifestyle, the Order has married couples and families. The Order is co-ed and has been from the get-go, with equal everything among genders. According to Order lore, Father Paul resisted this when he first got his vision of the Order, but he began ordaining women as well as men and allowing married couples to join.

For all its New Agey-ness, the Order has quaint rules about "courting." There are even some arranged marriages dating back to the early years of the Order's history, pairings decreed by Father Paul. For the rest of us in the looser years post-Father Paul, natural attraction gets to work in a circumscribed way. The spoken rule is that you have to get permission from Headquarters to spend time with someone to whom you feel an attraction. The unspoken assumption was that romantic energies will be heterosexual, and that a prospective mate will come from within the Order's pool of potential partners. As a result, "playing the field" varies: where you are located determines the field you get to play. While Order members in the U.S. are routinely moved around a lot and therefore have a chance to meet and mix, international relocations are more difficult, what with visas and language differences. We in European stations are relatively stable in our assignments and therefore stuck with the Order men and women we find *in situ*. I try, and fail, to imagine myself married to any of the women in the European houses. My one brief fling of officially sanctioned "courtship" with one of the women in the Cologne house, comes, by mutual agreement, to naught. Within a year, she splits and marries a Frenchman.

I'm in a jam. I know in my bones that I won't be turning into a Sunbeam any time soon. Without the prospect of imminent Ascension or relocation to another Order house, either of which would have sufficed to get me out of there, I begin to look askance at the other members in the Cologne and European Order community. The prospect of living with these folks long term, going into my thirties, single with no other mating prospects than the females in the immediate Order vicinity, is sobering. I want out, but I'm a long way from admitting it to anyone, especially in the Order.

A Word About Orders and Doubt

Unspoken rules and regs apply. In a community like the Order, with high spiritual and renunciate ideals, doubts tend to get tamped down. Especially as they try to rise to the level of being expressed openly. As for what you *do* say, the Order practices the tenets of the Science of Mind. You learn that what you think and say, good, bad or indifferent, will, lickety-split, become reality at some level, subject to an impersonal Law of Manifestation that is equally happy to provide you with a parking place in front of the bank when you need it, or a rotten hamburger. Order talk tends, therefore, to be unfailingly optimistic and positive, lest negativity creep in. Expressing doubts therefore borders on taboo, practically an existential threat. This has long roots in the monastic world and in communities where all members share a common spiritual teaching and practice.

One of those roots is the old biblical saw about the tongue

being a two-edged sword, an agent for both good and ill. All true, but it's the next octave of that teaching that puts you in the fire of change. The tongue is regarded as a way to get a handle on mental processes. In the Order, idle talk is discouraged, and chatterboxes get to spend days and nights in the chapel. All Order houses have at least an hour each day, usually before dinner, when the whole house is on silence. We are encouraged to spend time in silence in order to learn what happens when we shut up. We witness for ourselves what happens when we stop framing the world and all our concepts in language. This can be liberating.

Or the opposite. Tongue curbing creates opportunities for spiritual growth, alongside opportunities for self-delusion and emotional repression. From day one in the Order, in silence in the chapel for three days and three nights, I willingly start a process of shedding the mass mind and wriggling out of the assumptions of the world I have left. In classes on meditation, I am equipped with ways of rising out of my conditioning. I also begin suppressing doubts by always reaching for the high ideals embodied by the Order. By and by, I awaken to the fact that even this "elite" holy order has its own inevitable mass mind of assumptions about what's what. I also awaken to find that all this forced positivity has created a shadow made of everything I have suppressed in order to keep on the sunny side. It's exhausting. People who manage to thrive in such an atmosphere learn to deal skillfully and authentically with this issue.

31.

NORTHERN EXPOSURE

No one notices when I fall in love. A Swedish friend of the Order pays us a visit in Cologne soon after the birth of twins to a married sister in the house. I watch her handle one of the newborns and a paternal switch in me flips. Elsa is comfortable with my sudden attraction and not opposed to the idea of spending time together. To this end, she arranges a couple of "speaking engagements" for me in Stockholm, questionable in their premise that I would have anything meaningful to say to university-level sociology students. But these engagements are paid gigs. I arrive at her door with my heart on my sleeve.

Elsa shows me her Stockholm, the Venice of the North, constructed on islands wound through with canals. We go to a Tibetan Buddhist temple where she has a meeting of some kind. While she is busy, I meditate in the *puja* room with its wild array of benevolent and scary faces on the wall, and I jump when a monk silently appears at my side. *Would I like to meet Lama Nawang?* I say I would.

The little Lama leads me up a ladder to an attic loft which is his quarters. We have no common language. I speak no Tibetan, and he possesses no more than a few words in any Western language that I know. So we sit, I on a creaky chair, he in a lotus position on his army cot. Between us is a tiny Salvation Army coffee table with a pot of tea and a couple of cookies. We stare at each other until he breaks the silence.

"Drink Tibetan tea!" he says.

It has butter in it and smells of goat. Later I learn that it's yak butter. I take a sip and set my cup down. Lama Nawang's voice goes up twenty decibels.

"DRINK TIBETAN TEA!" I jump, startled by the penetration of his voice. He repeats this a number of times.

"DRINK TIBETAN TEA!!"

This is starting to not have anything to do with drinking Tibetan tea. We put down our cups and stare at each other. I have no idea where this is going. Lama Nawang's eyes become intense. He draws a sudden deep breath through his nose and holds it. Reflexively, so do I. He exhales though his mouth, and I follow suit. Another breath, deep and intense, and then another. Some are loud, released with a plosive burst of air. Reflexively, I copy him.

This continues. At some point, I stop copying. He is still initiating the breath each time, but now there is no more lag between his breathing and mine. This simultaneous, identical breathing is suddenly an intense communication between us. At first, Lama Nawang is "breathing" me, but as this ritual progresses, it's as if we're *both* being breathed.

Abruptly, our "meeting" is over, and I find myself in the lobby outside the *puja* room just as Elsa is coming out of her meeting. I'm still vibrating and awestruck that the tiny Lama could have such a profound effect on me just by breathing. That evening in an Italian restaurant, over a plate of *pasta carbonara,* as if reading my mind, she gently explains a couple of things to the lovestruck holy man gazing at her from across the table. For one thing, in her years of association with the Order, I'm not the first Order brother to fall in love with her. She tells me she is currently seeing a man. He has no particularly big spiritual aspirations, she says, but he has a big heart and really knows a lot about love. As the words linger in the air between us, I understand what she is telling me.

She reaches across the table and takes my hand in hers. I'm

a lovely person, she goes on, but my energy is too intense, too piercing, too hard to be around for long. I see myself through her eyes, and she's right. In my drive to take on the intensity I experience all around me in the Order, I have become an energetic loose cannon, untempered by feeling for other people. She is nobody's fool, and she has me pegged. Between the lines, I believe I hear a sweetly Swedish message that if I ever manage to loosen up, I badly need to get laid. But not by her.

So my grand quest for a mate fails. I return to Cologne and muddle through several months in a depressed fog, finding out something about my heart, which is broken. When my depression subsides, I ponder what Elsa meant about my piercing energy. I don't know why the question rankles me so much. It takes some months, but eventually I get an answer.

Breaking the Bowl
In the week between Christmas and New Year's Day, what Germans call the "week between the years," a handful of us travel to Rome to represent the Order at a mass gathering of the Taizé Community. There, thousands of pilgrims from every corner of Europe converge for two weeks of ecumenical convocations, culminating with a mass in St. Peter's with Pope John Paul II.

We are hosted by Signora Dellacroce, a poet and mystic and the mother of a member of the Order in the U.S. Between Taizé events, she gives us guided tours. We descend into torch-lit chambers in the Catacombs and wander through the Rome of the Popes and the Rome of the Caesars. We all put our hands into an opening in the face of a ceramic statue called *La Bocca della Verita,* The Mouth of Truth, into which jealous husbands would thrust their wives' hands to see if they have been cheating. We feel vaguely virtuous for having all our fingers when we pull them out again.

On New Year's Eve, we eat and drink, sing and dance in long, snaking lines through the rooms of the apartment. It's a high-energy moment. After midnight, we calm down from our tame little Bacchanal and, helpful Order brother that I am, I repair to the kitchen to help with dishes. Energy is still surging through me as I reach out to pick up a crystal fruit bowl to dry it, extra gently because I know it's an old piece. My hands barely touch the glass bowl and it shatters with a splitting snap. Stunned, I stand there with two handfuls of glistening shards as I face Signora Dellacroce. She takes it in stride, but I feel appropriately terrible.

Two weeks later, I am back in Cologne and a letter arrives from Rome. My Italian is just good enough to understand the poem it contains. Signora Dellacroce uses the *passato remoto,* reserved for events that unfolded back in the days of yore. It's an ode to the shattered crystal bowl, a generations-old family heirloom. The poem ends abruptly in modern past tense: *" . . . and hands, which should be busy healing, broke it."*

32.

THREE MYSTERY WOMEN

Holidays in Central Europe remind me of how far north I'm now living. Rome, a day and a night to the south of us on the train, is roughly the same longitude as Boston. Cologne is as far north as Labrador in Canada. My love quests to Sweden have taken me another giant step closer to the North Pole, where I find myself among people who are starved for light. On both of my trips to Stockholm, I manage to arrive on the day the ice breaks in the canals, and the sun makes a surprise appearance after months of darkness. Shafts of sunlight reach down like searchlights between the blocky downtown buildings. Pedestrians crowd into bright patches of sidewalk, tear open their coats and jackets, and expose chests and breasts to the sun in ecstatic end-of-winter ritual. The Feast of Santa Lucia is pure Nordic Solar Return drama. Into an utterly dark church come processions of singing, blonde, white-robed girls with wreathes of candles, lit ones, on their heads. People cry.

Back in dark old wintertime Cologne, Order services also have their beauty, a dash of drama derived from the interplay of Dark and Light, and I come to love the yearly procession of the equinoxes and solstices, especially the Winter Solstice. The low-ceilinged basement chapel in the Cologne house has the feel of a grotto, and our Christmas services are a mystic Christian Solstice ritual with hymns. We have serious choral singers in the house, so harmonies are worked out and Renaissance-tight.

143

The attendees from the public are our usual crew of locals, including a bald-headed former stage actor, a concert pianist named Ariadna, and our little Italian friend, Fabrizio, who has latched on to us and comes to everything. As midnight services are about to get underway, a trio of silent, utterly blonde, blue-eyed women slips into the chapel. Slightly angelic and ageless, they look like three stair-step sisters, all with the same page-boy hair. When they close their eyes, their white-blonde eyelashes are so fine they are almost invisible, making hardly any separation between their eyelids. After services, coffee is served. The three blonde mystery women sit a while, uncomfortable and wordless, not touching their cups or Christmas cookies, then leave.

Two days after Christmas, I am in the kitchen washing vegetables when a sister quietly tells me there is someone at the door who would like a word with me. I go downstairs to the public living room and recognize one of the blonde mystery women from the Christmas service. Again, the extremely blue eyes, at once assertive and painfully shy. An awkward silence surrounds her. When she finally speaks, her voice is an elfin High German lilt. Her name is Ursula.

"Would it be okay to sit together and talk?" She asks.

"Yes, sure, if you like."

"Do I have to call you "Reverend"? Clear subtext: *Are you going to hide behind your minister role?*

"I won't insist. You can call me Joshua." She pronounces it "YO-zua."

The moment is awkward. My eye catches on her hands, in particular her fingers, each segment conspicuously well-articulated. She tells me she has a brother in Cologne, but she doesn't really care if she sees him. Mainly, she wants to see me. Then she goes completely red in the face, silent, and embarrassed. Something hangs in the atmosphere that I can't decipher. It's as if she has dropped by in order to confirm something about me, but doesn't bother to tell me what it is.

We sit a while longer in strained silence, and when she leaves, I have no idea what this has been about. I have no idea that I am meeting my future wife.

33.

RIPPENFELLENTZÜNDUNG

Time accelerates in a movie reel of passing seasons. The Cologne house empties out with personnel changes and reassignments. One brother leaves for a vacation with his family in North Carolina and forgets to come back. Two sisters—not including the one who left to get married to the Frenchman—get relocated to the States. The married couple in our house is now pregnant with their third. When they get transferred out of Cologne, they fly to their new assignment in Shrewsbury, England, and I draw the job of transporting a motley collection of household items for their new dwelling by car.

It requires the combined efforts of a houseful of illuminated Order members, filled with the Light of Christ and Divine Intelligence, to strip the car of its front passenger seat and both back seats and invent elaborate lashing and tarping systems in order to make use of every possible cubic millimeter within and on top of the car. By the time I pull out of the driveway, the Order's red Audi sedan is filled to bursting with two mattresses bungee'd to the roof rack and crowned by three non-matching kitchen chairs. Once I get on the road, nestled in the wheel in the embrace of the family's household items, it takes me no time to realize I'm driving partially blind. With every side- and rearview mirror blocked by cargo, I have no way to see if my load is staying put, dangling over the side, or dragging on the road behind me. I regularly check the faces of passing drivers for signs of horror or wild gesticulations in my direction as they pass me on the *Autobahn*. In this condition, I cross Belgium, make the crossing from Calais in France, and thread the monstrous maze of London. My luck holds until I complete my delivery in Shrewsbury.

I make my way back to the coast. With hours to kill before the crossing, I walk the grounds of Dover Castle. I wander into the labyrinthine tunnels beneath the castle and emerge in freezing fog, wearing nothing but a thin jacket and a scarf as flimsy as a yard of toilet paper. Being one of the Elect doesn't guarantee common sense.

The crossing back to Calais is rough. Ferry personnel with mop buckets and disinfectant swab the decks while most of the passengers lose their lunch. Soon, even crew members have to stop and hang on to something solid as we pound through the waves. Through my nausea, a ripping sensation rises in my right lung as I cling to a bolted-down table. As I drive through Belgium, en route back to Cologne, chills commence. I can't quit coughing. Within an hour, I'm barking like a dog. The pain in my right side is searing. I've broken something, a rib maybe. When I arrive back in Cologne, I am diagnosed with *Rippenfellentzündung,* pleurisy, put on antibiotics and *krankgeschrieben,* paid sick leave, for six weeks. I'm definitely ailing, even after I stop my spasmodic coughing. I have indeed broken a rib, and the lining between my right lung and ribs is filled with hot coals. With my right hand, I feel the heat of my inflamed pleura radiating into the space around me.

It is one of the glories of the German socialized healthcare system that even low-paid wage slaves like me—at the time, I'm still teaching Turkish youngsters to speak German like I do—get paid time off when they are ill. An Order sister from the Bordeaux house tells of a curative week of acupuncture, homeopathy, and massage she spent at a healing center south of Stuttgart. Maybe this would be something for me. The healing center happens to also be the doctor's practice in a tiny village called Gammelshausen, headed by a Dr. Ulrike Gallmeier, assisted by a pair of sisters. In fact, this is none other than the trio of blonde mystery women who attended the Order Christmas service. Insurance will pay for it, and who knows what will come of it?

At my initial intake with Ulrike, a second person is present, someone we nowadays would call a "medical intuitive." This turns out to be Ursula, who dropped in unannounced at the Cologne house after Christmas. While Ulrike takes my medical history, Ursula meditates in a corner. Afterward, the two of them work out a course of remedies from the worlds of herbal, homeopathic, and Anthroposophic medicine, inspired by the teachings of Rudolf Steiner, acupuncture, and energy healing treatments. This is all new to me. The latter is particularly interesting to me. Ursula places her unusually warm hands on very specific places on my body and I, almost on cue, drop into an altered state, at once deeply relaxed and very alert. Imagery and emotions come and go. Afterward, I feel different, better. Strangely, the thought comes to me that I could learn to do this.

After my return to Cologne, my thoughts are magnetically drawn to Gammelshausen and the blonde mystery women in their healing center. I take a week-long silent retreat in France and return to Cologne via the healing center in Gammelshausen. In the kitchen, something passes between me and Ursula, and she begins to invade my thoughts. We exchange letters.

Things are still astir in the Order in general. The shipping off of the family to England was part of the first wave of reshuffling of the Order in Europe. In a short time, there are only four of us rattling around in the Cologne house like seeds in a gourd, when we get the word from Headquarters in San Francisco that we will be folding up the Cologne house and joining the Order community in Amsterdam.

Letters continue between Ursula and me, and the result is a logjam of feelings. I'm weary of being in the Order, but too conflicted about it to even admit it to myself. I'm afraid of having to weather the disapproval of my peers and superiors, not to mention other imagined spiritual consequences if I were to leave. It's too close to the deadly third rail of vow-breaking. The Order has moved on from the days when those who leave are condemned and excommunicated for deserting the cause. Still, I know there will be a backlash, and not all of it will be from fellow Order members. My internal guilt system is still fully up to the job of casting me into fear and doubts about my actions. After nine years of identification with this outfit, I don't know who I am outside the formal structures of the Order. I fear a free fall if I leave. This doesn't keep me from imagining some kind of liaison between me and the healer women, and between the Order house and the healing center. In addition, I'm now getting regular letters from an independent and strong-willed woman who has gotten under my skin. Letters that ask, *when are you leaving the Order?*

34.

AMSTERDAM, 1982

By now, I'm totally on the fence as to my life in the Order. I have no idea where this thing with Ursula is going, and I need new ways to cope with my contradictions. I'm a mess in Amsterdam.

Reading provides my imagination with daily calisthenics, and I've never been so grateful that I'm literate. The other face of literacy, writing, is new to me, and from my firstling attempts I understand that writing can also work like a probe for my subconscious. It becomes my way of finding out what I believe and a way to assemble my world of experience.

I live, cramped together with a revolving cast of ex-pat spiritual survivalists of the Order and their offspring, on a boat in North Amsterdam. In its glory days, the Vlaardingen VI was a ferry carrying goods and passengers among the West Frisian Islands. Now, it's a low-lying blue and white *woonboot,* a house boat chained to cement moorings in the filthy Buiksloterkanaal, which rises and falls and sways the living room chandelier like a hypnotist's watch.

My first night on board is filled with horror dreams. My Amsterdam-savvy boatmates point out to me that since my bunk is below water level, I have probably gotten a dose of psychic effluvia, the unprocessed subconscious phantasmagoria which infests the city's filthy canals. In adult education language classes at the *avondschool,* through our teacher's carefully enunciated Dutch, we wide-eyed, all-believing foreigners learn that the canals of Amsterdam's inner city have been dug uniformly "nine meters deep" (*negen meter diep . . . Ja?*): the first three are loaded with "sunken boats" (*gezonkene boten . . . Ja?*), the next three with household appliances and "dead bodies" (*dode lichamen . . . Ja?*), and the uppermost stratum is where all the bicycles are to be found.

I think the teacher is pulling our gullible foreigner legs with most of that yarn, but the last bit turns out to be true. When I go to buy a used bike, the sales guy tells me to come back the next day so he can fish a nice one out of the Herengracht canal and clean it up for me. That wonderful big raw-boned Amsterdam bike costs me a *snipje* and a *brametje,* local slang for the image of the "little snipe" on the Dutch one hundred-Guilder bill, and, less obvious, a "little Abraham" on the fifty-Guilder bill. (The latter is a scriptural reference in which Jesus tells the Pharisees that he has seen *Abraham,* and the Pharisees ask how this could be possible, since he is not even *fifty*).

Like my Samsonite suitcase that on my arrival in San Francisco joined the circulation of the Order's collective trunks and totebags, my newly refurbished bicycle gets stolen and joins the endless flow of bikes around the inner city. According to the mores of Amsterdam's bicycle world, this stolen bike initiation entitles me to a lifetime subscription to two-wheel transportation anywhere in the city. I try it a few times, and ride rusty unchained bikes for a few blocks before abandoning them for the next person. Instead of feeling cosmopolitan, I feel like a thief and buy another bike.

Bicycles are freedom in a compact city like Amsterdam. I branch out and explore my surroundings for hours. One evening, I wander into a "coffeeshop"[3] called de Kosmos and find myself in a darkened auditorium with perhaps a hundred people who are seated, listening. On the stage, I recognize Allen Ginsberg sit-

---

[3] In The Netherlands, where cannabis is "illegal, but not punishable," a "coffeeshop" is a tolerated cannabis dispensary.

ting on a chair, his body twisting and gyrating with each phrase as he reads from his long, famous poem *Howl.* He pauses intermittently to let a translator deliver the Dutch version, complete with identical physical gyrations.

Meanwhile, back at my new domicile on the boat, the only way to escape psychic contamination from our wretched canal is to raise my bunk above water level. For that task, our friend Josef, a man of arcane skills, is summoned.

Like the stand-in father of Jesus, Josef is a carpenter, but that in itself doesn't tell the story. Josef is an *Amsterdamse timmerman,* an Amsterdam carpenter, which is a unique species of craftsman. The defining talent of an Amsterdam *timmerman* is an ability to build and fix things in amazingly close quarters. This skill comes from working in narrow houses that have started out vertical but now lean against their neighbors like tipsy cigar box Dutch Masters propping each other up after a night of *borreltjes.*

In the inner city, many of the dwellings are "pulley houses." Staircases are too narrow and steep to get a large object—for instance, a grand piano—to an upper floor. The Dutch solution is to hoist the piano up the front of the building and haul it in from outside. A standard feature of a pulley house is an extra-wide picture window that opens beneath a sturdy arm protruding from the outer wall above the window. On the arm, the block and tackle of a pulley are mounted on a hefty hook. It takes a team of helpers and considerable balls to pull this off. The crew on the street yanks on a rope to set the piano a-swinging like a pendulum in heavy slow-motion high over the roofs of the cars backed up in the street. Meanwhile, the crew inside the apartment makes ready to catch the piano on the return swing as it sails briefly into the apartment through the open window. The indoor team has to brace themselves mightily in order to keep from being defenestrated when the piano reverses directions. Maybe some of the canal-corpses that I have learned about in Dutch class are piano hoisters snatched out of windows by swinging

Steinways that then landed on them.

Josef the *timmerman* has grown strong and stubborn schlepping bags of tools up near-vertical staircases to rooms that have settled into unique geometry. When he has jobs in the red light district near Centraalstation, drug dealers stash their wares in the wheel wells of Josef's parked Opel sedan while he works upstairs in an apartment, so as not to be holding in case of a shakedown by the *politie,* the cops. When he returns to his car from the job and climbs behind the wheel, the dealers dive under his car to retrieve their stashes.

Picture this: My cabin in the bow of the boat tapers at one end. All built-in structures must conform to the internal contours of the boat's shape. Forget about regular, repeating right angles. In nothing flat, Josef has crowbarred out the offending sleeping bunk, salvaging the boards and squeaking out the nails, which he then hammers back to straightness for re-use. Without a protractor or other measuring device, using only his hands, he feels deep into the cribbed angles of the interior bow and proceeds to reshape the salvaged boards with a crosscut saw, replicating the angles exactly. To cut them, he clamps a board almost vertically between his knees, as if working in a phone booth, while he saws with quick, precise strokes. Before my eyes, a new above-water sleeping bunk takes shape in my quarters. And next to it, a nifty compact built-in writing desk.

My first forays into writing take place in that canal-bound boat at that built-in desk. I try to emulate humorists like Kurt Vonnegut and, later, Mark Twain. Over-written imitations to be sure, but, by and by, they give me a feel for putting words together and for storytelling.

35.

What Comes Out of the Canal

Amsterdam is a libido cranker-upper, and almost every foray into the city on my big black Dutch bicycle is an adventure down the furry little rabbit hole of imaginary sex. My daily bicycle route to Elsevier Biomedical Press, where I work as a proofreader, invariably takes me right through the *Walletjes,* Amsterdam's over-the-top red light district. The curtainless front windows of the hookers' storefronts are in the Calvinist tradition—*feel free to look in because I have nothing to hide.* Even at eight in the morning, the red neon and subliminal vibrator buzz of sex shops and live shows leave enough residue to plaster every kind of sexual imagery to the walls of my imagination and keep it stoked all day. I'm thirty-two and haven't had sex since I was twenty-five.

Ursula has an old friend in Edam, up the coast from Amsterdam, and this friend's house becomes our rendezvous place. Several times, on some pretext, I requisition the Order's little station wagon and make the trek up the coast. These clandestine "dates" cost money for Ursula to take the train from Germany. Officially, I have no money, but a letter from my brother Bruce informs me that I have received $2600 from somewhere. Because of my vow of poverty, I ask him to be steward of it, so it won't be in my name. God and the IRS will have to deal with me later. Necessity gives birth to an elaborate scheme in which Bruce types letters in pretty darn good French to Ursula's friend in Edam. *Why French?* In the envelope is cash, U.S. dollars, to be converted into Dutch Guilders and given to Ursula for her travel expenses. Inexplicably, my brother's nom de plume is "le Frito Bandito." As per his instruction, *en français,* the money is to be used *exclusivement pour "l'Operation Pink Rose."*

Ou la la!

One Saturday in February, Ursula and I meet in Edam. Frost crunches under our feet as we clop along together through the streets with our hands and arms linked like a pair of Dutch skaters. A lace curtain of ice and algae covers the water in the canals, and the street lamps glow though the rising fog like a scene from a film noir. Our underlying drama has reached *Sturm und Drang* level. It's our usual impasse. For Ursula: *When are you leaving the Order?* For me: *How can I have it both ways?* We part ways, and each of us wanders off in the fog of our individual dramas.

I am bumbling half a block up a side street when I'm jerked out of my reverie. Ursula lets out a bloodcurdling shriek and, as the world falls out from under her, she walks straight into the canal. I race back to where I last saw her, but she has disappeared under the frosty algal bloom. I flop down on my belly and reach as far down as I can into the black freezing flow, manage to catch hold of the hood of her moss-green *Lodenmantel,* and pull her head out. Breaking the water's surface, Ursula gasps for air. Her screams echo like murder in the evening fog, so dire and penetrating that people leap up from their dinner tables and rush out of their houses, including her friend. Together we extricate her from the canal and, for the next two hours, we do what we can to warm her as she shivers violently. When she comes back into the present tense, I hold her and tell her I love her. Given the circumstances, we have crossed a Rubicon of sorts.

The green *Lodenmantel* is my undoing. The soggy, furry mess comes with me in the Order station wagon so I can take it to a dry cleaner. In The Netherlands, people, mostly drunks and kids, fall in the canals all the time, so there are procedures for removing the incredible filth that gets into the fabric. I end up having to explain the trip to the dry cleaner, and the extra expense, to people at the Order house, only to find out—surprise!—that everybody already knows about me and Ursula.

36.

SECULAR

After coming out to my Order *confreres* and *-soeurs* about my clandestine relationship with Ursula, I watch my status in the Amsterdam Order houseboat plummet. I wander for hours in the fields outside our section of Amsterdam Noord, agonizing over an unfinished letter to the Director General. In it, I spin out scenarios that would allow me to not have to decide between the Order and Ursula. In my final masterful draft, I lay out my vision of a liaison between the Order houses of Europe and the healing center in Germany. I plead my case for personal liaisons, even marriage, between Order members and "outsiders." For my troubles, the Director accuses me, starting in the opening paragraph of his reply, of abandoning my calling. *What if Beethoven had decided to stop composing, just because he was in love?* This questionable logic is flavored by an assumption, widespread in the Order: the only reason I have even the minuscule speck of spiritual attainment that I have is because I am part of the elite body of the Order. To depart from that body, so goes this logic, would cut me off from the Order's particular portal to Grace. In the second paragraph, my functions as an ordained minister of the Order are hereby suspended until I get myself sorted out.

Both the Order and Ursula are on my case to make a decision. Letters from Ursula accuse me of dawdling over a decision that should be straightforward if I truly love her. Meanwhile, word reaches me from a couple of sources that my case—the one about Order members becoming romantically involved with people outside the Order—is being watched closely within the Order. It seems I'm not the only one with this dilemma. For a brief time, I'm a Guinea pig. My situation has been discussed, apparently, in the Order's decision-making circles, maybe even the Esoteric Council. Regardless of what they decide, or what it portends for other lovelorn Order members, my days as a member of the Order are numbered.

We are taught in the Order to see the cosmic dimension of everyday life, the better to recognize God's presence in the world. Nothing is small, and I am no stranger to grandiosity. I'm thirty-three, the same age, I remind myself, as Jesus at the time of the Crucifixion. At nights in my boat bunk, alone with the tension and collision of impulses in me, I resist the temporary release of tears or masturbation. My mind winds endlessly through reruns of the same scenarios: either I toe the line and recommit to the Order, perhaps ask for reassignment to the States, and endure a period of sackcloth and ashes. Or I leave and take my chances with Ursula and try to land on my feet in a new setting. Other eyes may have seen other choices, but I lie there in full sight of God and the angels, like an insect impaled on pins, spreadeagled over the black-and-white version of my dilemma.

In the summer of 1983, a middle-ground solution is settled on: the Esoteric Council grants me a three-month leave of absence, a brief sabbatical in order to "resolve" my relationship with Ursula. Though everybody knows which way the wind is blowing, a paradoxical piece of kabuki theater unfolds. We all maintain the pretense that I will return to Amsterdam and the Order. I am given an envelope with four hundred Dutch Guilders—*severance pay?*—as I say my tearful goodbyes to my brothers and sisters on the boat. Then I'm driven to the Amsterdam Centraalstation. There, before I climb on the train, Reverend S., who escorts me to the train platform, kindly asks me to let him search my suitcase, just in case, in amongst my seven changes of underwear, I have mistakenly packed any books or tapes belonging to the Order.

From Centraalstation, the train of the *Nederlandse Spoorwegen* winds southward like a yellow centipede, cutting across the coiled semi-circles of canals and streets that shape the inner city of Amsterdam. Soon, we are traversing flat, open *polderland,* punctuated only by dykes and irrigation ditches. We roll through vast expanses of arable soil, reclaimed over hundreds of years from the sea by a people who would rather break their backs to create needed land than take it by force from their neighbors.

The Dutch-German border at Venlo is a cross-hatched maze of intersecting train tracks and high-voltage power lines. From the contrasting visceral feel of the two countries, my body knows where I am. Crossing into Germany from the relatively laid-back Netherlands, I go on alert for a moment, my breathing catches, and my right hand tightens. By and by, I fall back into the rock and rhythm of the tracks as I chew on a *kaasbroodje,* sip my coffee, and settle in for a day of travel. Outside my window, industry and office parks give way to green zones and farmland. I allow my mind to wander.

Despite the pretense surrounding my "sabbatical," I know I have left the Order for good, but I don't know how to shift gears. I wrestle with the notion that the Order, once so absolute and permanent in my psyche, could have been only a passing season in my life. In my train reverie, I feel into my shapeshifting spiritual path, still detectable somewhere down under my spiritual feet. It's the same path that announced itself to me when my best friend and I would lie on our backs under the nighttime Kansas sky, contemplating the vastness of it all. It is the same path that announced itself when I was busy getting high at every opportunity and then quickly handed me off to the yogis and meditators. It was the path of my collision with Aiko in Wichita a decade earlier, which led me to the terrifying Abbot. The same path that for ten years dressed me up in clerical garb and the sweeping mission of an esoteric order.

Ten years is a long time, a third of my life. It will take many more years than that to understand some things about the Order and to appreciate my time there. While the Order is not the world's only tiny conventicle of Light, it's the one where I first immersed myself, to the degree that I was able, in a community and the classic disciplines of spiritual life. Now, this path of mine has apparently changed its mind again. I change trains in Cologne, my former home, and wonder what lies ahead. Following the Rhine into Southwest Germany to my rendezvous with Ursula and the healer women, I am no longer the spiritual boy I was in 1972.

PART III
THE HEALERS
(1983 - 2000)

"Learn your techniques well and be prepared to let go of them when you touch a human soul."
~C. G. Jung

37.

MY ENERGY HEALING APPRENTICESHIP

Overnight, I become a member of an otherwise all-female household of healers in a village called Gammelshausen in the subalpine meadows and hills of the Schwäbische Alb south of Stuttgart. To a surprising degree, the healing center hums like a well-functioning Order house. As in the Order, everyone is mission-driven and focused, and everyday life has a touch of wonder about it. There are regular meditations and a no-nonsense work ethic. The house itself carries a charge. The feel is one that I learned in the Order to call a "spiritual transmission," the strong sense that there are invisible spiritual guides about, and that transcendent things are happening through the place. When I arrive, I tell myself that this is another way of being in the Order.

After my agreed-upon three-month sabbatical, I write to the Order's Esoteric Council to officially request "secular status," which is granted. I am now released from my vows, free to fulfill my calling, whatever that is, outside the Order. After ten years of being moved around the map and thrown into new situations with no preparation in the Order, I believe, mistakenly, that I should be able to land on my feet in this new identity with no trouble.

I am there to be with Ursula, but it's not a regular romance. The transition to the healing center is like stepping from one moving train to another. By virtue of being there, I am exposed to a culture of healers. Although nothing is said, this is the informal beginning of my apprenticeship in energy healing. It starts with the fact that I'm thirty-three and only now finding out about my own basic needs as a human.

The healing center is also the village medical practice, so every day sees a stream of Ulrike's patients with its run of flu shots, work accidents, and moms with kids. I have little to do with this side of the healing center's operation, but an old, rural house like this needs constant upkeep.

Every household decision takes vibrational qualities into consideration, and all food and other products that come into the house have to pass muster. When the job of painting the workshop room falls to me, I drive to Eckwälden to buy orange-oil-based pastels obtained from Wala, a company specializing in healthy, plant-based products. The town is a stronghold of the Anthroposophic world of Rudolf Steiner followers. With their gray hair, Birkenstocks, and beet-dyed homespun sweaters, the local "Anthropops" are as identifiable from a hundred paces as Mormon missionaries. Those who can afford it renovate their houses in Anthroposophic architectural mode with doors and windows fashioned without right angles, giving both the houses and the Anthropops themselves a rooty, hobbit-like feel.

The Anthroposophic paint I buy in Eckwälden is like nothing I have ever seen before—a thick lavender-colored gravy, luxurious and fragrant with citrus oils. Its smell awakens me viscerally. I have a strong urge to tip up the can and drink it straight, but I settle for letting it drizzle down on me in a fine mist as I roll it out on the ceiling. The strong urge triggered by the paint grows. I finish rolling out the first coat and make a beeline for the kitchen. There, I root feverishly through the refrigerator until I find what I'm looking for. When Ulrike walks in, I am finishing off two cups of heavy cream, guzzled straight from the plastic container. She is unflustered and speaks softly. "That must be something you deeply need, Joshua," she says, "Did you leave me any for my coffee?"

At night, touch opens the floodgates of grief in me. Ursula holds me, and I sob for hours. An ocean of uncried tears pours out of me in wave after wave. My transition out of the Order has taken me into darkness. I don't know who I am or what I'm about. This is the free fall I feared.

By and by, I land. My grieving subsides, and I settle into the daily routines of the healing center. Commonplace household tasks open an aperture on the nature of energy and healing. I'm fascinated by the coal-fired *Dauerbrenner* stove in each room, a miracle of German engineering, which I learn to tend. Egg-shaped coal nuggets drop, one at a time, into the firebox, and its internal mechanisms keep the thing burning efficiently and indefinitely. When the plums ripen in the small orchard behind the house, a massive canning operation gets underway. *Weckgläser,* the German equivalent of Ball jars, are filled with preserves, and sealed shut. I'm shown how to squirt a bit of alcohol on top of the pectinated fruit and ignite it with a fiery cotton ball held in place with tweezers from Ulrike's practice. As the flame sucks up all the oxygen and creates a vacuum, the lid, with its rubberized gasket, clamps right down and seals the jar. I am in an open, almost child-like state, and these revelations come to me as a series of ah-has.

Ursula teaches me the fine art of energetic wasp herding. In Germany, screens are nonexistent to keep out the little wasps who are magnetized by the sugar that permeates the air at canning time. These little critters are a friendlier bunch than their cranky North American relatives, and while these healer women are on good terms with them, it doesn't mean a wasp with a sweet tooth gets to stay in the kitchen. I learn to position myself so the wasp is between me and an open window. Then, using my hands like oars on a boat, I "splash" it with waves of energy. I find that if I keep my hands loose and my wrists mobile, I can more easily move energy out into the room. The wasps feel the waves of etheric movement and obediently follow the currents as I "herd" them in the direction of the open window. They approach the opening, find the fresh air, and "zoop!" Out they go!

Hornets are less obliging. I find one in our attic apartment and figure the same strategy ought to work to usher it out. I get the hornet between me and an open window and begin splashing him with energy. This particular hornet feels the energy waves I'm directing at him and turns to face me, looking straight at me with however many eyes he has. This is disturbing, and when the stalks of his antennae begin to undulate in a rhythmic wave directly at *me*, I'm transfixed where I stand. The hornet lifts off and lands a foot closer. Reflexively, I shrink back a foot. Insistent, he lifts off again and backs me up another foot and continues, unyielding, until he has herded me out of the room.

1983, Gammelshausen: Ursula sleeping in a hammock.

38.

FALLING APART AND

FALLING BACK TOGETHER AGAIN

During the week, the healing center sees a constant traffic of patients from the village. On weekends, there are workshops and extended visits from Ursula's students. Some of them are young people with strange energies. A number of them report that things like glass tabletops and wristwatches have a way of breaking in their presence. I remember Elsa's words to me in the Stockholm restaurant about my own unruly energies and my shattering moment with Signora Dellacroce's fruit bowl.

One morning, I'm seated at the breakfast table next to a young Dutch woman who has been staying at the center for a week of healing, much the same as I had done during my recovery from pleurisy. Amid the clicking of coffee cups and saucers and the scrape of the butter knife, the girl falls abruptly silent. Strange psychic weather builds around her. She stares, trembling, at her toast, then comes unglued. Her coffee cup is first to hit the floor, followed by her toast and egg cup. She bangs the table with her fists, catching the upturned tines of her fork which flips in a high arc off the table and rattles to the floor. This upsets no one at the table. I put my hand on the girl's shoulder and stay with her. In a surprisingly short time, she comes back to herself, breakfast resumes, and life goes on, as if this kind of thing were standard fare in this house. As I pay attention to the girl, I realize in that moment that all eyes are on *me*.

167

Apparently, I have passed some kind of test. From that day on, I start getting called in to work, in tandem, with Ursula. With this, my apprenticeship in hands-on healing work takes a concrete step. At first, it's pure imitation because I know next to nothing. I watch Ursula closely. Myriad shapes and geometric patterns tumble out of her well-articulated hands, gestures that speak the language of energy movement, now spiraling energy out of her client's body, now combing with raked fingers, fluffing and smoothing the field, followed by tiny flicks of her fingers as if shedding drops of water. I find myself mirroring her, sensing her inner postures, and where she positions herself within herself.

Somehow, it's all of a piece with things I absorbed in the Order, a sense of ritual, and the way energy will follow intention and visualization. I find I already know something about grounding and maintaining a sense of safety and containment for the person on the table. I am clearly the student here, but there is a synergy in our work together. Ursula's clients drop into new depths within themselves.

Little is said. Over the summer and into fall in Gammelshausen, I witness a hundred versions of the breakfast table fall-apart-and-regroup phenomenon in what looks to me like a series of small initiations. Ursula has an ability to zero in on places in her clients' bodies and energy fields that are holding charges and patterns that are ready to release. At first, it's uncanny to me, more like witchcraft, or magic, in the same category as energetic wasp herding. By and by, patterns emerge, and the witchery begins to make sense to a part of me that seems to know about these things. It's an adventure.

39.

AN IRISHMAN IN DENMARK

I theorize about Ursula's generation. *Why have so many of her contemporaries become healers and trauma specialists? Why have so many developed extremely rarified spiritual sensibilities and gifts? How is it that so many have come to specialize in sound healing and the use of gongs, bells, and singing bowls?* In every case, the answer in my mind is this: World War II burned away the psycho-spiritual middle ground of Central Europe and, for many, survival has meant either becoming utterly cynical and materialistic, or finding their spiritual life. No in-between. On a continent with so much need following the war, every kind of healer was called into action, from doctors, psychotherapists, and clergy, to those who know how to mend the torn etheric networks of bodies and souls with the subtle healing arts.

Ursula is a former music teacher and church organist, and she later becomes a *Heilpraktikerin,* a naturopath, with a subspecialty in homeopathy. Her own therapy brings her into contact with psychics, mediums, and energy healers. Her intuitive gifts grow. At a seminar on death and dying in Düsseldorf, she meets thanatologist Elisabeth Kübler-Ross and approaches her about becoming her assistant. If she's serious, Elisabeth tells her, she should drop everything and come with her right now to the airport and fly with her to Helsinki. Which Ursula does. She becomes a student of healers in the United Kingdom and Northern

Europe, and finally she emerges as a practitioner and teacher with a full practice and a modest but loyal following. By the time I, still a member of the Order, come for my week of healing in Southwest Germany, Ursula already has her wings.

At the Gammelshausen house, the workshops are Ursula's domain. She puts aside her role as medical intuitive and steps into the foreground as teacher. She offers a hybrid of color, crystal, and sound healing exercises with gongs, Tibetan bowls, and dissonant little chimes on leather cords. There are deep breathing practices, intermingled with emotional release sessions in the ecstatic, cathartic, mattress-pounding style of the Human Potential Movement and the Esalen Institute. Underpinning it all is a detailed and organized body of knowledge of the human energy system.

Gradually, I come to understand that this enclave—part doctor's practice, part home, part healing center in a tiny Schwabian village—is part of a loose network of healer-types in the United Kingdom, Central and Northern Europe. Among the subset of these energy healers that Ursula, Annette, and Ulrike belong to, the common link is a certain Bob somebody, an Irishman living in Scandinavia, whom they see as their teacher. Since I am now hooked up with Ursula, she puts in a request on my behalf that I be allowed to come with her to Bob's classes. There, at the Psykisk Center, Bob's base of operations in Ringkøbing, Denmark, nine kilometers from the North Sea on the west coast of the Jutland Peninsula, I come to recognize that I'm not in the Order anymore. I have entered a new world of spiritual development.

40.

A Clairvoyant Irishman is Still an Irishman

I'm ambivalent about spiritual teachers at this point in my life. I know from experience how uncomfortable it can be to be around them. The teachers in the Order had an energy and intensity about them like nothing I had ever experienced. In their presence, I mistrusted all my impulses and experienced confusion over even their casual comments, which I took defensively as reflections of my spiritual state and shortcomings. When I hear that Bob Moore is "very clairvoyant," my reaction is cautious. Being X-rayed by someone who will see the confused state I'm in is the last thing I want.

The title of my first class with Bob Moore is something about energy healing for partners. As Ursula's partner, I get to jump to the head of the line of people waiting to come into Bob's classes.

We queue up as Anni Moore, Bob's Danish wife, collects workshop fees and greets the participants. She has seen the coming and going of hundreds of Bob's students, and the line stops frequently while she catches up with old friends. As handfuls of Danish Kroner change hands, I overhear Anni's tongue-in-cheek question to a pair of Norwegian classmates in line ahead of me: "So what's it like to pay all this money to have a nervous breakdown?" Everybody laughs. Anni is mischievous by nature, and more so from living with Bob. It's ob-

171

viously an inside joke in the crowd that comes here. I wonder what she means.

I'm sitting in a conference room with Ursula and thirty-eight other people, wondering what to expect. My ears scan the room for recognizable languages. There is British-accented English, some German, some Dutch, but mostly it's the muddy sounds I come to associate with Danish. A large pair of Bang & Olufsen stereo speakers is aimed at the class from the front of the room. In the corner, a skeleton, "Mr. Mickelson," hangs suspended on a teetering stand. None of Mr. Mickelson's bones appear to be from the same body.

In the fullness of time, a stocky man wearing slightly elven shoes with turned up toes walks up the center aisle to the front of the room. He positions himself behind a swiveling office chair, where he almost appears to be hiding as he leans over its back and supports his weight with his hands on the arm rests. Thick-lensed glasses give his eyes a bulgy look under his thick eyebrows. He wears a curious blue-gray smock that reaches almost to his knees. As a newcomer, the thought comes to me that this is the gardener here at the Psykisk Center. In an introvert's mumble, he asks everybody to please turn off lights when they are the last ones leaving a room. He goes on to add that it's all right to wear swimming suits in the indoor pool if we want to. Without a segue, and in the same slightly mumbled English, he is now talking about *chakras* and etheric energy movement around the body, all in great detail. To which he adds, "of course, the whole thing is so much easier to understand if you can *see* it." Which, it turns out, he can. This is Bob Moore.

After the end of our third day of class, which is focused on energy exercises for couples, I get lost in the meandering house and accidentally walk into Bob's living room. There, in a stuffed chair under a bright standing lamp, sits Bob, holding a magazine one inch in front of his eyes, reading it through his Coca Cola bottle spectacles and a thick magnifying glass. Bob, it turns out, is almost legally blind, partly the result of being exposed to four-hundred volts of electricity when he was in engineering school. The sight of him reading like that brings tears to my eyes, and I wonder exactly how he is able to do what he does.

Clairvoyance comes in many shades. One morning in class, I ask a question about some specific sensations I'm having during an energy exercise. Without a hitch, he asks me to think back to events that took place when I was twelve, almost thirteen, and to realize that they are still having an effect on me. There, in a room with thirty-nine others, in a strangely private way that no one but he and I are privy to, he points to the death of my mother. It is a form of respect I see hundreds of times over the years with Bob.

Every other person in the class is a psychotherapist, it seems, and then a mixed bag of nurses, doctors, bodyworkers, energy healers, geomancers, and shamanic types. There is an old guard of Bob students, which includes Ursula, who have followed Bob's classes in Denmark, Switzerland, and the UK.

"Seeing" energy is not a big deal with this crowd. We learn exercises and partner treatments that all seem to be in the service of personal development. Everyone in the class at least talks a good game as they read off reams of energetic impressions every time they tune in to the energy field of a partner. My energy sensing is nothing encyclopedic like these all-stars. Compared to them, I'm an energy-sensing slug. I get impressions, all right, but they are basic, along the line of "full," "depleted," "charged up," "relaxed." Bob tells us, "I can teach you to see energy movement in about two weeks, but it'll take you the rest of your life to understand what you're seeing."

More happens. "Bob exercises" are a species of body-energetic meditations that thin the veil between my conscious mind and a numinous land of memory and insight. He teaches an abundant variety of energy practices involving the use of sound and geometry and very specific shades of color. On a magnetic whiteboard Bob hangs large sheets of colored paper from the Pantone system used by paint stores. The shades he recommends are highly specific. In terms of how they affect the human energy field, for example, there is a palpable difference between Pantone® 325 and Pantone® 326.

I learn new skills. I gather my attention into a loose bundle of energy, feeling, and awareness, and aim it at specific places in my body. I learn to park my attention at specific positions on my body and let myself sink down through the energetic strata to what's underneath. From there, I learn the art of taking journeys in my body. In one such exercise, my navel serves as a point of departure for a Magellanic circumnavigation of my body, traveling my skin's surface on the midline. My attention is a slow, persistent ladybug crawling southward, following this invisible songline between my body's East and West, over the ridge of my pubic bone into the switchbacks and bulges of my penis and scrotum, across the plain and crevasse of my perineum and anus, to the tip of my tailbone, slowly up the ruck of my backbone to the base of my skull, then up and over the top of my head and down between my eyes. Then, I head south again, down the slope of my nose, managing somehow to stay between my nostrils, and down over my lower lip and chin. From there, it's a slow-motion glide until I'm safely back at my navel where I started. Along the way, I get diverted, plenty. There are dives and detours as I forget what I'm doing and find myself in the Timbuktu of memory and the *terra incognita* of my inner life. Getting lost is part of the game. I am a pilgrim in my own body.

One morning, we start by finding a specific point on our foreheads, five fingerbreadths above the tops of our noses. The idea is to bring our attention to this "Five-Finger Point" and allow this little vortex of energy movement to draw our awareness into itself which, by and by, it does. After sinking into this position, we move our attention in turn to specific pairs of points at our hips, precise locations at the corners of our big toenails, and the tops of our pubic bones before returning to the Five-Finger Point on our foreheads. Each of these energy-active positions has its own signature and feel. In the course of sinking in, my lower body relaxes, and I enter a place of utter stillness. The Order brother in me has no trouble seeing these exercises as spiritual practices without a religious overlay, close kin to the classic disciplines of the inner life, right next to prayer, meditation, and contemplation. The student in me recognizes a perfect laboratory for learning how energy works.

The inner world I am entering has its own laws. Exercises bring up memories and sudden flurries of emotion, as if they have been lodged in my body, waiting to emerge at the right moment. Night exercises plant seeds for dreams. In one meditation, I have the sensation of running headlong into a wall. It's so physically jarring that I reach up to touch the point of impact on my skull, stunned that a meditative practice could bring up such a visceral experience. In a tumble of images, I see a mountain in front of me, and despair grips my chest. The next moment, I am stuck forever inside the mountain, which is made of my fixed ideas about myself. Suddenly, I'm a Chinese man, sitting by a stream, watching the bank slowly crumble into the flowing water. The insight washes over me that *nothing is fixed.* Everything, including myself, is in the process of becoming something else.

I'm reminded repeatedly of the episode with the Dutch girl at the healing center in Gammelshausen, when she seemed to fall apart and then fall back together again, reorganized, in less than an hour. Anni's provocative question about paying all this money to have a nervous breakdown comes to mind. We come away from a week-long class with thirty or forty such meditative energy exercises that stir our psycho-spiritual innards. On the last day of classes, we join the stream of cars of our classmates heading out of Ringkøbing. One by one, cars pull off the road so drivers can fall apart for a few minutes before continuing on.

41.

FIND OUT IF IT'S REAL

After every class with Bob, phone calls in careful English flash across Northern Europe as students anxiously grill each other about exercise steps:

"Has Bob said four fingers above the top of the nose?"

"No, that is wrong. Bob has said *five* fingers."

"I am sure he has said four fingers."

"No! Absolutely not! Bob has said five fingers!" There is genuine angst about just how many fingerbreadths to believe. Friendships fray with the unspoken understanding that nothing in your life will ever be right again if you get this or that energy position wrong. The precise locations of energy positions are front of mind for many of Bob's students, but I'm not sure that Bob sees it that way. From my experience in the Order, I recognize the potential to make an absolute, rigid doctrine out of anything. The other side of Bob's teaching is the care for the inner experiences that arise from doing the exercises. These experiences belong to you, he is fond of saying, and he encourages us to trust the authority of our own experience.

Energy healing lore is filtered through Bob's unique spoken English. Born in the 1920s in Northern Ireland, his first language is English, but it's very foreign to my American ears. For some of his Scandinavian students, Bob is the only English speaker in their lives, so they assimilate his odd, endearing verbal mannerisms and make them their own.

In Bob's mouth, "girl" becomes "gyarl," "car" becomes "cyar," "intuition" becomes "in-too-AY-shun," and "human" becomes "thyoo-man." And, in my favorite piece of BobTalk, the "umbilical cord" becomes the "umbiblical cord—where you were attached to you-know-who before you were born." I never find out if this is just an Irish Gaelic gloss on English pronunciation or a specialty all Bob's own. It makes for strained listening.

For many in the classes, the only way to make sure they don't miss a single detail is to take verbatim notes. These notes are then used to produce massive typescripts consisting of endless sentences and unparagraphed floods of BobTalk. To that end, the perimeters of the conference room are littered with small tape recorders, thickets of cables, and a host of microphones on miniature tripods lined up like rows of tiny cannons, all aimed at Bob. Every thirty or forty-five minutes, the class is punctuated

The exact location of energy positions were taken very seriously.

by the irritating plastic click of dozens of devices turning off and being reloaded with fresh cassettes.

One day, Bob has had enough. "This room is so full of the energy fields o' your bloody recorders that I c'n hardly see you! Instead of trying to write down every word, *try listening!"*

Bob is a workhorse. After teaching a class of forty for a week, he's up and ready for several private sessions, starting at seven. After one class, we stay an extra night so we can have a private audience with him the next morning. I'm full of insecurities, fresh out of the Order that has defined my life for a decade, newly hooked up with a woman who, for all I can tell, is part of a benevolent coven of healer witches.

Bob's chair is draped with a *flokati*. His eyes bulge large, magnified though his fat glasses. I try to present my various quandaries so he can tell me what to do. Bob listens carefully, letting me wind down a bit. When he finally speaks, it's in the slow, private, confidential voice I'm getting used to in classes, a mumble laced with an undercurrent of Irish music.

"The way I see it, Jim (by this time, I've changed my name back), it's probably best you've come out of that organization (referring to the Order). You were doing yourself no favors by staying in a hierarchical structure like that. You really need to take responsibility for your own life, and how're y' goin' to do that if there's always someone telling you what to do and what to believe? I know you spent many years in that group, but you have to prepare yourself for finding out that a lot of it was an illusion."

I go blank inside. I'm like a person in the sixteenth century hearing for the first time that the Earth is not the center of the universe. The proposition that the Order, or a lot of it, has been an illusion jolts me into something foreign. I don't know if I'm willing to just throw the Order into the dustbin of my personal history as if it was a teenage infatuation. Being a member of an elite body of spiritual adepts with a divinely guided hierarchy is part of my cherished inner narrative. Through the years, I had plenty of opportunities to see the clay feet of the Order's high and holy. And to their credit, the wiser priests and teachers went out of their way to climb down from the pedestals, with everything from well-timed farts to moments of genuine self-revelation. Still, the power structure was a key to life in the Order. I've come to Bob to ask him for guidance, and he is telling me to break this need for someone to tell me what's what, to grow up spiritually. I feel what a kite feels when its string is cut, suddenly at the mercy of the wind.

Our session comes to an end. Bob tells me and Ursula to go knock on the door of his apartment. Maybe, if we ask nicely, Anni can be persuaded to give us a cup of "the black stuff" before we hit the road.

Anni is obliging. "Would you like anything in it?" She nudges a bottle of imported Mexican mescal in our direction. A worm lies curled up like a tiny fetus on the bottom of the bottle. It's eight in the morning.

"Is the worm real?" I ask.

Anni almost smiles. She cocks a wry eyebrow at me over the top of her red-framed plastic reading glasses as she pours a shot into each of our coffee cups and shoves the bottle across the table to me. Her look says it all. *Well, Jim . . . there's one way to find out if it's real.*

42.

NOT YOUR GURRA

Never underestimate the power of magical thinking and cognitive quirks in groups of spiritual people bent on following a leader. This is something Bob understands. Not only does he not match the popular image of the enlightened teacher swaddled in a flowing beard and robes, he resolutely resists the spiritual father role that his students, myself included, are all too willing to project onto him. He proves to be utterly unwilling to be in that kind of arrangement with those who come to him insisting on being told what to do.

"I'm not your gurra!" he says to our class. "The whole point of these practices is that you come to the point of answering your own questions." It's everything he tried to get across to me in our private session about stepping out of authoritarian setups and learning to trust my own experience.

One person who doesn't try to make Bob into her gurra is Ursula, who has her own sources of knowledge. If she gets a session with Bob, it is in order to compare notes on what she herself has already reeled in with her intuitive faculties. I can see the special regard Bob has for Ursula. She has endeared herself to him as one of only a few students who don't try to put him on a pedestal.

Back in Gammelshausen, regular workshops continue, mostly led by Ursula. Occasionally, there are presenters from outside the

Bob Moore orbit. One regular is a friend of Ursula's, a semi-famous medium from England. In this woman's sessions, the air thickens as she goes into a semi-closed trance and channels a discarnate teacher, either verbally or in the form of automatic writing. In the role of translator for the German speakers who attend, I am privy to many of her private sessions. The workshop goers treat the medium's words like Gospel, and I see how much authority is conferred onto persons who are able to "get" an intuitive download about something or someone.

Mediumship is accepted as a valid way of knowing things at the healing center. At some point in her spiritual life, Ursula began channeling information and teachings from guides from other dimensions. If a workshop is due to start at 8 o'clock, Ursula sits down at 7:40, goes into meditation, and gets the whole workshop, from soup to nuts, in a single intuitive download. It's wonderful, one-of-a-kind stuff, and it has a profound effect on the people who come to see her.

Bob Moore teaching at the Psykisk
Center in Ringkøbing, Denmark,
circa 1984.

Shortly after I arrive in Gammelshausen, in a curious swerve, Ursula tells her guides to turn off the guidance, at least for a while. She's feeling a strong need to find out who she is in this process. After watching how some mediums get run ragged by the entities they channel, this move on Ursula's part strikes me as a healthy thing. It's a dilemma that many mediums find themselves in—being so joined at the hip with their discarnate partners that they lose track of who is who. In Ursula's case, on command, the visions dry up as her guides stop funneling information to her. Ursula continues to lead groups, but instead of channeled stuff, she serves up what is coming from her own personal sense of things. After a time of adjustment, this empowers her. This all goes great until she announces in a workshop that she has stopped channeling the content.

The room falls silent, and all eyes are on Ursula. Everyone's expression says, "Come again?"

"If you're not getting it from your guides, where are you getting it from?" asks a group member who has made considerable changes in her life through the years, based on Ursula's channelings.

"It's coming from me," says Ursula. This is a huge letdown. As a tribe, and for good reasons, Germans are wary of persons claiming personal authority, but many in the same set of people say *Ja und Amen!* if they are told it's *channeled.* Some long-time students get upset and quit the group. After all, if it's not channeled, if it's just coming from someone who's sitting in the room with you, what good is it?

The SNAG

After her sabbatical from the guides, Ursula goes back to channeling class material. Workshops are a hit once again, but by that time in the Gammelshausen healing center, something is different. I'm in the picture now, and we are giving the workshops together. My years of regular spiritual practice in the Order have given me a certain presence, and being male in this predominately women's domain sets me apart. The Order vibe still clings to me, even as I try to wriggle out of that identity. That, and being Ursula's partner, has imbued me with a certain credibility in the eyes of the workshop crowd. Passing the fall-apart test with the Dutch girl in the kitchen and my subsequent informal healing apprenticeship have been my entry into a support role. As it turns out, I'm a good person to have around when people fall apart or fall into canals.

I'm perceived by some workshop attendees as a co-intuitive on somewhat equal footing with Ursula, but I know better than to believe that. On workshop days, Ursula and I meditate together, and I give my two cents' worth about the content. But no, Ursula has already gotten the whole thing from her guides in her meditation.

Despite the fact that the house belongs to Ulrike, the village doctor, the de facto line of authority in the Gammelshausen house unmistakably runs through Ursula. If she wakes up one morning with a vision that we should paint the workshop room lavender, that's what ends up happening. There is nothing like the rigid structure of the Order, and still it becomes clear that the others in the healing center rely on Ursula's ability to get guidance in meditation.

At least in that respect, it's life in the Order all over again. I'm so used to living in a hierarchy that I glide into a familiar default mode of acquiescence. For a while, this seems to work. There are advantages to being seen as a "safe" man, labeled in people's minds as a SNAG, a Sensitive New Age Guy, but I pay a price for getting "over yin-ized" and passive. Bob's warning about not accepting such setups definitely rang a bell for me up in Ringkøbing, but that bell is barely audible down in Gammelshausen.

43.

DECISION

Life's rhythms set in, and I settle into life in a tiny village in Southwest Germany. The old house requires regular attention, and my informal energy healing apprenticeship continues. Periodically, we drive our boxy red Renault R-4, which we have named Marcel, to visit Ursula's mother in Soltau several hours to the north, then up the west coast of the Kansas-flat Jutland Peninsula of Denmark to Ringkøbing to take a class with Bob. It's a time of rubbing elbows with a wide variety of Northern European healer-types who all speak English like Bob.

On one trip, we rent a thatched bungalow nestled among the white sand dunes on the North Sea coast near the town of Hvide Sand. There, we collect several fist-sized stones, rounded and smoothed by the tides, and stow them under the driver's seat. Recalling the long-ago day when the terrifying Abbot summoned the Abbey into his pocket so he could reinstall it in the new Abbey in Detroit, I declare these to be our *Reisesteine,* our "travel stones," collected specifically to hold the memory, the vibrational record of Marcel's travels, to be transferred later to another car when Marcel dies.

Ursula has turned off the faucet of channeled material from her guides and then turned it on again. As a relative newcomer, I am naïve about the deeper power dynamics in the healing center, but this sudden decision on her part, followed by her equally sudden reversal, has had an effect on everybody. With the fresh flow of other-dimensional guidance through Ursula, the subtle order of things is reestablished. On the surface, daily life resets.

In the autumn of 1983, Ulrike, the doctor, closes the medical practice for a week and *abseils* off to attend a personal growth workshop on her own. Newly self-assertive and empowered, she arrives back in Gammelshausen and throws all of us out. It's a sudden, bitter break up. Ulrike is unyielding, and Ursula is shattered. By the end of October, we are packed and gone.

Our landing place for the nonce is a friend's apartment in Munich. Up until now, the position and resources of Ulrike's medical practice in Gammelshausen have provided the healing center and all of us living there with stability and community visibility. Now, in our inner city apartment with its high ceilings and winter drafts, we are without work or income. Old friends of Ursula stop by for *Kaffeeklatsches* and ask for healing sessions. They drop hints that there are plenty of people in that part of the country who want workshops. This is encouraging but, still stunned by the reversal in our fortunes, we pass a bleak winter in Munich, the metropolitan heart of Bavaria.

Insecurities seep from me like grease from a cheap Bratwurst. Internal Inquisitors, some wearing Order garb, raise dark eyebrows and examine me silently about my choices. In less than six months, I have left my Order life for a woman I barely know and moved, with my seven sets of underwear, into a scene at an alternative healing center that disappears overnight. Any sense I once had of being "reassigned" has dried up and blown away. I feel more like I've been banished.

I struggle with how to talk to others, to my family, and to the moral establishment in my head, about my relationship with Ursula. After living in the Order, with its quaint but antiquated code of courtship and marriage within the fold, I am preoccupied with my self-image as a sanctified man. I may have escaped the insular world of the Order, but I'm twenty years behind the curve of modern attitudes about cohabitation. I flounder. It's 1984, and I am conflicted about living unmarried with Ursula, and if she were to get pregnant, *what then?* The idea never enters my head that she and I are free to choose the path of our relationship. On a trip to Denmark, I propose.

That Ursula is now engaged to an unemployed foreigner eight years younger than she is seems to bother no one in her family. Ursula's sisters welcome me with open arms. Ursula's mother places me at the paternal head of the table at dinners and makes sure I get the biggest serving of meat, a post-war holdover custom.[4] I jump into honorary male roles, unfilled in this family of women since the death of Ursula's father. I feel genuinely loved and accepted, even as I remain in my status as a "good foreigner." In some confusion as to the origins of the name "Gilkeson," I am introduced at my future mother-in-law's seventieth birthday as "Ursel's Icelandic fiancé." Getting married represents grounding and stability for both of us and, before long, the obvious thing to do is to fly across the pond to introduce Ursula to my family.

---

[4] The rationale for this custom was that the menfolk needed their strength in order to go out and "rebuild Germany." This custom overlooks the fact that with so many men dead or missing after the war, it fell to the women to literally pick up the pieces. They were called the *Trümmerfrauen*, rubble women. Ursula's mother was one of them.

44.

DRUID HONEYMOON

When we have our civil wedding in Munich in the spring of 1984, my father and step-mother don't make the trip. The ceremony takes place at the *Münchner Standesamt,* the Munich City Hall, on the edge of the English Garden. A month later in June, my brother Bruce makes the journey from Wichita to attend a wedding ritual with our teacher, Bob Moore. He lands the role of escorting Ursula's mother and sisters to the event, takes the wheel on the *Autobahn* from Soltau to Ringkøbing, and hangs in there remarkably well in German, which earns him the undying admiration of his new in-laws.

The dinner that follows our blessing by Bob is a potluck, bohemian affair. Friends gather around us with candles and songs in the thatch-roofed home of fellow Bob-student Eva, who bakes us a Danish wedding cake. The moment is heartfelt, the people genuine.

We're borderline broke, except for the bit of cash that comes my way from my grandmother's estate. The money feels unreal, and the Munich housing market promises to eat it up in no time. So instead of returning to Germany from Denmark, we turn west at the port city of Esbjerg and ship across the North Sea to Newcastle Upon Tyne in England. Ursula is being called by the Druids, and since I have no better intelligence, we point our arrow toward the Scottish Highlands. There, we ferret out an empty croft house overlooking the northern tip of Loch Ness. We have just enough to rent it for the summer. The place is called "Balliemore," Gaelic for "Big Town." This "big town" consists of our wee four-room house, wired for electricity, but not hooked up to the mains. Ballimore is also completely outfitted with indoor plumbing, but it's a summer of drought and the well is dry. Not a drop flows inside the house.

Time is elastic. We haul water, rehabilitate the little house, meditate, write by candlelight, and ride the emotional roller coaster of living together. Marriage is an alien state for both of us. It's 1984. I'm thirty-four and Ursula is forty-two. She has never expected to marry at this juncture in her life, more accustomed to herself as an independent person.

Ursula is a starchild. She wants to dive into the telluric currents of the Druidic underworld of the British Isles. Forays to the north take us to Findhorn, a community famed for extraordinary vegetable gardens, grown with the help of nature spirits. To the south, we make pilgrimages to the Isle of Iona, Stonehenge, and St. David's Head. In Wales, we visit a pair of old-timers from the circle of students around Bob Moore. He is an old Scotsman with a stentorian voice and great brambly eyebrows. His elven wife is half his age. They are fervent Celtic mystics, utterly steeped in the lore of secret Earth energies. Together, they make regular pilgrimages to the power vortices in the surrounding countryside. In their kitchen, we sit under a wall map of the *chakra* system of the UK and drink tea out of mismatched cups. With great pride, they recount the auspicious day when Sir George Trevelyan, author of *A Vision of the Aquarian Age,* installed them as the Stewards of *Ysgyryd Fawr,* Holy Mt. Skirrid. Midway down its long sloping ridge is a curious gash which our hosts inform us was cloven by the Mighty Sword of Archangel Michael. After we dine on black bread, cheese, and whiskey, they invite me to walk across their living room and feel the energy of the ley line, a palpable earth current, that diagonally bisects the room. Sure enough, when I pass over the room's middle the energies vibrate and wave perceptibly.

For my part, I'm still in the aftermath of exiting from the Order, weary of lofty spiritual ideals and otherworldliness in general. I want to drink beer and play golf. Ursula finds out quickly that I am not the priestly counterpart she has hoped for. She has learned to deal with the demands of her own spiritual calling without the additional challenges of living with a husband, and here we are, married.

After three months in Scotland, we depart Balliemore and cross the Channel back to the Continent. In France, the clutch on our ancient Renault, Marcel, begins to slip, and in the city of Reims, Marcel can no longer climb hills. Again and again, we nearly make it up a steep incline, only to falter, and roll backwards down the hill like Sisyphus's stone, each time coming to a providential stop in front of the tiny garage of a Renault mechanic. The ADAC, the German equivalent of the American AAA, puts us up in a hotel, buys our dinner and breakfast, and a tank of gas. It gives us a line of credit to have the machinists repair our *embrayage*. We return to Germany on literally our last *Pfennig*.

New Learning Curves

After bunking for a couple of weeks, courtesy of Ursula's sister, with a commune of *sanyasins,* followers of Bhagwan Rajneesh (later known as Osho), in Munich, I find work teaching English at a language school. We find an apartment in Freising, a bedroom community of greater Munich, and I commute every day. The language school sends me out to firms whose employees are required to deal with international business. Assignments take me weekly to big insurance companies and to the Dornier Aircraft Company, famous in World War II for building the giant "flying boats" with a dozen propellers.

My life is one steep learning curve after the other. There are things I just don't know about in the world. For my work at the language school I get no paycheck. Instead, funds are transferred electronically each month, popping up by magic in my ac-

189

count like overnight mushrooms after a rain shower. One day, out in the city, at liberty between classes, I walk into a branch of the Deutsche Bank and withdraw all but three Marks from my account. The rest of the day, I walk around with the wad of cash bulging in my pocket like an erection or a lucky talisman, feeling the numinous wonder of it. Toward the end of the day, I go into another branch and redeposit it. The small inheritance from my grandmother that got us to Scotland felt unreal, and this is the first time after ten years of living under a vow of poverty that I have had money of my own.

Paternal yearnings rise up in me, yet I am blind to reality. We never do anything to prevent pregnancy or even talk about having a family. But Ursula, who is forty-two, knows long before I do that we are never going to have children. When it comes to having babies, her biological clock has finished ticking, and her eyes are on spiritual matters. The realization takes longer to land with me. After work, in the anonymity of the Munich subway, I park myself on the metal benches with my language teacher's briefcase on my lap for a desk. There, I let trains pass me one by one and write long spidery letters, blotched with tears, to children I will never have.

45.

An African in Bavaria

In 1985, I find out after the fact that my father has suffered a heart attack. He didn't want me to worry, I'm told, and he has recovered well after a pacemaker was installed. I write back to say this is something I *want* to worry about. The heart attack points out the obvious: I am way out of position to be of any use to my father if an emergency should arise, not to mention the fact that the two of us have hardly spent any time together since I first left home. Better late than never, I want to be a son.

Up to now, I've been a member of that species of ex-pat that derives a great deal of satisfaction from how well they can live in another country. I quietly celebrate my little milestones of acculturation when Germans don't automatically identify a telltale American accent in my speech. I love it when they ask, "Are you Norwegian? Are you Dutch?" In my own mind, I have achieved a certain exotic status.

A year later, I return to Germany after traveling to my brother's wedding in Mexico, and the weight of a decade of being a foreigner lands on me with both feet. Speaking English with my family for a couple weeks has reminded me that, good though my German may be, I am only able to express about seventy-five percent of what I want to say. But it's about more than language. I go to Hugendubel bookstore on Marienplatz and make straight for the foreign bookshelves. There, I find a copy of a new bestseller, *The News From Lake Woebegone,* by an

American humorist I've never heard of, and devour it in a wave of nostalgia. Hungry for more, I ask Ursula for books by Mark Twain for Christmas. She obliges me with a hefty compact volume, onion-skinned and leather-bound like a Bible. *The Complete Works of Mark Twain*—in German. I dutifully plow through classics like *Die Abenteuer von Tom Sawyer und Huckleberry Finn* and *Leben auf dem Mississippi.* In his notes, the translator explains that he solved the problem of rendering American hillbilly English into German by using a rural Swiss dialect. It has a surreal effect on me.

To my great disappointment, I haven't truly "gone native" here in Europe, the way I thought I could when I was younger and prided myself on being a man of the world. Here I am, living in a language, a culture, and a marriage that require me to cross an inner bridge every day, and it's wearing on me. The book is a sweet gesture, but it does nothing to scratch the deep itch I'm feeling. I'm far from home.

I'm not only homesick. I'm also tired of this chapter of my life. I'm pushing forty with no job skills except for my tattered resumé as an autodidact, uncredentialed, professional speaker of English, and a fledgling energy healer. We have by this time moved from Freising to Mauern, a village hidden away in the hinterlands, out where fox and squirrel kiss each other good night. It's what Munich people, in their urban sophistication, call the "Bavarian Congo." The rent is cheap, and we have a whole house to ourselves. But we're both "Prussians" in the eyes of the locals, which is how people in the Bavarian Congo refer to anyone who isn't from there, like the way the Amish refer to outsiders as "English," regardless of where they're from.

I quickly tire of being asked where I come from by the villagers in Mauern who have never been around a foreigner. When we first arrive, I borrow a ladder from a neighbor who just cannot wrap his head around the notion that I'm an American. He mishears me each time, thinking I'm saying I'm from Africa.

"Wo kommen'S denn her?"

"Ich bin Amerikaner."

"Afrikaner sind'S!?"

"Nein, Amerikaner."

"Afrikaner?"

"Nein, ich bin A-MER-I-KANER!"

"Soooo . . . Amerikaner sind Sie!" he says, whacking his forehead in disbelief with the palm of his hand. *"Wo gibt's das denn? Saperlot!!* I'll be damned! Whoever heard of such a thing?"

The news makes the rounds, starting at the local *Stammtisch* at the local pub where the old-timers meet every day over beer, that there's a Prussian from Africa living right there in Mauern.

46.

YANKEE GO HOME!

I'm professionally adrift. Energy healing, as a profession, is a world of self-ordained practitioners, since there is no one besides you to tell you that you're ready. But the notion of setting myself out in the world as an energy healer on no one else's say-so but my own is a bridge too far. I'm growing as a practitioner and have the occasional paid client for energywork sessions. And I've grown habituated to my support role in the workshops Ursula and I hold in our musty little house. But nobody is beating a path to my door. I sense Ursula's desire for a fully equal partner, but I never truly believe myself to be that. Instead, I'm swamped by my inner clash of homesickness, professional unfulfillment, self-doubt, and uncredentialed limbo, which eclipse the progress I'm making.

The feeling snowballs. I make an exploratory journey to Freiburg to check out an educational program run by disciples of the psychologist Carl Rogers. But that would mean committing to a long program in far-away Freiburg and then ending up with a German credential in Rogerian counseling psychology. *Is that truly what I'm about?*

On my outdoor lunch breaks between English classes in Munich, I stare longingly at airplanes taking off from Franz-Josef Strauss International Airport. I force my eyes to make out the airline logos on the planes' tails and wonder where in the world they are heading. Air travel, always filled with mystic

194

overtones for beings who can't fly, becomes my metaphor for transformation. You strap yourself into a sealed capsule in one world and emerge like a butterfly in another. I'm already traveling to new places inside myself and need a metaphor equipped with wings, jet engines, and landing gear to make it stick. In meditation magazines, I read advertisements for American schools of Transpersonal Psychology. This speaks to me of legitimacy and a way to do healing work under some institutional authority.

School brochures from American institutes pile up on the kitchen table: California Institute of Integral Studies, Institute for Transpersonal Psychology, the Boulder Graduate School. All of them require an undergraduate degree, which I lack since being dropkicked out of the University of Kansas a semester shy of graduation. I write to the KU Office of Admissions and find out that all I have to do is petition to be reinstated. In due course, KU accepts my petition to come back as a "non-traditional student." I also get a welcoming echo from the Boulder Graduate School, a Colorado-based version of the Institute of Transpersonal Psychology. They tell me I can enter their graduate program as soon as I have my B.A., along with preparatory classes in psychology. Fair enough. It is the beginning of 1989, and I'm high on the prospect of getting back to the U.S.

This proposed relocation is completely unilateral on my part and comes out of the blue for Ursula. Her whole life is in Europe. We have built our life there, and she has no desire to uproot herself. Up to now, we have ignored the fact that being married to someone from another country means that at least one of you will always be a foreigner, no matter where you live. But she never thought that *she* would be the foreigner. The prospect of striking out to the New World puts Ursula in a bind. This is emphatically not her choice. Suddenly, all bets are off.

By the spring of 1989, I am enrolled at KU, and small parcels are piling up on my step-sister's downstairs couch in Lawrence,

Kansas. I send books and small items by slow boat from the tiny Mauern post office where they have never before seen so much international business. In August, I fly to the States and prepare for fall semester. I rent a house on the southern edge of Lawrence. The Midwest heat and humidity almost knock me over, but the nighttime electrical storms are thrilling, reminding me of the Wichita summers of my childhood. On the bedroom wall, I tape a postcard with a picture of a little bird in flight and wonder what this is doing to Ursula, in limbo now in Stuttgart, still undecided. Days, I run the gauntlet of immigration paperwork for her visa without knowing for sure if she will be joining me.

Classes commence and still no word. I'm wired and the world is jumpy and surreal. International news is filled with mixed signals. On the front page of the *Lawrence Journal World* is a photo of Mikhail Gorbachev. I trance out, staring at the crimson birth mark on his forehead. One evening, the newly installed phone rings. Through the crackle of static, I can't tell if Ursula is laughing or crying. She has jumped over her own shadow and caught a flight to Chicago, only to be detained by immigration authorities. Her visa photo, it turns out, is showing the wrong ear. Dead weary from the long flight, she has no choice but to wade through the process of getting her identification in order before she will be allowed into the country. Ursula arrives in Lawrence in September, less than three months before the Berlin Wall comes down.

47.

JUST START

It's a new life. In my eleven years abroad, I have acquired what linguists call the "German mouth," the particular facial and speech musculature that develops from speaking German day in and day out. I'm told I speak with an accent, but I'm feeling the relief of speaking American English without having to curtail my vocabulary for non-speakers. In time, I will acquire the American mouth again, but that can wait.

I find myself in a new stratum of Lawrence, known to locals as "Larryville." Besides being a Jurassic Park for old hippies from the sixties, Lawrence is a quintessential university town, fertile ground for intellectual and social experiments. I become a regular at Paradise Café, where the "No More Hard Times Special," a bowl of rice and beans, paired with a chunk of cornbread with butter for under five bucks, sustains many an old beard farmer in bib overalls. At street level, I run into characters I remember from when I was here my first time around as a student. "Tan Man"—I remember him when he was "Tan Boy"—still rides his bike, shirtless and in shorts, regardless of the weather. I recognize the same sprinkling of old radicals and poets and even a couple of the town's endless walkers, still pacing the uneven sidewalks of East Lawrence, mellower now for the Prozac they get. They never left. Beneath it all, Lawrence also has a deep historic substrate of Free Thought and the anti-slavery movement of the nineteenth century. Full name: The Free State of Lawrence, as opposed to The Slave State of Lecompton, just down the road fifteen minutes away. Instead of Main Street, the principal downtown thoroughfare of Lawrence is named Massachusetts, the home of the abolitionists who founded the city. Liaisons run deep here.

Who knew that I would take to being a student? I'm pleased with my spiffy new German briefcase, my bus pass, and meal ticket at the Student Union. I spend my days on campus and in the computer lab, where I type my essays and short stories on word processors. For the first time in my life, I'm getting As on tests and papers. I'm a "non-traditional" student, twice as old as most of the people in my classes, even older than some of my professors. I also have a German wife at home who, as it turns out, is not languishing away her days, pining for the Old Country. Ursula takes her new circumstances admirably in stride. The local NPR station plays classical music, and a KU choir performs a Christmas concert that earns a solid B by her well-honed standards. And she already has a modest practice as an exotic foreign energy healer woman.

In the early 1990s, busy with KU and reacculturation to life in the U.S., I barely notice that Lawrence is a good place for an alternative healing practice. While Ursula builds a practice through word-of-mouth contacts, I fret. The narrative I'm running on—the one about completing educational prerequisites in order to legitimately practice energy healing—is flimsy. I'm skittish about starting a healing practice of my own, but I also have a vague plan. Twenty-three years after starting as an undergraduate in 1967, I walk down the Hill in cap and gown with the graduating class of 1990, a forty-year-old Bachelor of Arts with a major in Germanic Languages and Literatures and a minor in Italian, well-nigh useless if I don't become a language teacher again. I have added courses in psychology and sociology, prerequisites for entering Boulder Graduate School, my pathway to becoming a transpersonal psychotherapist.

I take a reconnaissance trip to hip, alpine Boulder, Colorado, to scout out job possibilities. There, I meet the principals of Boulder Graduate School and come away with a less than solid feeling about the whole enterprise. Sure enough, well in advance of the time when we would decamp to Boulder, a form letter arrives from BGS, informing the world that the school is going belly up. Financial stress is claiming another fledgling alternative school.

Bob Moore reserves an hour a day for calls from outside Denmark, and when I call during that time slot, hoping for some clairvoyant advice, it's as if he's been waiting for me. I lay out my wretched situation and fall into the deep silence of his listening. I only know he is still on the line because I can hear his breathing. As I listen to myself talk, I see how my insecurities have generated this legitimacy crisis. When he finally speaks, Bob does an end-run around the problem I have created for myself.

"The way I see it, Jim," he says, "if you had gone into that program in Colorado, it would have been a fiasco. Why don't you just start your practice?"

I thank him and agree it's time to start. I hang up and immediately wish I'd asked Bob what exactly my practice is.

48.

A Healer in Lawrence, Kansas

We settle in a modest house in a modest neighborhood in Lawrence. Under the blue windy sky, we entertain friends on a patio decorated with a snowy fleece of cottonwood seeds. And the wind! From the moment of arriving back in Kansas, I am again united with this constant childhood friend. The summer southwind roars like a gentle chesty lion over the enclosure of our little backyard, bending the branches of a giant cottonwood, rustling its leaves. I close my eyes and imagine the surf of a vast upside down ocean of air breaking above our heads.

In Ursula's world, gardening is somewhere between a mystical practice and a competition sport. This begins with attending to the backyard nature spirits. Whatever she plants gets permission to indulge in quick giantism. From popcorn, meditative collaboration with the spirits grows backyard corn with quartz crystals entwined in its roots. Old maids bear fruit like Sarah in the Old Testament. At Ursula's urging, sunflowers reach deep into the earth to accumulate telluric powers and rip their way upward through cracks in the patio with so much momentum that they bolt upward, displacing chunks of concrete, and find sunlight by looking over the top of the house.

From long dowel rods strung together with fishing line, Ursula fashions the skeleton of a teepee, bedangled with crystals. More crystals seed plant starts at the base of each dowel to lure Big Energies. She whispers magic to each one, egging them on in a sprint to the top of the teepee. A Morning Glory Race! I'm reminded of kudzu vine, imported from Africa as a solution for erosion in the southern U.S. The kudzu grows like crazy. In no time, it's out of control, devouring houses and roads, creeping up telephone poles and crashing power lines with the accumulation of weight. The Morning Glory Race in the middle of our backyard is a dead heat, but the vines keep going, ignoring gravity and the supposed finishing line at the top. Instead, they twine their way to the apex of a seven-foot volcano of green leaves and dazzling flower trumpets and overnight produce a tousled geyser of gaudy blue racers gushing into empty air.

It is difficult in these pages to adequately describe Ursula's contribution to the healer scene in Lawrence and nearby Kansas City. She has a profound, often unsettling effect on the small circle of people that come to her for healing sessions and to the workshops we lead. There is a shamanic quality to her work.

Ursula is a reminder that healers come in all kinds of packages. They are a diverse lot of mold-breakers. Some healers are sweet as a coconut pie, some bristly and off-putting. Some are refined, meticulously professional, and others are loose cannons, some self-righteously health-conscious, while others smoke like chimneys and ride on motorcycles in black leather. One autumn afternoon in a Kansas City attic apartment, I receive a powerful healing treatment from a man in his late sixties who looks exactly like Ronald Reagan. What they all have in common is an active quality that expresses through them and affects others. Call it a talent or a spiritual gift. As with natural-born leaders, artists, and teachers—especially the ones, like Ursula, who have taken the trouble to develop their gifts—you sense it in their presence.

A regular workshop venue opens in the home of a psychotherapist in Kansas City, and we become part of the regular rota of weekend workshop providers there. My apprenticeship continues with lessons about teaching groups of healer-types.

One of the common occupational hazards in the energy healing workshop milieu is people's projections. Once a client or weekend workshop participant decides that you are a spiritually realized teacher, it's a hard tooth to pull. I remember how many father projections Bob Moore had to deal with from his students, myself included. A variation of this happens with couples who come to be seen this way, and many of our workshop attendees see Ursula and me as an ideal spiritual couple. This creates a raft of unspoken expectations that are hard to dismantle. The truth is, I have only superficial confidence in my own gifts. I don't know in my own heart of hearts if I am a healer or a teacher in my own right. Meanwhile, the still small voice in my head whispers a steady stream of messages about imposters. It's not Ursula's fault that I don't feel myself to be on equal footing with her, but I suffer from it.

1992, Lawrence, KS: Even this grainy photo tells the story: Ursula had a serious effect on sunflowers.

49.

FIRST PRACTICE AND BREADLESS ART

I have completed the self-assigned exercise of finishing my undergraduate degree, designed to segue into the next phase of my education to become a transpersonal psychologist, but that has been derailed. For her part, Ursula has precious little regard for the professional credentialing process that I'm so obsessed with. As much as I have observed her over the years, I still don't know how she does what she does. She parachutes into Lawrence, a reluctant immigrant, and shakes a healing practice out of her sleeve on no other authority than her belief in what she is doing. Boulder Graduate School, where I have pinned my hopes for professional legitimacy, is folding, and the whole scheme that returned me to the U.S., pulling Ursula along with me, turns suspect.

Money pressures mount. I wander from one temporary job and season of breadless art to the next, all in the name of "keeping the Ruble rolling" until I create some kind of healing practice.

Jumping Over My Own Shadow

As far as Ursula is concerned, I'm going at it all backwards. Her way is to self-legitimize by finding what she feels called to do, getting the intuitive signal that she's ready, and then finding the least restrictive way to do it legally. And to make things worse, I now have Bob on the other end of the telephone line in Denmark, telling me to forget all that credential stuff. All I need to do is jump over my own shadow.

I give it a shot. A friend in the Kansas City cadre of healer-types offers me the use of an empty room in the Myrtle Fillmore Center, named after the co-founder of Unity Church. I set up my massage table and do a few energy healing sessions. This goes a couple of months, but nobody comes back a second time. I'm forced to admit to myself that what I'm doing is an imitation of how Ursula works. I've adopted her hand gestures, moves, sequences, and explanations. I have learned how to move energy around in another person's body. I have healing gifts and a certain presence and spirituality about me, but this, all by itself, does not a make me a healer with a practice. No amount of visualization and intention-setting creates a difference.

Meanwhile, Ursula grows her practice, and I meander from gig to gig. Between her work and what I scrape together from odd jobs, we pay our bills. Workshops provide a bit of extra cash. In our weekend energy healing classes, we minister to a circle of regulars. My role increases. I teach more and find I have some facility for getting complex ideas into bite-size pieces. It's an unexpected source of enjoyment for me, and this, in turn, breeds a new confidence.

Penthe Publishing

Ursula's first treatment room is upstairs in Lamplighter, Lawrence's metaphysical bookstore, owned by a former pastor and his wife. David and Mary, the owners, learn from Ursula that I can read and write and edit, and that I need work. Soon, a call comes from an elderly woman who has made a deathbed promise to her husband: she will see to the publication of his unfinished manuscript. The bookstore owners have pitched me as the ideal ghostwriter to complete the work on *Death Without Fear,* a book of "afterlife research," channeled by spiritual mediums. The widow entrusts her husband's manuscript to me, and I set to work. As I read into the manuscript, I envision seance circles of blue-haired ladies in dimly lit Earl Grey Victorian rooms fun-neling messages from the dear departed.

Ghostwriter, indeed. The late author, until his death a lec-turer for Edgar Cayce's Association for Research and Enlight-enment, becomes my familiar spirit. I feel him standing over me, dictating as I work, and I discover in me a chameleonic ability to adopt his voice as I rewrite and organize. When the refur-bished manuscript is not accepted for publication by any of the publishing houses that go for afterlife lore, his widow pays me to learn the ropes of home publishing. I establish a small press. I'm sheepish about charging her for all the work this entails, but it's her way to fulfill a solemn promise, and she is all gratitude.

I create a jerrybuilt design of the layout of *Death Without Fear* with a pre-Windows version of WordPerfect at KU's com-puter center. When I hand the "galleys" to the owner of a local family printing business, he takes one look and invites me into his office. On his desk between us is a bound book which he shoves my direction.

"Open that book and riffle the pages at the corner. Watch what the page numbers do." I riffle and watch. You could have stuck a pin through the center of those page numbers. They don't move a single nanometer.

"That's the first book my dad set, by hand, over forty years ago," he says. "Now take your pages and riffle them." The numbers dance around nervously. Point made. Despite my danc-ing page numbers, the printer abandons all principle and prints the book, featuring cover art by a stateless visionary artist Ur-sula and I have met in Frankfurt. *Death Without Fear,* by Har-vey Humann, is published in 1992 by a new small press in Lawrence, KS, called Penthe Publishing.

In the months that follow, I learn that small presses, even amateur operations like mine, have their niche in the literary ecosphere of a college town. The main qualification is a will-ingness to do the work and make no money doing it. *Sign me up!* A friend from my first years at KU, Denise Low, is all ears when

I tell her about my small press. I know that Denise is an astrologer and author of some kind, and I soon learn that she is an English professor at Haskell Indian Nations University and well on her way to becoming Kansas Poet Laureate. For a time and a season, I'm her publisher, and Penthe Publishing gets involved with the microscopic but prolific world of Lawrence local writers. I bask in my role as a midwife for other people's publishing projects and get to rub shoulders with "real authors." I'm still in the closet with my own writing, but I nurse a fond wish that someday I would find a publishing midwife to do the same thing for me.

I take my small press seriously. With each new project, I get more sophisticated with typesetting, layout, and design. And each new project is my last. By the time a new book is born, maybe to be read by one or two hundred people, I'm ready to swear off book publishing. But it's a drunkard's oath. No sooner do I take delivery of thirty boxes of newly printed books and get a whiff of fresh printer's ink, I start spinning plans for the next book. When I call Bowker, Inc., the official source for ISBN numbers, so that Penthe's books can be scanned in bookstores and catalogued by distributors, I ask for one hundred numbers to be assigned to my small press. I can feel the woman smiling on the other end of the phone line.

"Let's see you do ten," she says. "You can always come back for more." In my career as a micro-publisher, Penthe publishes nine books.

50.

SOUTHWIND

In 1993, I pluck up my courage and apply to work as a massage therapist at Southwind Health Collective. I have absorbed enough massage technique through Ursula that I can do a decent session in the long-stroke style of the Esalen Institute. These are the old days when there's a not a school of bodywork and massage on every corner. In the unregulated Kansas of the early 1990s, I can rent a room, set up a table, hang out a shingle, and call myself a massage therapist. It's also a time when therapeutic massage is starting to become a thing outside of hospital and physical therapy settings, but people in general don't quite know what to do with it. There is much still clinging to the popular idea of massage that carries a whiff of prostitution.

Southwind, the first massage and bodywork practice of its kind in this college town, is a band of women dedicated to promoting their work and educating the public. They work hard, and each of them has managed to create a regular clientele and make a living. It's different for me. When I first come on board, you could have held a convention of all the male massage therapists in Lawrence in a phone booth and still had enough room left over to do a massage. Many days, I sit at the front desk, answering the phone, making appointments for my female colleagues. These are popular massage therapists, and, unlike me, they book out. One day, a woman on the phone has tweaked her neck, and she's desperate to get relief that day.

"Who else at Southwind has openings?"

"I have openings," I say. *I'm not just the receptionist.*

"I don't know . . . I've never had a massage from a man."

I aim to please. "Would you like me to call around and see if I can find you a female therapist with an opening?"

"Would you do that? Yes, please! My neck is killing me!" She hangs up. I call around. All the go-to female therapists in town are booked. I call the woman back. After she sits a moment with the grievous news, I add, "Well, if you'd like to take a walk on the wild side, I have an opening this afternoon." She is miserable enough to say yes and comes for a session. In the process, she discovers that I'm not an incipient rapist disguised as a massage therapist, and the world becomes a better place. She becomes a semi-regular client. This begins to happen more.

The more experienced therapists at Southwind are certified by the American Massage Therapists Association, and they have their noses to the winds of change in the professional massage world. Though not yet required by any law or oversight committee—Kansans suffer no regulation willingly—we collectively decide it is time for everyone at Southwind to get credentialed. By then, there is a National Certification Board for Therapeutic Massage and Bodywork that will issue us certifications if we can meet their minimum requirements. This entails passing their exam and swearing in an affidavit that we have done a certain number of hours of massage work, thereby proving that our touchwork is not lethal.

It's early 1994, the last year we can be grandmothered into this basic national certification without having gone to a massage school. Together, we study *Milady's Theory and Practice of Therapeutic Massage* and subject each other to inquisitions about the arcana of muscle origins and insertions, correct draping procedures, and endangerment positions. Our test-prep group expands to include two non-Southwind members, Ursula and a woman named Diane, who has tired of her work as a clinical social worker and is now Ursula's prime student in energy healing.

When the big day comes, we caravan *en masse* to Kansas City. We show up with our best game and take the exam in an auditorium packed with hundreds of others trying to slip in under the wire of grandmotherment. There are trick questions: "Which palm is facing forward in Eastern Anatomical Position?" This refers to the body posture shown on acupuncture charts and in Asian medicine in general. Afterwards, we repair to a nearby Vietnamese restaurant to drown our sorrows, certain we have all flunked the test. We later learn that the NCBTMB's exams always feature several trial questions, just to gauge how they fly with test takers, but which don't count on test scores. It takes weeks to find out that we all passed.

Credential magic. I'm official! The thin confidence of a piece of paper that I can hang on the wall puts a puff of wind in my sails, and my practice becomes a practice.

Having clients helps. I enter the professional world of bodywork with a few routines that at least don't cause anybody grievous damage, while wondering what in the world to do with the energy healing training I have. It's always with me in the background as I work, singing harmony with my massage strokes. It's a start.

Ten thousand hours of meditation and Order-house silence and doing endless somato-energetic exercises in Bob Moore's conference room all turn out to be good for something. Abilities grow in me, but not necessarily the ones I expect. Touchwork turns me into a tactile listener, a human stethoscope, a sonar probe, privy to things my mind misses in the silent ocean of movement under my hands and forearms and elbows. Palpation, paying attention to what's happening under the surface I'm touching, is an altered state of consciousness. I'm like a person passing by a glass-fronted bank on a sunlit day who learns to look through the glare and reflections, gradually making out the shapes inside.

Close attention to the work of Tom Overholser, the second male massage therapist to arrive at Southwind, affords me an entry into deep tissue work. My energy skills are growing, too, but despite an ability to wax eloquent in workshops, I'm inept at talking about that side of things with clients, so I keep this to myself.

51.

IN TOO DEEP

My early attempts at short fiction still sit, fizzing in my drawer like clumps of unprocessed uranium, still radioactive enough to cause a blip on my inner screen when I come near them. They remind me that I secretly think of myself as some kind of writer. I spend hours collecting and polishing my workshop notes, trying to make something intelligible out of a hash of marginalia. I mine my experiences from the Order, Bob Moore, and Southwind and create angles on the learning of energy healing that are at least interesting, if not useful. It takes me two years of this to admit to myself that I'm writing a book.

When I tell Ursula what I'm up to, there is not much response. She has heard my big ideas before. The idea of learning energy healing in any way except directly from a teacher strikes her as slightly suspect. But my admission to her gets my serious side in gear. I learn what it is to be pulled from bed before dawn every morning by a nagging muse, and the writing comes in binges. The discipline does me good, and a slow sense of momentum builds.

In my way, I'm teaching language all over again. It's another octave of teaching English to aircraft techies and German to Turkish teenagers. I find I have something to say to people who get involved with weird things like energy healing, and when I say it to them, it comes out in stories. The result is a salad of practices and treatments, loosely joined by vignettes and philosophical connective tissue. I give my opus the grandiose working title "The Longing of a Drop of Water for the Ocean," after a lecture by Sonja Becker on homeopathic salt. Gradually, a manuscript takes shape, a body of sorts, a Frankenstein assembly of my pet ideas in search of an electrode of some kind to jolt them into life.

The Health and Wellness Fair at the Holiday Inn features talks by Southwind's founder and a host of other presenters. It's a New-Agey marketing carnival with booths, books, and free samples of herbal elixirs and healing salves. As I make the rounds of talks and demonstrations, I'm huffy and indignant, a nose-up snob with a gimlet eye and a definite opinion about how this healing stuff ought to be presented. Surrounded by an adoring crowd, a guy in flowing Aladdin pants, obviously not from Kansas, gives a crystal treatment to a seated woman. He waves his arms around in her aura while announcing to the room that she is now healed. All but a few of the energy healing books on the display tables strike me as humorless, poorly written, flakey and overly mystical. I vow to myself to write a down-to-earth book about energy healing.

My gestating Frankenstein of a book seems to install etheric markers in my aura, visible to those with eyes to see. On our next trip to Denmark for a class with Bob Moore, he picks right up on it. Typical of Bob, who is reticent to a fault, he bides his time before saying anything about it. In class, I ask a question utterly unrelated to writing a book. As if he hasn't heard me, and apropos of nothing I can see, he quotes Omar Khayyam: "The moving finger writes; and, having writ, moves on . . ." Bob then goes out of his way to make it clear that he will not be writing any books himself, but when I do, I should write from my own perspective, not his.

My friend Dennis invites me to join a group that meets weekly at the Kansas Zen Center. We don't call it a "men's group." This is in the days before the "official" Men's Movement á la Robert

Bly and movements like the Mankind Project come along to bless such gatherings with all the approved templates for being modern men. We call our group "In Too Deep for Suicide." *What, exactly, do we mean by that?* The members are an assortment of specimens from late-sixties Lawrence, some KU faculty, a couple of hip local business owners, a co-founder of the Kansas bioregional movement, a future Abbot of the Kansas Zen Center, a Sufi realtor who resembles Mr. Natural in Zap Comix, and myself.

We gravitate to a handful of topics. The Alphas do most of the talking, the Betas listen and nod. I do some of each (does that make me a Gamma?). After a couple of years of this, it's time for something new. We decide that each of us would have an entire meeting—*two whole hours*—dedicated to telling our life stories. We agree on procedures: 1.) The teller talks. 2.) Everybody else shuts up and pays attention.

It's a miracle. Over the course of eight or ten weeks, we hear each other's awkward and triumphant and stupid and unresolved yarns. Everything is on the table. Upbringings and identity crises, marriages and divorces, periods of poverty and dumpster-diving, sexual wanderings, grand causes and failures. Having witnesses who just listen is a doorway into the over- and understories of our lives. The hearing is as healing as the telling. When it's my turn, I find I have a million stories in me, and I'm hot to tell them.

Between the in-too-deep-for-suicide men's group, my massage practice, and my yet-unabandoned small press, my circle widens. One evening, I find myself among an erudite group of university people at the home of the head of the Department of Classics at KU, who is also the Abbot of the Zen Center. I'm seated across the table from a skinny environmentalist named David Abram. He is holding forth on matters of philosophy, environment, language, performance art, and uncanny encounters with animals. He tells of travels in the outback of Nepal and Indonesia, trying to meet shamans. His ingenious go-to ploy is to perform sleight-of-hand magic tricks for villagers, who invariably take him straightway to the local medicine man. Abram is working on a manuscript about it all, something called *The Spell of the Sensuous*. For once, my first thought is not to wonder if this is might be something for my small press. Instead, I think . . . *if this guy can get published, why not me?*

52.

THE ELUSIVE THIRD POSITION

As a writer, I'm a lot of boat without very much rudder. Too complicated, too prone to shoot off in all directions at once, trying for some global manifesto of energy healing. Readers of early drafts are entertained, but it's all hypothetical. It doesn't connect.

My bodywork practice at Southwind is not much better. Neither my massage nor my energy healing work have discovered each other yet. Under my hands, physical bodywork and energy work are like strangers living in the same boarding house, who only encounter each other at the breakfast table when neither one is fully awake. By now, I can give a good, workmanlike massage with the standard array of stretches and strokes from European massage. Then, I can go all energetic, connecting energy-active positions on my client's body, moving energy around in their system. *But what of it?* I am largely replicating the outward moves and gestures I have absorbed from watching Ursula and my more experienced colleagues. I can place my hands on the solid realm of bones and muscles and make out the wispier world of energy, moving ghostlike behind the scenes. I don't know how to bring the two worlds together. Moreover, I have no clear idea of *why* I would want to do that. In my mind, it's still either tissue or energy, so I keep them at arm's length from one another.

A chiropractor in Kansas City invites me to an open house at which he demonstrates basic techniques in Upledger Craniosacral Therapy, a light-touch manual therapy that is gaining currency in the bodywork world. A small group of us gather around to watch as he works his way around a woman lying on her back on the massage table. Early in the treatment sequence, he demonstrates a lumbosacral release. The maneuver defies verbal description, and seeing it for the first time, even with explanations, is downright bizarre. What I do understand is that this is a gentle means of decompressing a juncture in the lower spine, giving relief for what we used to call lumbago. He holds this position for a couple of minutes in silence. For all its unusual appearance, this miniature treatment is a tidy procedure, accomplished with astonishing grace and efficiency, and the woman on the table is visibly relaxed and relieved. The open house ends with wine and cheese.

The main effect of the open house demo in Kansas City is that when it comes time to look for continuing education to renew my national massage certification, the Upledger Institute makes the choice easy. Their introductory course in Craniosacral Therapy will be held that summer in Sarasota, Florida. I go for it.

Ursula is gone that week on travels of her own, and it's liberating to be off by myself on an adventure. Everything is dirt cheap because August in Florida is the middle of hurricane season. In the steaming hot days before the course, I rent a car and binge-golf—thirty-six holes a day and lots of beer. I camp at Turtle Beach and decide to not shave for the week. At night before crawling into my sleeping bag, I go for naked swims in the lazy Gulf surf.

My introduction to Craniosacral Therapy is a treat on multiple fronts. The instructor, Roy Dejarlais, is a breed of teacher I haven't encountered before. Astute and scientific, he knows the names of things, while demonstrating generous respect for the unseen side of life. I see all kinds of subtle energetic overtones with Craniosacral Therapy, but Roy insists that this is not energy work. *Roy,* I think, *this is nothing but energy work!* He stays on his side of the track, studiously sticking with what we all can agree on. "One thing I like about teaching anatomy and physiology," he says, "is that no matter if you are a fundamentalist Christian, a Buddhist, a Muslim or an atheist, flexion is still flexion, and extension is still extension."

Roy passes nickels around, and we place them on the backs of our hands and the tops of our heads, the better to appreciate what five grams of force feels like. It's force all right, but barely palpable. "This, ladies and gentlemen, is the amount of force we will be using in many of the basic craniosacral treatment forms we will be learning." Just like the woman in the Kansas City chiropractor's open house demonstrations, we workshop participants find ourselves responding. Headaches clear, back pains lessen, and even the most uptight harried practitioners melt into the tables in relaxed puddles.

I grow new synapses as I listen to Roy. This business of using targeted but extremely tiny amounts of force is compelling. Roy talks tissue. I think energy. All the while, a new thought takes form in me: *something special happens at the cusp of structure and energy,* but as yet I have no name for the phenomenon. Dots connect. My note taking gets frisky. I come away with new anatomy and hand skills and, just as important, a new, poetic look at the physical body, and the way it heals itself.

I come to realize that I have found the elusive "third position" I've been half-consciously looking for between the density of physical tissue and the wispiness of the energy field. I have the image of grasping the solidness of a water pipe in a house and, simultaneously, feeling the rush of water flowing through it when an upstairs toilet is flushed. It is at this cusp between physical structure and energy that I learn to focus my touchwork. I later find out that it even has a cool esoteric name: the *physical/etheric interface.*

217

There's time to kill in the humid evenings between class and the Early Bird Specials at Sarasota seafood restaurants. I wander into a bookstore and browse the few books on energy healing. I'm living in the secret gestational throes of my book idea. I've admitted to myself that I'm writing one and that it will be on my down-to-earth take on energy healing. There, on my liberating junket to the wilds of Sarasota, Florida, riding the brainstorm that comes on me while sitting in Roy Dejarlais' craniosacral class, I decide now is the time to get serious and finish my manuscript.

Donna Eden and Carolyn Myss are the current heavy hitters in books on energy healing. I like them both, and they are clearly a notch above the schlock I encountered at the Health and Wellness Fair in Lawrence. I thumb through tables of contents and forewords, and the far-off mountain of publication swings into view. I browse further and find, drawing my eye like a magnet from the end cap display on a row of environmental books, the newly released title *The Spell of the Sensuous,* by David Abrams. The little skinny dude beat me to it!

53.

Energy Healing

Back at Southwind, new things start to happen on my massage table. The majority of my clients come for massage, and our sessions take their predictable form. But a few of my clients seem to have been waiting for what I'm now doing. At least they are open to trying something new, especially if it helps them feel better.

The first step is to help them be comfortable with my hands resting on their body, seemingly doing nothing, instead of the near-constant motion of a standard massage. My training with Ursula and Bob Moore in finding energy-active positions on the body has sensitized me enough to track energy movement. Now, I set about tracking micro-movements in my clients' tissues, often so subtle that I don't know if I'm following their physical body or the energies moving through it. One woman tells me she feels me touching her "inner body," and she seems completely at home with the idea. In other sessions, my attention is magnetically drawn to specific places in my client's body, and when I get that area between my hands and follow the tiny movements I find there, I feel my client drop into a new relaxation. Soon, I'm letting all my clients' bodies "speak" to me this way.

The combination of energetically-sensitive touch, rudimentary craniosacral techniques, and following tissue movement brings up unforeseen responses. Some clients drop into deep meditative states. Others spiral through cathartic emotional releases, followed by deep relaxation. In sessions, clients report cascades of unexpected memory, as if intense long-ago experiences have condensed into quite specific corners of their bodies and nestled in there, forgotten until this mode of touch helps the memory resurface. A woman comes into my practice complaining of a stiff neck and emerges from our session with a giant smile on her face. In an accent I can't identify, she recounts how, while lying on the table, she has vividly relived a concussion she sustained on an obstacle course during Army basic training. With a fully-loaded backpack on her shoulders, she climbed to the top of a barrier, slipped, and fell on her head. This landed her in sick bay for two weeks. Her big smile was because this got her discharged from the Army. After our session, her neck problems fade away.

I take further training in craniosacral work which provides more procedural and theoretical scaffolding. Exposure to the Zero Balancing® teachings of Fritz Smith further confirms what my hands have been telling me for a couple of years. Insights come and crystallize into basic precepts. *Follow the body's micro-movements, and they will lead you to what is ready to change. Held, unmoving places in the body often have too much energy in the tissue, often from a physical or emotional injury. Release the excess energy and emotion held in the tissue, and the tissue has an easier time normalizing.*

With time, a session with me becomes an unnamable blend of massage, stretching, craniosacral, and subtle energy therapy. It comes to me that I am able to put a person into an altered state of consciousness through my touch. My task is to create an approach that speaks to a broad range of human experience. I work in freehand improvisations of touch and technique, while my mind chews on questions my hands already know the answers to: *Is touchwork a trigger for spiritual experience? Is energy healing a pathway to inner growth?* My hands say yes.

I can hardly believe my audacity as I shop book proposals around to publishers. Especially when one of them takes my pitch seriously and asks to see a whole manuscript. Energy healing is gradually becoming a thing, crossing over the threshold of public awareness, and Marlowe & Co. of New York wants a piece of that action. Who knows?—maybe this massage therapist from Lawrence, Kansas, will be the next Donna Eden. I receive a contract and a four-thousand dollar advance and orders to work over the manuscript with an editor. I don't know any editors, so they give me a name, Hal Zina Bennett. I'm told he has worked extensively with authors from the Human Potential Movement emanating from the Esalen Institute. Big names like Gabrielle Roth and Stanislav Grof. It's late 1998 and I finally have my midwife. *I'm playing with the Big Kids!*

I print out my manuscript and send it off to Hal. His wife, who works with him in their publishing business, wants him to turn it down—it's too much of this and not enough of that for her. She's right. It's a train wreck. But he reads it, and two weeks later we're on the phone.

"Do you have the manuscript in front of you?" he asks.

"Got it." I said.

"Turn to page 124, second paragraph, third line."

"Got it."

"Let's begin the book there," he says. I stay calm, but a big cartoon exclamation point flashes neon in the thought bubble above my head.

"What about the first eight chapters?"

"Maybe you can work them into support articles for the book. Or you can just throw them away, if you like."

I'm gobsmacked. This is not starting well. *Am I about to work with someone who doesn't like my first eight chapters?* "Just curious, Hal, why do you want to begin there?"

"Because that's the first time you actually start talking to the reader. Everything before that is just writer's warm-up."

So we pitch the first eight chapters, take everything else

apart from top to bottom, and I revise the whole book. It's like nine months of psychotherapy. Hal has me kill my darling pet formulations and circumlocutions. He painstakingly shows me how to stay connected with the reader every step of the way. He cajoles, he badgers, he asks really dumb questions. One week, I redo a single passage five times for him. And still, he corners me.

Energy Healing *was published in 2000. One of my students literally read it to death.*

"I still don't get it," he says. Now I'm triggered. *Who is this guy anyway?* I've never laid eyes on him, and probably never will. He's somewhere in California.

"What the fuck, Hal?! Either I'm the worst writer in the world, or you're just plain dumb!" I go overboard, just to spite him. I write it one more time, spell everything out, step by step, as if for a clueless child, and hit "send" one last time.

A reply comes back in less than a minute. "There! That's what I'm looking for! Now you're present and talking to *me*! Good work!" I've never thought I could love a book editor, but I love Hal in that moment.

Energy Healing: A Pathway to Inner Growth goes to press as the world braces for the worst. This is the end of 1999. The media, especially in spiritual circles, is awash with apocalyptic Y2K predictions. There is a flaw in the essential software that runs the world, a Shadow in the system. Chaos is predicted. Computer glitches will cause disruptions in utility and food services, banking and transportation services. Meanwhile, famous psychics redraw the map of North America, but something about it is off. Florida and Maine are still sticking out like toes on Dr. Suess characters, but the West Coast is a receding line along the Rockies. The psychics predict a time, maybe to coincide with the coming digital collapse of Y2K, when the San Andreas Fault and the San Juan de Fuca Plate give way and a third of the continent slides off into the Pacific. We joke that all we have to do is sit tight, keep the faith, and we'll all have beachfront property in Kansas. All the same, better safe than sorry. We stock up on essential supplies and buy a portable toilet.

54.

SHADOW, SHADOW

I'm on a roll. *Energy Healing: A Pathway to Inner Growth* goes to press around the time of my fiftieth birthday, set to be released just after the new year, Y2K permitting. I'm having a season of success as a massage therapist, and my book deal, sweetened by early praise for *Energy Healing* from Elmer Green, the Father of Biofeedback, is swelling my self-esteem. For my birthday, I hatch the idea of hosting a party to which I invite everybody I know: family, work colleagues, artist friends, golf buddies, men's group, the well-behaved and the bohemian in my life. All these people represent different parts of me, I tell myself. Up to now, I have habitually kept them apart for fear that they would be incompatible. Now, I'm feeling bold, curious about what will happen if they rub up against each other.

The party goes off without incident, but something niggles in me. The more attention and praise I absorb, the more I sense a shadow rising in me. Having a published book in the works burnishes the image I project into the world as a healer and teacher. At the same time, a quiet inner message sounds in me about being an imposter. Ursula and I are seen as an evolved healer couple, and I've always assumed that our spiritual relationship would allow us to zip-line over our differences. But here, at the end of the century, those differences are feeling more and more complex. I stand before my friends and Ursula like a

224

man in a fine suit, knowing I'm wearing badly torn underpants underneath.

Ursula's shamanic work consumes her. She takes regular retreats into nature, called by the spirits to the desert Southwest for up to six weeks at a time. There, she gets instructions from her guides and comes back with copious handwritten notes.

I wander. When Ursula is off on her spirit-guided travels, I discover my own rhythms. I work. I write. I play golf with friends and drink oceans of beer. I hang out at Paradise Café until closing time with friends, both men and women. A change is taking place in me and, deep down, I dread it. I fantasize about being free, being other places, with other people. At the same time, I cling to the identity and approval I get from being a good boy, a good former Order brother, a healer husband with a wife whose spiritual connections guide the way. It's a variation of the very problem Bob tried to alert me to when I left the Order. *You really need to take responsibility for your own life, Jim, and how're y' goin' to do that if there's always someone telling you what to do and what to believe?*

I leave home on February third, and I don't come back. It is twenty-seven years to the day since the evening I was pulled into the chapel of the Nashville Order house for a surprise initiation ceremony. I sit in my tiny red car, my eyes closed and burning, my emotions in a blender, mortified at what I'm doing to Ursula and my life. I pause at the end of the driveway for several minutes. I literally don't know which way to go.

After couch-surfing and wandering for three long weeks in the shock of my separation from Ursula, I rent a basement room from a member of the Zen Center men's group. In photos of myself from this time, I see an intense salt-and-pepper-bearded Sarastro, forehead exploding with energy, newly hatched and vulnerable. In my basement, between sessions huddled with a Jungian analyst, I enter the painful *sadhana* of separation and divorce, and I begin to guess the lonely answer to the question of who in this world I belong to, namely, nobody but myself.

Too agitated to sleep, I drive a nocturnal circuit of East Lawrence alleys, always ending up behind the house of my Southwind colleague, Tom Overholser. There, I hide my car in the shadows, gingerly lift the Styrofoam cover of his hot tub, shed my clothes, and slip in for a solo soak under the stars. Mornings, I become a denizen of Milton's Cafe in downtown Lawrence. There, I rendezvous with myself over scrambled eggs and coffee, journaling and writing. In the distress of this time, it's a daily exercise in remaining mobile within myself, flexible of psyche. Anything to make good on an agreement I make with myself to maintain some kind of exchange between my head and my heart, between my depths and my surface.

Outwardly, my bodywork practice at Southwind is still in full swing. Within me, I can still touch what I have distilled from my time in the Order and with Ursula and Bob Moore. Under it all, however, I feel my time in Lawrence coming to an end.

2000, Lawrence, KS: My friend Charles Gruber took this photo of me during my basement year.

55.

CONTRA-DANCE AND THE WATER WORLD

In time, enough smoke clears after my exit from my marriage for me to look around. Events dodge and swirl, and lives overlap in a contra-dance of connections, romances, and real estate deals. A college friend of my brother, a woman named Laurie, with a bushel of hair like a gray tumbleweed, turns out also to be friends with Ursula's student, Diane, and her husband, Gary. They are all part of a network of Kansas environmentalists that includes Laurie's husband, Bill Ward, a brilliant lawyer for the Environmental Protection Agency. When I tell them I have known Bill Ward longer than any of them—we lived next door to each other as little boys in the early 1950s in Wichita—there is enough small-world quickening in this revelation to make us muse about how we all fit together somehow.

Over the years we have known each other, Diane and I have danced around a simmering attraction to each other, and the attraction is growing. It's not a welcome thing. The tangle of relationships in a small community makes it complicated, not to mention the fact that she has been Ursula's student.

Attraction grows. Diane returns from a family trip to Colorado. We talk at length, and it's clear to me that she is both excited and perplexed. Diane speaks in paragraphs and compound sentences, and it takes me a while to put together a picture. It centers on a water treatment she has received in a thermal pool. The way she describes it, with hand gestures and sound effects, I imagine it like this: the practitioner wraps Velcro® floats around her legs for flotation. She relaxes, weightless, like a leaf on the water's surface, as he wordlessly moves her through a series of stretches and dance-like maneuvers. It's a silent aquatic ritual, an intimate, moving, trance-like water-tango. He turns and her body unfurls, snapping like a whip in slow motion, spiraling out from its core, and then collapses in on itself. The session ends, and the first thing out of Diane's mouth is, "where can I learn to do this?" That night, a dream reveals painful truths about her marriage.

Diane enrolls in a workshop on intimacy and sexuality in Northern California, only to find out at the last minute that is has been cancelled. It's too late to cancel her flight, so she takes it. A client informs her that the would-be workshop venue is right down the road, rurally speaking, from Harbin Hot Springs, a clothing-optional hot springs retreat center. Online photos show it nestled in a box canyon among voluptuous teddy bear brown hills and stands of live oak and madrone. She has definitely heard of Harbin before. It's the world epicenter of the strange, evocative water-tango she experienced while in Colorado, a meditative, therapeutic form of aquatic bodywork called water-shiatsu, or "Watsu."

It's a natural fit. Diane is a bona fide nature ecstatic, turned on by the faces in flowers and driftwood whorls, and attracted to moss-covered boulders that she can crawl over like a salamander. A former cell biologist, she is easily drawn down the rabbit hole of a microscope into intercellular universes, captivated by internal communication switchboards of slime mold and networks of mushroom rhizomes on the floor of a forest. As a Pisces, she wants to swim in any body of water larger than a wash basin. She stays a week. Watsu sessions from Harbin's Health Services staff confirm her first impression. This crazy aquatic therapy blends nearly everything she values in the worlds

1993, Kansas City: Diane's 50th birthday. With her best friend (and my childhood neighbor), Bill Ward and me.

of nature and therapy.

Her week at Harbin ends. Diane returns, but only long enough for us to get more attracted, and more perplexed. The School of Shiatsu and Massage located at Harbin has a professional program for aquatic bodyworkers, and she will be turning right around and heading back for a total of nine weeks of intensive classes in Watsu.

On visits home between classes, Diane describes her experiences in florid detail, and again, my imagination does the rest. In my mind, I see her being slalomed through the warm water like a rippling strand of seaweed. The graceful swishing and stretching is interspersed with periods of silent floating cradled in the arms of her "water-tango" partner. When she opens her eyes, she sees stars through the broad leaves of the spreading fig tree that umbrellas the pool. She hears a question. *Would you like to go under?* When she doesn't say no, she feels a firm nose clip being fitted into place. With few words, silent signals establish between them. Soon, she can sense when to take a breath before being dropped beneath the water's surface where the swishing and twirling continue in a silent underwater dance.

It's more than Watsu. Something in the Harbin land and water speaks to Diane, compelling. She tells of encounters with residents of the Harbin community. The staff that tends the hot springs and takes care of guests is a tribe of unique, creative souls, and Diane finds an instant affinity with a number of them. There is a sense of coming home.

By now, I am well acquainted with the turnings of Diane's inner gyroscope at this critical juncture in her life. More long phone calls and more watery images from her telling: I imagine a switch flipping in Diane's nervous system as the streaming of warm water along her body morphs aquatic sessions into pre-natal journeys in amniotic fluid. Time goes away. For long minutes, she can stay under forever. Finally breaking the surface, she feels herself being slowly brought to rest at the side of the pool where she weeps equal tears for the life she is leaving and the one opening before her.

During one of Diane's visits, we have dinner at La Tropicana in North Lawrence. We stroll the levee by the Kaw River and have a frank moment. Our hearts open, and we glimpse possible futures. When we part, I know she has found her element and, as things stand, our unstated desire to be together is no match for it. I continue solo.

56.

WESTWARD BOUND

I live in my basement grotto, working hard to find my footing as a singleton. I worry that Diane is gone for good, but I accept it. We have only glimpsed possibilities, but we've made no plans, no promises. Besides, to the newly separated, monogamy is an unnatural state, and neither of us is in a hurry to hitch up with anyone. For the time being, she's off learning Watsu in a clothing-optional enclave in California. *More power to her*, I say to myself. In my imagination, I wonder if I might find a few women in Lawrence who want to roll around naked with me. In my way, I try, but after ten years in the Order and seventeen years of marriage, I lack polyamorous skills. Nothing clicks. In a lull in communications with Diane, I can only surmise that distance and circumstances are going to do us in before we even get started. All I can think of to do is *feng-shui* the basement.

I map out the *Bagua,* the energy sectors of my underground grotto: Creativity, Helpful People, Career, Spiritual Growth, Love and Marriage, Health, Money, and Fame. I spruce up these sectors the best I can, declutter them and arrange them in a way that pleases my eye. But no matter how I turn it and slice it, the disused storage closet that juts into a corner of my main room just stares at me. It's smack dab in the middle of my Love and Marriage sector. I can take a hint.

I use a heavy, broad-tipped screwdriver as a crowbar and pry open the jammed door to the concealed roomlet. It's a dank, narrow vault with seeping, cracked cement for a floor, dimly lit by a single failing forty watt light hanging by a wire from the ceiling. Cobwebs dangle like Spanish moss from mold-encrusted wooden shelves lined with dusty shards of terracotta pots. I suspect there are plenty of spiders hiding in the corners.

For a whole day, I sweep the walls and ceiling and scrub the secret room's floor on my hands and knees like Cinderella, surrounded by the talking mice in my head. Order house lessons come back to me. *If you want to raise the vibration and the feeling of a place, clean where nobody ever looks.* Out come the rotting shelves and broken pots, in comes fresh air from a fan. I caulk the floor cracks and brush the walls with a layer of water sealant and then two coats of citrus-based sky-blue paint. Forty watts of light become seventy-five, and the new bulb now sports a clean fixture. I smudge with sage and then again with frankincense. This I continue into the rest of my grotto room, circulating stagnant energy out of the corners into the center of the room, where it can be transformed into Light. While Diane learns Watsu at Harbin Hot Springs, I take charge of my surroundings.

My labors pay off. The act of scrubbing out, fumigating, and delousing the Love and Marriage Sector of my grotto brings on a palpable change in me, like a psychic bone self-adjusting itself with a small click. I explain it to myself as an energetic healing of the space I live in. Something within me calms. Diane emails me with news that she will be in town the following week, and she wants very much to see me.

Diane comes back for a month in the summer, pendulating between her family and our trysts. When she returns to Harbin, I'm transported back to a time on the Vlaardingen VI, the Order's houseboat moored in a wretchedly filthy canal in North Amsterdam, when all I could do was to lie awake, watching the cinema in my head, spinning out endless reruns, hitting every octave of longing. Everyday life is a challenge.

Diane is now a resident member of the Harbin community, which, thanks to the Internet, is becoming known to more than the hip San Francisco elite as a special healing retreat. She has become a qualified Watsu therapist and a member of the Health Services staff. Endless email volleys pass between us. We're lovers now, but lovers who talk a good game of non-monogamy. We're shucking off the shackles of domesticity, right? Hey, we're both middle-aged and divorced, and we can choose who we want to be with. Marriage, in the traditional sense, is a relic of a bygone age. No single partner can ever be all things to someone else. If you're not going to try to raise a family, why tie yourself down? This is the story we tell ourselves.

We're lovers but, inconveniently, we're also in love.

On her visits, Diane stays with me in my *feng shuied* grotto for a few days at a time. Then she's on the plane again, back to her beloved Harbin, and I go back to my unsettled sequestered life. This gets old. Lawrence no longer feels like my home. There's a James Taylor earworm singing in my head, telling me that sometimes it's enough just to be on my way, enough just to cover ground, that home is inside me. I'm unhappy here, and I need to get moving.

My little car crawls westward on a High Plains journey through a haze of memory, emotion, and road reveries. I drive a red Geo Metro, a car with only three cylinders—that's all it has ever had—a small, unpowerful, thin-skinned capsule on wheels that gets you where you're going a little at a time. I have had a life-long romance with long road trips in tiny cars. There is something about settling into a solo trip in a small car that allows my deep sensorium to drop down enough through the driver's seat and chassis to comprehend the car's weight. From there, I kinesthetically reach down and down to where my tires meet the road, then through the cracker-thin veneer of civilization laid out between me and the unfathomably huge landmass below, gradually expanding until I understand the shape of the world.

Two worlds, both lost to me now, rise up behind my eyes, and then collapse behind me. The Order is a distant dream, a thing that happened to someone else. As the road rolls under me,

2000: Crossing the desert on the way to California in a three-cylinder car.

I'm engulfed in memories of Ursula and our last visit with Bob Moore in Ringkøbing. By then, I'd admitted to myself (but no one else) that I'm writing a book on energy healing. Not long after that, Ursula and I visited her mother and sisters in Europe. We were poised to take a side trip to Denmark, but, fully in line with his statement "I'm not your gurra," Bob suddenly had no time to meet with us. The subtext was clear: *You've got your wings, and it's time for you to fly. You've got the essentials of these teachings, so go and make them your own.*

Diane and I are now lovers, but a stable relationship is anything but a certainty. What lies ahead is unknown. The skies of Nebraska and Wyoming arch over my solitude like a vast cobalt tent. I pass through Salt Lake City, where I spent a year of my Order time. The Mormon Temple, once the tallest building in downtown Salt Lake City, has now been replaced in that capacity by financial offices. Statues of Mormon pioneers and the Angel Moroni remind me that I have reached the Edge of the West. On my stereo, Will Ackerman's "Ventana," recycles its questing theme like a bird riding the thermals, but never landing, never resolving, a wind that lifts me out high over the bottom of a vast inland sea towards an impersonal Pacific. I cross Bonneville Salt Flats and arrive in Wendover, Nevada. There, I pause at an inner precipice to let my spirit catch up with me and my tiny red car. I gather myself, alone now, and shove off.

PART IV
THE LIFE-ARTISTS
(2001 - 2015)

Lebenskünstler: (German, literally: life-artist)
"Imagine making art, not with paint or clay, but with life itself as your medium."

~*Anonymous*

"It's not suppression of American madness that we need, but rather the forming of it. And form means art. Art as formed madness."

~*J.H.*

A Full Moon ceremony at Harbin Hot Springs.

57.

THE WATER MOLECULE

After a night at the home of my editor Hal Bennett in Ukiah, I take a deliberately slow route down to Calistoga and slalom through the ninety-two curves in 9.2 miles of Highway 29 leading northward to Middletown. I cross from the prosperous wine country of Alexander Valley into Lake County, the poorest county in California. The welcome sign at the edge of Middletown gives the same number for the town's population as its feet above sea level, and I imagine a small world where tiny elevation-adjusting earthquakes occur whenever there is a birth or a death. At the convenience store at one of the town's only two stoplights, a local woman gives me directions to Harbin Hot Springs. It's not hard to hear the change in her voice when she mentions the place.

Water Molecule
Harbin is an untested place in my mind. I have no idea what will unfold here. Diane and I are still in the "what if?" stage of our relationship. Over dinner in Harbin's restaurant, she uses a word I've never heard before: "biomimicry," modeling our human structures and ways of living on natural patterns. Out come a napkin and a ballpoint pen. Diane, the former biochemist, sketches two circles, each with the letter "H" inside. A third circle contains the letter "O" and forms a triangle with the other two. Even sketched on a napkin, the angles are specific. They de-

239

pict magnetic valences that hold it all together. We are looking at a water molecule.

"Imagine a pair of small houses," she says. "They could be yurts. These two circles are hydrogen atoms. Now imagine a larger house. That's the oxygen atom. H_2O. Yours, mine, and ours." When the napkin shreds, we rearrange cups and saucers on the table. Again, Diane adjusts the angles, just so. In the middle of the triangle, she places a glass of water, symbolizing a Watsu pool.

Worlds Below
It's April of 2001. I am literally between worlds, with one foot still in Lawrence, and one not planted anywhere. I feel displaced, a guest in a strange paradise. While Diane is busy with bodywork sessions, I hang out by the pools and explore my natural and human surroundings. I take impromptu guided walking tours with a variable cast of old Harbinites. Some recount episodes of Harbin history, and others conjure up visions of the sacred land and waters under our feet and the nomadic peoples who have come here since time out of mind for healing and ceremony. These walking meditations are forays into spiritual archaeology, where eras of human activity stack on top of each other like layers in a cake. I'm taken to meditate at a giant fist of rock rising out of the land, a power spot called "Indian Rock." By and by, a rough picture of Harbin's past forms in my mind.

Surface impressions of Harbin are a mix of West Coast New Age culture and romantic glimpses of bygone eras. Historic photos in the Stone Front living room show fashionable early twentieth-century guests, brave souls who endure the days-long journey from San Francisco in sweltering stagecoaches to get there. These city dwellers have come to rusticate, take the waters, hike the hills, and play gentle games of croquet in full-length skirts and straw bonnets. They appear sweetly oblivious to the worlds lying below.

Despite the nostalgic trappings on display in the public areas, Harbin is situated on an energetic and geothermal power spot. Invisible fires burn underfoot. Lake County is a place of volcanic activity, geysers and hot springs, and Harbin's are part of this underground system. A few miles up Highway 175, Calpine produces electricity for the entire region from subterranean thermal rivers. An ancient inland sea of 100-million-year-old water, a swimming hole for plesiosaurs, is trapped miles below. It makes its way to the surface for the first time in its history through the seven springs that flow into the pools at Harbin. Diane shows me a tiny foot bath outside the hot plunge. Unlike the other springs, it is rich in naturally-occurring arsenic, good for preventing athlete's foot.

I become fascinated by the world-apart feel of Harbin. I'm reminded of places I have been that have a palpably different feel from their surroundings, like the Isle of Iona off the west coast of Scotland, the Findhorn Community, and the grottos of Rio Chiripo in Costa Rica. In its way, coming onto Harbin property is as distinct a departure from the everyday world as stepping into Order Headquarters in San Francisco, or the Psykisk Center where Bob Moore taught in Denmark.

Dating back to a time when everyone traveled on foot and met each other in person, or not at all, Harbin land became an intertribal hub of great significance. Even though Europeans came and brought an end to the traditional life of the Lake Miwok, the underfoot tradition of the land and water continues. We stand at a small waterfall near the Harbin Market, and I hear how Pomo, Wappo, and Lake Miwok shamans would enter trances and use openings on Harbin land, especially the springs, as portals into the spirit world, then return and minister to their sick in the healing waters. *Is Watsu a present-day continuation of this tradition?* On a winding uphill road I would drive countless times in my years at Harbin, is a flat turnaround at the elbow of a hairpin curve, a site where elderly tribal members would live in order to prepare themselves for their transition beyond this world. Regional street and place names retain Miwok and Pomo names like Konocti, Callayomi, and Tuleyome. To the south is Sonoma County.

Vivid painted faces on signs, Harbin's equivalent of gargoyles, prohibit open fires. No candles, no incense, and no campfires are allowed. A single smoking deck with a bright red fire extinguisher is situated near one of the parking lots, well away from centers of activity. Harbin's fire history is a matter of record. In 1894, the Victorian patrons had to evacuate when the hotel burned down. Harbin burned again in the late 1920s. Newspapers reported "fires of unknown origins" following rumors of an impending "Negro invasion" when Harbin was purchased by a Black social organization in Lake County, where the KKK was active. In 1943, on September 12th (a date that would recur in Harbin's fire history), wartime Harbin closed with plans to reopen the following spring. Four days later, it burned down. In October of 1960, Harbin went into foreclosure because the owner had defaulted on loans. Six days later, Harbin conveniently burned down again.

Multiple cycles of burning and rebuilding marked the coming and going of entrepreneurs with visions of how to use the Harbin land. Meanwhile, all around it, Lake County was styling itself as "the Switzerland of America." The Harbin Springs Health and Pleasure Resort, where health-conscious, stringently moral Victorians came to take the waters, was replaced by a parade of short-lived organizations: a weight-loss spa, a hunting and health club, a boxing camp, and a gay country club. In 1968, Harbin was purchased by the Frontiers of Science Fellowship, whose founder claimed to have been abducted by a UFO and then returned to the Earth with a mission to enlighten the world. He founded the Harbinger University, "the psychedelic country club of the nation's hip intelligencia." It lasted eight months before falling into chaos and disbanding. Harbin is a powerful place, if not always focused.

242

The Founder

The history lesson continues. Enter Robert Hartley, later known by his spiritual name. Ishvara is a Harvard-educated real estate investor. He has already financed two Summerhill-type alternative schools and become heavily involved with Gestalt Therapy. Together with two others, he sets out to find land for a Gestalt center. When Harbin comes on the market in 1972, they are interested, but his partners balk when they see how run down the place is. Harbin fits criteria in Ishvara's mind, however, and his low-ball offer is accepted. When his would-be partners back out, he finds himself in sole possession of Harbin Hot Springs, unaware that over the next twenty years, it would become a special refuge, revered by thousands of people.

One of Ishvara's criteria for the land is to have no close neighbors, so that residents can be naked without upsetting anyone. He believes that nudity is conducive to spiritual growth by helping people to transcend societal norms. As the crow flies, Harbin is barely thirty miles from the Order's retreat center near Santa Rosa, where I was ordained and took my life-changing naked swim twenty-three years before.

Down in Middletown, Harbin is referred to as "that nudist colony." Locals suspect it is a non-stop sexual free-for-all. This coincides with my years in the Order in Europe and the mass suicides in Jonestown. Lake County residents have relatives who died in Jonestown and want nothing to do with another cult.

But the waters are magic. There's plenty of work for young people whose walkabouts take them north from the city, back to the land. At Harbin, they can work a few hours a day in return for a place to hang out where no one can find them. The swimming pools are restored and filled with water straight out of the ancient aquifers. Massage therapists pull their tables alongside the pool and work for tips.

Ishvara envisions a New Age mini-society and tries for an amalgam of the best of religiously-based and secular commu-

2002, Freeport, The Bahamas: Diane and me with a couple of new friends.

nities. He works on a manuscript called "Living the Future," in which he applies New Age principles to societal problems. In it, he presents his vision for an offspring community, separate from Harbin, and finally, the establishment of a New Age University. These ideas flow into the founding philosophy of Harbin. Spiritual practice is encouraged, but according to each individual's choice, not following a leader or a teaching that everyone in the group must adhere to. For me, this is in stark contrast to my former life in the Order, and to attempts by Bob Moore's students to create a unified orthodoxy out of his teachings, despite his insistence that he was nobody's "gurra." Harbin is a crazy quilt of personal beliefs and spiritual traditions. On the secular side, there is enough structure to ensure that the place isn't ruled only by those with the loudest voices. Models for utopian communities are available, but Ishvara believes that people do best in an atmosphere of both freedom and responsibility.

Ishvara plays the stock market. Between the computer screen of his lucrative day-trading and his deepening energy yoga practice, Ishvara operates behind the scenes, living in a simple house in the woods on Harbin's property. He multiplies Harbin's funds. Under his direction, the old resort gatehouse becomes the entrance where an entry fee is collected from guests. Over the years, Harbin becomes a hot tip secret, a place where San Francisco hipsters can come for the water, the land, and the laid-back, slightly outlaw vibe. And you can go naked if you want to.

58.

TESTED

When I get there, Harbin seems, by my standards, like a sufficiently low-commitment community, so I apply for residency. At
my interview, I'm vaguely encouraged when I hear Harbin described not as an intentional community but as a "circumstan-
tial" community, whatever that is, where I can choose my level
of involvement. I like the sound of that, and I decide that I can
live at Harbin on my own terms.

On one of my walking tours of the Harbin land, my guide
tells me that before the White Man arrived, nomadic Pomo and
Miwok bands made camp here as they passed through on their
seasonal migrations. He makes a point of telling me that there
was general agreement among them that this land was only for
healing and ceremony, and not to be lived on. The spirits of the
land were too easily offended, the energy vortices too strong. No
one, it was said, could live full-time on such land without becoming strange. Diane and I live at Shady Grove, the former
Camp Venture, a ring of nine cabins owned by Harbin, but several miles away from Harbin Hot Springs itself. I'm happy that
we are living "off property."

It's bodyworker testing season. In the usual scheme of things at
Harbin, candidates for residency spend three months doing
whatever tasks need doing—that is to say, making beds and
cleaning toilets. But I've come at a time when Harbin is expe-

riencing a swell in the number of guests, and there are not enough massage therapists to meet the demand. It's known that I am some species of bodywork practitioner, and since bodywork is one of the tasks that need doing, I ask to be evaluated for the Health Services staff.

Harbin is proud of its reputation as one of the best places anywhere for bodywork and takes its health services seriously. Healers who do best here are those who can roll with emotional upheavals that can get stirred up in guests by their exposure to the land and waters of the place. This is something I don't understand when I first arrive, but which I come to understand much better over my fourteen-plus years on staff. When guests come up from the high-pressure San Francisco Bay Area and from all over the world, just the process of getting to Harbin encourages them to decompress. This, in turn, has the effect of unwrapping deeper, forgotten inner patterns. A couple of days of taking it extremely easy, camping, soaking, and maybe a magical romantic chance encounter with somebody appealing, can prime a person for the next step in their healing process. It takes newcomers by surprise to enter a landscape that tips them toward their deep inner process, where dreams and memories, insights, synchronicities, and spiritual connections come into the foreground. What starts as escape from the rat race can lead to upheavals and life decisions. The land and waters of Harbin offer all of this.

Like all practitioners, I must run the gauntlet of being evaluated by the gatekeepers of the bodywork staff. This consists of giving sessions in each bodywork modality I want to offer to the Evaluation Committee, a trio that always includes Ishvara. As near as I can tell, his qualification to evaluate a bodywork therapist starts with the fact that he is the owner of the place and has distinct opinions about what makes a good bodywork therapist, a Harbin bodywork therapist.

My first evaluations go well with a couple of Harbin old-timers, one from England, and the other a French-Canadian from Montreal. They are obviously dedicated to quality control and to protecting the good reputation of the bodywork staff. One of them clearly disapproves of the decision to consider a new residential candidate like me for the bodywork staff right off the bat. My bodywork is apparently Harbin-quality, but she makes no secret of her conviction that everyone, in order to have the "full Harbin experience," should start at the bottom of the totem pole and work three months at whatever job is deemed necessary. Having already once in this life been a novice in an order, I'm quite familiar with hierarchical bottoms, and I'm not overly crushed to forgo this privilege at Harbin.

Following these two sessions, I'm feeling confident as I go into the Health Services office to wash my hands. There, I find both of the desk staff standing with their ears pressed against the wall opposite their desks. On the other side of the wall is the massage room where Ishvara is evaluating a new candidate for staff. An explosive yelp pierces the wall, and they turn and smile at each other. The yelp is followed by a string of yelps. In my mind's eye, I see "Curly" of The Three Stooges in a stomping fit of "Whoop!-whoop!-whoop!"-ing. The desk people count the whoops, nod to each other with approval, and smile reassuringly in my direction. The whoops are a good signal. They see the question mark on my face.

In the sweet way of some Northern Californians when talking to the newly arrived, they remind me that I'm not in Kansas anymore. Ishvara, they explain, is a dedicated kundalini yogi. Kundalini yogis are the Pentecostals, the Holy Rollers of the yoga world. They shake and flinch and cut loose with vocal bursts like a person speaking in tongues. Ishvara's high-power energy yoga practices give him a preternaturally sensitive nervous system and hair-trigger reactivity to energy changes. From the number and intensity of *kriyas,* or spontaneous energy bursts Ishvara has in the course of a session, the desk staff is able to predict the outcome of an evaluation. If the *kriyas* are loud and long and many, the office staff listening through the wall give each other a thumbs up. *This new massage therapist is going to get a high ranking!* But passing is not a given for everyone who gets tested. If an evaluation session is over without cascades of *kriyas*, and especially if the prospective therapist comes back into the office with tears in her eyes, they commiserate. But they know she won't be coming on staff.

They tell me not to worry—I'm going to do just fine with Ishvara when I test with him the following day—but their looks say *if you can handle the* kriyas *and whatever else Ishvara might throw your way.*

The next morning, I'm met in the massage office by the man himself. He is a thin seventy-something, half a head taller than I am, fresh out of the pool, and naked. We walk to the massage room on the other side of the office wall and, without preamble, he says, "I hear you have a published book. You probably think you're hot shit." *Is he deliberately trying to rattle me?* I explain that, actually, I'm painfully aware of the book's shortcomings, which keeps my shit pretty much at standard temperature. He's satisfied with that answer—thank God he isn't dealing with someone with an inflated ego!

Professional ethics prevent me from disclosing details of my evaluation session. Suffice it to say it is unlike anything I have ever experienced. Looking back, it turns out to be my initiation into a new world of bodywork. I survive my evaluation. Ishvara is satisfied with the session, and he seems to think I have the makings of a Harbin bodyworker. I receive a decent skills ranking from the evaluation team, which means only that I get to work on the bodywork staff. I have zero seniority, and I have brought zero dollars into Harbin's coffers. In the Byzantine Harbin ranking system, this puts me near dead last in my composite ranking. When it comes to getting shifts, this means I get to sign up for shifts only after everybody else has had their pick.

59.

HARBIN PSYCHO-DIVERSITY

"There will come a time when you can even take your clothes off when you dance."
~*Frank Zappa*

Everyone has their own Harbin. Diane and her water family soulmates are living proof of the Aquatic Ape Theory. They would live full-time in the water if they could. They ripple through the water like seaweed and float like bars of Ivory soap. They can stay underwater forever, and I wonder if they have gills. I myself am made of other elements. The warm water makes me drowsy, and I get water-logged and sink to the bottom inside of fifteen minutes.

Diane's loves and causes converge at Harbin. Her background in the sciences and the environmental movement, her time as an energy lobbyist, clinical social worker, and energy healer—all these coalesce in the water. She has not only found the professional love of her life, she has also landed at the international nexus of a hydrophilic tribe of aquatic bodywork practitioners, organized by the Worldwide Aquatic Bodywork Association, WABA. (I have to explain to my brother that this is different from the Wichita Area Builders Association.) Diane's welcome into the "water family" takes place at a time of peak activity in a global network of aquatic bodyworkers, with outposts scattered throughout the world. Like a minor religion, aquatic bodywork inspires visions of healing and a better world. In Israel, a practitioner is granted a momentary suspension of border security protocols for his independent peace initiative of teaching Israelis and Palestinians to float each other in the Red Sea.

Diane's transition to the Harbin community is of a piece with her decision to become a full-fledged Watsu practitioner. For her, it's a match made in heaven. Harbin's land and waters infuse everything with larger-than-human energy and meaning, especially these water sessions. Diane is where she wants to be, out in the elements, and doing healing work in the most perfect environment she can imagine. To top it off, many of the guests who wander in and out of Harbin have come primed for healing. Whether they know it or not, the energy vortices and the spirits of the land and the waters open people up to their inner processes in unpredictable ways.

People in Motion

I soak in the warm pool and ponder the social phenomenon of nudity. On the surface, Harbin is easy to describe in terms of its exoticness and excesses. The clothing-optional piece never fails to titillate. Midwestern friends automatically imagine a non-stop writhing orgy. But this ignores the fact that lots of "regular" people come to Harbin, regular people who didn't mind being around a few naked hippies. Myself, I'm somewhere between a regular person and a former holy man who used to take off his clothes and run around naked at night.

There is something about being naked in the pools and in casual hanging out together that makes for egalitarian relations not based on money or status. Ishvara's conviction that nudity is conducive to spiritual growth by helping people to transcend societal norms is borne out in and around the pools. Every day I watch city people arrive at Harbin and drop the trappings of their social roles and status. First-timers fret about what it will be like to be naked around all these strangers. *What if people see*

251

that I'm overweight? Won't this lead to some kind of sexual entanglement that I don't want? What would my mother think? I was raised to be modest! But the water feels great. So do the sunshine and air. Layers drop. Once a guest is in the pool, the average time it takes to shift gears—and shed the bathing suit—is about ten minutes.

I see people in motion. Harbin is a stop on the migratory circuit of international nomadic types who spend their year in slow rotation from one hip, high-energy spot to another, from Yelapa in Mexico to Breitenbush in Oregon, from Bali to Burning Man. Pot-trimming in season earns some migrants a gangsta wad of cash that pays for a *pied-a-terre* in Chiang Mai or Botany Bay for part of the year. In autumn, the grand annual encampment of Ancient Ways descends on the Harbin meadow to hold its yearly pagan observances, and the Warm Pool takes on a green tinge from the number of full-body tattoos refracting through the water. Teachers of Tantra and a rainbow of spiritual practices and therapies are hosted in Harbin's Conference Center, built in the 1970s by the Human Awareness Institute. On weekends, the pools become a throbbing head soup.

Harbin is a good place to rub shoulders with the broad psycho-diversity of our country and the world. My first impression is that I am walking into a flourishing scene like none I've ever encountered before. It's as if all the spiritual practices and memes in the world have been dumped out into this place and allowed to mingle.

Time slows almost to a standstill. It is not a world where things happen. It's a Taoist valley, a place where events arise out of the void, and then dissolve back into it. You can meet timeless types at Harbin, people who have nothing on their mind. They come and go, enigmatic, at home in the moment, content. They don't strike me as stoned so much as having reached a kind of meditative stillpoint, a place where the world stops, and they can get off, just like the song says.

Harbin is a magnet for sun worshipper subcultures—sun-gazing ascetics with hair longer than their bodies, spiraling face-down in the warm pool like ecstatic sea creatures. In the pool and on my massage table I meet all nationalities, races, and genders, people with cryptic tattoos and piercing in and on every fold and bulge of their bodies. People who look like they have stepped out of Middle Earth. People who practice ancient Earth religions, UFO cultists, celebrities, and inventors of perpetual motion machines, alongside combat veterans, and businessmen freed of their three-piece suits. Once, after giving a bodywork session to a guest, I receive a DVD as a tip. On it are detailed blueprints for a contraption that generates energy out of thin air. In the restaurant, I share a table with a breatharian who eats food, but only for the taste. I meet a movie star-handsome young man who is a new Harbin resident like me. He is named after his great-great grandfather, the nineteenth president of the United States.

There are uncanny encounters. Harbin is like a Rorschach blot, a place like the planet Solaris in the Andrei Tarkovsky sci-fi film by that name, where the contents of your subconscious are mirrored back to you. It's a clothing-optional Taoist valley where I find shadow figures from my subconscious soaking right next to me in the Warm Pool. The Girl from Ipanema walks by on full display, suntanned and lathe-turned in the Pilates studio. True to the song, she looks straight ahead, not at me, non-connectile. But not always. For reasons unknown, someone might catch my attention and continue to stand out from the crowd in the restaurant or the pools. I don't always know if I even like the looks of this person, but they have caught my eye all the same. Half an hour later, the same person is on my table in the massage room. This happens more times than I can count.

A person I do not want to run into is Ishvara. The experience of being evaluated by him has made me wary of having anything to do with him. His partial hearing loss makes for disjointed conversation, and, in the odd logic of living in a Taoist valley like Harbin, this discomfort means that we are constantly running into each other. At first, I see him coming down from the pools and I take an alternate route. But Harbin is a small town, and I have something to learn about this. One day, instead of diverting, I try spiritual judo. I walk up to Ishvara and give him a big hug. That seems to do an end run around our mutual awkwardness. In time, a simple, rudimentary fondness grows between us.

I'm busy at Health Services and with my relationship with Diane. Our cabin at Shady Grove, the former Camp Venture, is a far cry from the water molecule we imagined on the restaurant napkin when I first arrived. Our cabin is, in fact, more of a one-and-a-half person house. Despite the cramped conditions, we are able to practice a miniature version of the "yours-mine-and-ours" water molecule, and we do well with it.

Across the horseshoe of cabins from us, on the other side of a concrete slab called the "landing pad," lives Harbin's taxi driver, Jim, a kindly seventy-something man who picks up guests from Bay Area airports and bus stations. When Harbin acquired Camp Venture from the UFO researchers of the Frontiers of Science Fellowship, old Jim came with the deal. He regales his passengers with intergalactic lore. The Mother Ship will be returning for him any day now, so he apologizes ahead of time in case he's unable to take them back to the airport.

My work at Health Services is my window on Harbin as a social and spiritual hub, a place where, as Tolkien put it, "many paths and errands meet." Summer passes, and I witness the particular role that Harbin plays in the lives of people who come there. A highly visible journalist for a major TV network who comes to me for bodywork sessions confides to me that no one in her world knows that she comes to Harbin. Her family and colleagues would be scandalized to know she visits a "nudist colony." Harbin serves as her special place, her secret refuge. There are many like her.

One morning at the drowsy end of summer, I arrive on "Mainside" to find Harbin pervaded by an atmosphere of brooding. Residents and guests move about in a restless silence as if listening for something. It's the the agitated stir of animals with noses to the wind and ears pricked just before an earthquake. There are outbreaks of irritation from otherwise mellow people. About midday, we catch ripples of news and learn of big airplanes being flown deliberately into big buildings. This is followed by a shockwave that rolls across the entire country. Within days, waves of guests begin to wash up at the retreat center, people who are clearly taking refuge from the turbulence. The world comes abruptly to Harbin on September 11, 2001. Here we are, three thousand miles from the site of events which will change our world, and many of us feel that we are suddenly on a psycho-spiritual frontline.

Circa 2013, Harbin Hot Springs: Diane giving a Watsu session to our friend Kim.

255

60.

ON THE HEALING STAFF AT HARBIN

Harbin has been a well-kept secret up to now, but the Internet and word-of-mouth change that. The tragedy of 9/11 opens a door, and through it comes a surge of guests from the East Coast, Europe, and even Russia. They are not West Coast hipsters or UFO cultists or sun worshippers, but Harbin touches a deep need in them all the same. They need something not city, not beating to the harsh metronomes of business and rush hour, not colored by life in a crush of population. They find a place in nature where they can spin down into the person they are under their roles. City people stop talking midstride, grab the arm of their travel companion, and point at one of the mule deer that wander freely here. During a bodywork session, one of these docile creatures noses its way into the massage room and stops to lick my client's bare feet before proceeding to eat the flowers in the vase. It is an event filled with religious overtones for this guest. A mother skunk ambles across the lower parking lot, and a woman with a thick Slavic accent asks me what it is.

I see the effect of the land and waters on guests most dramatically in bodywork sessions. Since my time at Southwind in Lawrence, I have had an ability to track the subtle movement of energy in my clients' bodies and follow the dynamics of their inner processes. I can't say for sure where this instinct comes from, but whatever it is, it blooms at Harbin. My bodywork "specialty"

is my own mash-up of massage and light-touch work that com-
bines craniosacral and subtle energy therapies. All of this, prac-
ticed in a rarified setting like Harbin, can evoke strong experiences in persons who open to it. I take seriously the reminders
that this is healing land, and part of my job is aligning with the
forces here.

In Harbin's pools and bodywork rooms, I enter a new
world. I'm no longer an Order brother, no longer the student of
a teacher. Countless times in sessions, something is touched in
the core of my client, and I come to the edge of my concepts and
technical skills. I have no choice but to trust that deeper healing
processes are afoot. Over the next fourteen years, at the nexus
of Harbin's land and waters, and the healing spirit of the place,
I find my wings as a healer.

Most days are filled out with sessions of routine strokes and
stretches, standard fare in a massage and bodywork practice,
whether at Harbin or in Lawrence, Kansas. On other days, the
stars line up differently. I put my hands on human diversity itself:
a lithe sun worshipper who flings herself full-naked and dripping
wet onto the table, *Here I am!*; a Chinese amputee whose energy
body vibrates palpably where his leg once was; a bald man who
asks me to work his gnarled purple abdominal scars from a gun-
shot wound; people who disappear into a deep meditative state
the instant I touch them; round-eyed American Buddhists who
hang colorful Tibetan *tankas* on the wall during our session; and
shamanic types who bring parts of dead animals—in one memorable instance, roadkill—and invoke their totem spirits to ac-
company our healing work. We are not in Kansas.

I learn a new layer of my craft, oddly thankful for my
bizarre initiation into Harbin bodywork when I tested with Ishvara.
In my mind, that encounter melds with my trial by fire at the Gammelshausen breakfast table long ago when I first witnessed the
young Dutch woman who completely fell apart emotionally, and
then fell back together, miraculously reassembled. Now, in the
wake of 9/11, these moments only become more frequent.

257

I become increasingly bone oriented. That is to say, I have taken to orienting to what is going on at the juncture of a person's skeleton and the energies that move through their skeleton. I am strongly influenced by osteopaths and touch healers such as John Upledger and Fritz Smith. I discover a certain knack for this kind of work, and I develop this set of skills.

What does this look like? After getting comfortable and settling into a receptive state, I set my hands on on my client's body, typically in a way that is both very light—like a leaf riding on water—and very connected. From this position, right at the interface of physical structure and energy movement, a world of impressions often becomes available to me. Like a spider sitting utterly still at the center of her web, I sense the micro-movements, holding patterns, and imbalances in my client's body. In this state of awareness, sensing something as unsubtle as a dislocated bone is easy.

My hands learn the thousand ways human flesh can feel at the cusp of its structure and the energy that moves through it. Inflammation radiates heat through the back of my hand. Depletion feels empty and draws energy through me like a slow vacuum cleaner. Pockets of emotion and condensed experiences packed away in energetic cysts feel charged and chaotic when they are active. The aftermath of hallucinogens can leave a nerve-jangled feeling. Botox-injected facial tissue feels like it has spun glass in it, making me afraid I will crush it even with the lightest touch. Hormones changing their religion in persons undergoing gender reassignment give their bodies a feeling that is hard to describe. Each of the thousand ways has its own feel under the surface, under the chatter. I discover the touch equivalent of the visionary Teilhard de Chardin's words: ". . . perceiving the irresistible development hidden in extreme slowness, extreme agitation concealed beneath a veil of immobility . . ."

Often, the theme is trauma—from blunt impact, whiplashes, falls from horses and ladders, falls from Grace, to surgeries and emotional and sexual abuse—that lodge in a person's flesh. I marvel that people survive being knocked around so much in their lives. Something has changed in me since Southwind: women now seem to feel safe in my presence. In sessions, it's not uncommon for some to pass through body memories of rapes, incest, and terminated pregnancies. They release excess energies that have been locked into the tissues of their bodies, reorganize, and come out the other side. The basic therapeutic and spiritual skills of "holding space," and of staying centered and grounded, are lifelines, essential skills for the work of accompanying a person through difficult, even existential knotholes. My trust in these processes grows.

Trade-offs

In spite of being nearly bottom-ranked on the Health Services staff, I get to work right away. I'm willing to fill in for other therapists, so work increases, and I climb in the rankings. I work as many shifts as I can, getting paid every day for the previous day's sessions, if there have been any. I walk out of the Health Services office with a pay sheet folded over a small stack of bills, held together with a paper clip. Often, two quarters are taped to the outside of my pay "envelope," a quaint reminder me that this is a cash economy. My collection of paper clips and quarters grows.

We're all independent contractors at Health Services. Rent is cheap in Harbin housing, a patchwork of communal houses sprinkled around Middletown, including our little house at the former UFO camp and cabins and trailers on Harbin property. From the corner of my eye, I see residents commanding wages sufficient only for living at Harbin in a company-store arrangement. The prevailing attitude coming from the management is that living in Paradise ought to more than compensate for the lack of employee benefits and decent pay.

Most accept the trade-off. Harbin is still a slightly outlaw place, after all, where residents can be as off the radar as they want to be and live the liberation of disconnecting, at least temporarily, from their past. It is also a place of rebirth and rechristening for many. In *The Harbinger,* the Harbin newsletter, there are frequent notices of name changes. These usually come in three flavors: spiritual names—often Sanskrit, given by gurus—which name spiritual qualities to be embodied in this life; botanical-zoological-mineralogical names that sound cool and often identify a person with a totem spirit; and original one-of-a-kind names, artistic twirls of self-reinvention, like an author's *nom de plume.* There are people at Harbin whom I only know by their assumed names. Standing in front of the mailroom cubby-hole I share with my friends Paramahansa and Acorn, I puzzle over letters addressed to unknown individuals. *Who the hell are Oren Leadbeater and Hildegard Fendritch?* Having lived with a spiritual alias for more than a decade in the Order, I have long since gone back to being Jim.

Circa 2013, Part of the Harbin community at the Resident Center.

61.

THE ACCIDENTAL TEACHER (TAKE 2)

Harbin's allure as a world-apart for guests is unmistakable, but it's an island, and I soon find out that I am not a good islander. I'm not good at hanging out. I'm also not good at living on Harbin's company-store economy. I have debts, and I'm not sure I can even make enough of a living there to sustain myself.

In bodywork sessions, guests ask me if I know anyone in the Bay Area who works like I do. I can only think of one practitioner like that: me. I take their names, and when there are twenty of them, I start to look for an office in Marin County. A non-compete clause in my contract prevents me from having a practice within fifty miles of Harbin, but Marin County is well outside that range. In 2002, I rent office space in San Anselmo, one of the hip little towns off Highway 101 in Marin County. There is something resonant for me with this location. From a university philosophy course, I remember the words of Saint Anselm of Canterbury, who said, "God is that than which nothing greater can be imagined." The "that than which" formulation was the hook that stuck this quote in my mind. It's funny the way the mind works: I take the plunge and open up shop in San Anselmo.

My bi-monthly trips to the Bay Area are made possible by a new friend, Steve Robinson, a Harbin regular who lets me sleep on the couch in his apartment in the Sunset District of San Francisco. Friday and Saturday evenings, I drive from San Anselmo into the city, and we tour the gaggle of eateries around Ninth and Irving, a block away from Golden Gate Park. Steve loans me his Yamaha acoustic guitar, and I start playing music again.

I thrive on these commutes between my Harbin life with Diane and my bi-monthly weekends in San Francisco and Marin County. Small doses of city energize me and provide exactly the right contrast from my life at Harbin. And, critically, I earn enough money to not be one of the chronically impoverished denizens of Harbin. Then, even at Harbin, new opportunities open. I begin to offer classes in energy healing at the Harbin School of Shiatsu and Massage. A few classes in, I'm asked if I would fill in for the school's teacher of craniosacral work, an Australian citizen who is having visa problems.

I have no interest in doing a knockoff of the Upledger Craniosacral Therapy I have learned, or anything else with a "brand name." My background in energy healing and my years in the Order are always lurking in the background of the healing work I do. I sense all these streams trying to converge into something of my own, and the effort of writing *Energy Healing* has taken me a further step in that direction. Instead of attempting a rehash of teachings I have received, it's time to attempt my own distillation. *Creation instead of imitation.* There are numerous branches of the craniosacral tree, for example. *Why not add one myself?* I decide to put into words how I myself work. Hunched over a clunky black laptop in a cramped airplane seat on the way to Jackson, Mississippi, to be with Diane's newborn grandson, I craft a lesson plan for a course I call "Energy-Active Craniosacral Work."

My most regular teaching venue is the Harbin School of Shiatsu and Massage. Shortly after I arrive, construction begins on five domed structures that will house the school in a surreal nest of classrooms and school offices, wrapped around two Watsu pools. Teaching in the domes is a lesson in acoustic architecture.

The shape creates surround-sound. I speak and hear my voice behind me, as well as every cough, pop, and paper-crinkle coming from the class. I learn to place myself in the sweet spot in the center of the dome as I lead my class through exercises.

The guiding design principle of the Watsu Center has decreed that everything should flow, like water, and means the total exclusion of ninety-degree angles. Every piece is custom-crafted, which means that nothing can be simply replaced by going to Ace Hardware. When finished, it's reminiscent of the houses on the planet Tatooine in *Star Wars*. In my mind, it's a cock-up waiting to happen, a cluster of swirled Dairy Queen blobs perched on a hilltop, about to melt into the valley below. The Watsu Center reminds me of the scene in *Zorba the Greek* in which an elaborate trestle is built to cascade newly-cut tree trunks down a mountainside to the town sawmill. The priest consecrates it with holy water, and no sooner is the apparatus blessed and the first giant log sent whizzing down the mountainside, than the whole thing collapses. At that point in the movie, Anthony Quinn (Zorba) breaks into dance and cries, "Did you ever see a more splendiferous crash!"

The Watsu Center: Three of the five Harbin Domes. No right angles.

62.

THREADS

My classes expand. Bodywork is viewed as a desirable profession in Northern California, and student enrollment is at a peak. Part of the trend at massage schools is to include instruction in energy healing. Most every school has classes in Reiki, for example, but I have something different to offer. Having a published book on the subject gives me some cachet with school directors in the Bay Area and Sacramento where I pitch my classes.

School directors are often bodyworkers themselves, so job interviews typically include a table session. My hands-on sessions are done fully clothed, so it's an easy thing to set up a massage table in an empty classroom. In one interview session, the school director lies on her back with a vinyl-covered bolster under her knees. I sandwich part of her torso between my hands by sliding a hand under the small of her back while my other hand rests on her abdomen. Unbeknownst to me, a loose silk thread from the waistband of her panties has crept out over the top of her loose-fitting pants and snagged on my fingernail. When it comes time to retract my hands in order to move around the table to place my hands on other positions, I don't realize that the thread has come with me. At the conclusion of the treatment, I open my eyes to a sprawling web woven from a single sky-blue strand of fine unspooled thread. My eye traces the glassy thread, glistening like a skein of spider silk in a morning meadow. It exits from the top of her panties, stretches to her right hand, up her arm, and loops around her right ear, perilously close to catching on her earring. Not willing to disturb my potential employer with this news while she is in the process of reentry, I quietly wind up the thread, follow it out of the silken labyrinth I have created, and gingerly tuck the fuzzy ball under her waistband. After she is done simmering on the table, our interview continues, and I'm hired, even after I tell her about my adventures with her underwear.

For a stretch that lasts almost ten years, I teach a patchwork schedule of classes at several different schools. Classrooms vary from cozy living rooms to open, echoing mass-gathering halls, to geodesic domes like the Harbin Watsu Center. Every one of them is equipped with the very same set of muscle and bone charts hanging on the walls, and the same over-handled, frequently dismembered life-sized model skeleton—anatomically correct and manufactured in Germany—impaled on its metal stand and teetering like a drunk in the corner, waiting for its moment in the spotlight.

Bodywork schools attract unique sorts, mostly women. I watch for diverse learning styles. Studious middle-aged career-changers sit upright and take notes laced with stenography symbols. Empty nesters who haven't been out in the workforce for decades fear that they have gone brain-dead from raising children. There are lovely oddball ragamuffin twenty-somethings with dreadlocks and highly refined nervous systems, who dress like elves and don't do chairs. Instead, they sit in yoga poses in the corner and appear to be completely elsewhere with their attention. They take no notes and waste not one nanosecond reading the manual I have painstakingly produced. After I demonstrate a treatment sequence, however, many of these students render it perfectly and look like they have been doing healing work all their lives.

I hit my stride as a teacher, gratified to be teaching my own synthesis of the work I do, the journey that began for me with meditation and led me into the Order, then finally to Ursula and Bob Moore in Europe, my piecemeal education in "manual medicine," and an intense journeyman period at Southwind and Harbin Health Services. Classes feed off my hands-on practice. My writing feeds off my teaching. Class notes become chapters for a new book about the intersection of energetic practices and psycho-spiritual development. The first decade of the new millennium points me this direction.

Ancestral Energies
During one class in Davis, California, my usual lodgings are not available to me, so I spend the nights at the home of my cousin Mimi in Granite Bay. She has taken on the mantle of family genealogist, having rescued from oblivion our grandmother's research of sixty years before. One evening, I return to my bedroom to find, laid out without comment on my bedstand, the carefully scissored strips of a newspaper article: *Bob Davis Reveals: Origin of the Sweet Family, Famous as Bone Setters, White Point Beach Lodge, Nova Scotia, 1934.* The article is a florid description of a clan of bonesetters to whom Mimi and I are apparently related through our grandmother, Susan Wright Sweet Gilkeson.

The Bob Davis article triggers a small avalanche. After reading it, I wonder what may have come tripping down the generations in my DNA from these Welsh immigrant ancestors that might have predisposed me to the profession I have followed in one form or another for the last thirty-five years. Then, as if on cue, more lore about the Sweet bonesetters starts falling out of the sky.

In class, a student, Ruby by name, with the features of a beautiful elf from *The Lord of the Rings,* comes bounding up to the front of the classroom clutching a book. Ruby herself is the human equivalent of a bright red rubber band in a box of paper clips. She has ransacked the library of her late father, himself a craniosacral therapist, and come up with a slim bound red volume called *Principles of Manual Medicine,* by Phillip E. Green-man. On the first page of the preface my eyes fall on a capsule history of manual medicine in North America, which mentions by name my ancestors, the Sweet bonesetters.

Pilgrim

There comes a point at which I admit to myself that I am writing another book, and by 2008, I'm full at it with a kind of personal manifesto of energy healing, organized around fifteen principles of energy healing and spiritual growth. My working title is *A Pilgrim in Your Body: Energy Healing and Spiritual Process.* In an ill-considered attempt to associate my book with a celebrity, I send a draft to a well-known figure in the energy healing world and ask her to consider writing a foreword. *Note to self: Never, never send out a manuscript with a request like that to anyone whose work you have not read yourself.* In an unpleasant encounter, I am upbraided for taking liberties with the established terminology of energy healing, the language of *chakras* and *nadis,* appropriated from yogic texts in Sanskrit and freighted with millennia of ancient Vedantic doctrine. The silver lining is that the encounter stimulates a rewrite of the manuscript, using only generic terminology. Losing the old venerable language means jettisoning the myriad preconceived notions that modern, very informed students come with and affords me a way to depict an approach to energy healing based on direct experience.

Before moving to the West Coast, I had an astrological consultation with my old friend, Denise Low. She cast a new chart for me, using my new California location as my birthplace, instead of Wichita, Kansas. My new astrocartography yielded an interesting shift. The move westward, Denise informed me, would be enough to nudge my rising sign over the line from Cancer into Gemini. With my new Gemini rising, I would be more in the public eye than ever before. Not hugely famous necessarily, just a little more visible, more public with some of the things I do.

This turns out to be the case. My writing and classes on energy healing have a modest resonance, and in the small circles I operate in, people seek me out. Meanwhile, my first book, *Energy Healing,* makes the rounds and grows a readership that includes a Danish woman named Pia Fallentin. Pia has originally trained as a concert pianist, which turns out to be breadless art. She eventually studies Medical Anthropology at the University of Copenhagen and takes an interest in energy healers, of all things. Pia organizes grants—one of them from a manufacturer of hearing aids—for an extended research junket in order to write her thesis. First, she goes to live with a tribe in the shadow of Mt. Cotopaxi in Ecuador, where she subjects the native healers and shamans to Danish scientific rigor. The second leg of her research journey takes her to the wilds of San Francisco, where she rents an apartment in the Mission District. From there, she makes regular forays to my small practice in San Anselmo, and a couple of times, she ventures all the way to Harbin Hot Springs to observe me in my native habitat. She has found me by virtue of my book on energy healing, my bit of Internet presence, and the fact that I studied with Bob Moore in Denmark.

As a researcher, Pia is deathly afraid of "going native," a fate worse than death for the disciples of Franz Boas, the Father of Anthropology. Going native is when the researcher loses her objectivity—like virginity: when it's lost, it's lost—and starts taking on the beliefs of the people she is researching. In Pia's case, I wonder if she may have stepped over an invisible line when she starts coming to me for personal sessions, instead of just interrogating my clients about their experiences.

Pia finally finishes her medical anthropology thesis on energy healing, and I'm right in there with the Ecuadorian shamans and research statistics from my practice. If you ever care to read it, warning: it's in Danish. I'm honored to be mentioned.

In 2009, I'm ready with my second book, *A Pilgrim in Your Body: Energy Healing and Spiritual Process*. It's a trifle dense for casual reading, but every bit the manifesto I am hoping for.

AT SKABE MENING

GENNEM KROPPEN

*En antropologisk analyse af det ter-
apeutiske møde mellem healer og klient*

Af Pia Fallentin
Kandidatspeciale
Institut for antropologi
Københavns Universitet
Vejlder: Vibeke Steffen
Februar 2014

2014: The cover of Pia Fallentin's master's thesis on energy healers. Also pictured is Dierdre Davis, a Harbin resident who served as the model for illustrations in A Pilgrim in Your Body.

63.

BURNOUT AND NEW FRONTIERS

Much as I love the attention I'm getting, I worry. Most students like what they learn with me, but purists in the worlds of bodywork and energy healing find my work to be different from what they learned. I straddle traditional lines between bodywork and energy work, healthcare, and spiritual practice. I borrow from numerous disciplines, but, being more interested in what happens when you blend them and allow something new to emerge, I don't pledge undying allegiance to any of them. Throughout it all, I'm haunted by the fear that I am an imposter. This is a default mode, formed partly in embarrassing Show-and-Tell disasters in grade school. In me, just under the surface, a towheaded boy looks down at his sneakers, painfully shy when pressed to get up in front of the class. Then, once the boy pulls out the cork and gets going, his inner crazy bone acts up. He's hard to shut up and needs to be silenced and physically dragged back to his seat. Neither mode engenders confidence. Fortunately, my teaching style has advanced somewhat beyond that by the time I get in front of the bodyworkers in my classes.

For most of a decade, I teach hands-on and meditative skills to bodyworkers. I drive and drive between classes in a three-hundred-fifty-mile triangle that takes me from Harbin to the Bay Area to the Sacramento Valley and then back to Harbin. Before or after each teaching gig, I see clients for individual sessions, and this makes for long breaks in the continuity of life. My work life is at high tide when I turn sixty in the same year as the publication of *A Pilgrim in Your Body*. I love the classroom and the opportunity to open doors for gifted young people who are waking up to their healing gifts. But increasingly, every class has a faint whiff of burnout, like an overdriven Chevy Biscayne with no water in the radiator. My teaching gets sloppy. I grow tired of hearing the sound of my own voice droning on and on about the same subjects. In my head I hear the words of a Southwind colleague who once said, "You know you're in a rut when you can take your hands off the wheel."

At the end of 2010, I call it quits at all the schools at once. Something else is calling me, namely mentoring individuals and small groups of practitioners who are done with their schooling. I want to work with people who are already in practice, have made some mistakes, and are ready for the next tier of questions. I shop this idea around to students from old classes, and in 2011, the first energy healing mentorship group begins in Marin County. Almost simultaneously, out of the sky falls an invitation to teach in Copenhagen. To this day, I don't know exactly how it has come together, but I suspect the collusion of lingering Bob Moore connections in the persons of Gitte Larsen, the director of Healingcenter Aarhus, Marianne Garst, who is involved with a state-funded research project on the efficacy of energy healing for cancer survivors, and my book. And also Pia, who becomes my guardian angel when I come to Copenhagen, no doubt out of her eternal gratitude for letting her research me for her master's thesis.

My first class in Copenhagen is a mixed bag. It's one thing to teach energy healing to hip young Californians who are cool with things that don't always make sense, as long as those things resonate intuitively and mostly feel good. Here in Denmark, it's different. I know from my eleven years as a foreigner in Europe that critical thinking is a basic ingredient of education here. Deeply mystical Northern Europeans, who will talk at great length about trolls and nature spirits and flashbacks to former lives in Atlantis, will also question any unsubstantiated pronouncement about the human energy field. In Denmark, energy healing has to have hands and feet. My first workshop in Copenhagen is a long way from perfect but, somehow, I'm invited back to Scandinavia three more times.

I have quit at all the bodywork schools where I have been teaching, but this doesn't mean the schools all go along with the plan. The school director at Massage Therapy Institute in Davis, a former Harbinite, talks me into staying, and I relent. It was more than a case of her saying "pretty please." I'm a teacher at heart, and it doesn't take long for me to start missing the classroom.

64.

TENSIONS

Harbin lives atop a volcano of competing forces. Fire and water collide beneath the surface of everyday life. The building of the Watsu Center marks an uptick in the perennial clash between the Harbin-as-a-spiritual-community faction and the Harbin-as-a-business faction. Aficionados of New-Agey architecture groove on the surreal Watsu Center domes. But those who wonder what the spirits of the Harbin land and water think about the whole thing abominate it. Harbin has always been a place of healing and ritual. Now, it is also a cash cow. In the name of being open to one and all, there is no cap set on the number of guests who may be there at any one time. The physical and spiritual carrying capacity of Harbin land is tested, and the ancient Indigenous injunction against living full-time on this land rings like a wind chime in the background.

In an active place like this, with construction and building maintenance teams always at work somewhere on the property, residents get their share of injuries. I become something of a go-to person in Health Services for residents who get clonked on the head or jam a finger on the job. As often, bruises and strained muscles come from ecstatic gyrations at the weekly "Unconditional Dances." One evening, I'm summoned to the Watsu Center, where one of the aquatic bodywork instructors has tripped over the guy lines on her camper. She has bashed her head and fears she might have sustained a concussion. After I work on her and sit with her until she is no longer dizzy, I hear about the string of quirky accidents that have happened there of late. Slips and falls, injuries, flat tires, a door slammed by the wind into a student's face. Computers are acting up. Information is scrambled after they are rebooted.

I hear more about the situation from Connie, the school's office manager. She lives on the Pomo reservation outside of Middletown. In the midst of this flurry of mishaps, she looks up from her desk one day to see the tribal medicine man walking up the road to the School. He is an elder, so she listens. He reminds her that this is healing land. What is going on here is upsetting the nature spirits, and no Tribal Member ought to be complicit. He orders her to quit working at the School. Connie refuses. *Instead of coming up here all high and mighty and telling me to quit, why don't you help?* The medicine man considers this, goes away for three days to consult the spirits, then returns. They will do ritual at the Watsu Center to align it with the nature spirits and then watch to see if they settle down and quit taking it out on the people and computers there.

It happens. The spirits calm, and the accidents cease. But notice has been served. Harbin must come into accord with the land or risk more pushback from the spirit world.

Catastrophic Predictions

Harbin lies in a transition zone between the arid inland terrain of California and Nevada and the rainforests of the Pacific Northwest. Plant life is rugged, able to withstand months of dry conditions, followed by weeks of non-stop rain. Unlike many Harbin residents who flee to Bali or Hawaii when the seasons turn, Diane and I stay year-round. In our early years at Harbin, fifty annual inches of vertical rainfall are the norm, most of it in the months between Halloween and the Ides of March. Friends to the north boast of a hundred inches in the same time period. Except for holiday family trips to the Midwest, we stay through the winter and witness the other side of Harbin's mysterious charm that unfolds in a hushed cloud of constant rain falling like strings from the sky.

In 2012, the snow pack in the Sierra Nevada, which accounts for roughly thirty percent of California's water supply, plummets and drought conditions spread. By April of 2015, levels have dropped to five percent of the annual average. Governor Jerry Brown issues the state's first-ever mandatory water restrictions. Every three days at our circle of cabins at the UFO camp, a water truck arrives to fill our tanks, which were once fed from St. Helena Creek. New habits form. Drought habits. With a bucket at our feet to catch water for flushing the toilet, we take "Navy showers," like my father tried to teach my brother and me to take when I was growing up, turning the water on only to rinse off. Signs hanging in Harbin bathrooms read, "If it's yellow, let it mellow. If it's brown, flush it down." Everywhere in Lake County, there are fire hazard signs showing clock faces with dials turned all the way to the right, marked red for "extreme."

A visiting former member of the Findhorn Community in Scotland teaches a group of Harbin residents how to listen to the spirits of the land. They fan out in search of plants willing to communicate. When they reconvene, they have all received the same message: *the land needs to rest.* The Findhorn woman goes to Harbin management and predicts a reckoning if Harbin doesn't change its relationship with the land. Of course, the spirits are speaking to more than just Harbin.

In 2015, fire season comes. Scruffy dry patches of St. John's Wort and *Yerba Santa* line the dusty frontage road by our cabin. The air, once the best in California, hangs, hot and acrid, and smells of cinnabar. Along the horizon, thin white plumes of smoke stretch wooly fingers into the sky. Most of the fires are small, attended to by small planes dropping their loads of magenta-colored flame retardant. On September 12th, a do-it-yourselfer on Cobb Mountain decides to save a few bucks by wiring his hot tub heater all by himself. The results are disastrous.

CODA
WILDFIRE COUNTRY
SEPTEMBER 2015

Well, nothing ever happens in this little town
Unless you count the day that the whole place
burned down
People were staring a hole in the sky
Hoping that black cloud would pass them by
But it swept through the middle of our little town
In a hundred minutes flat, it burned
Paradise down
The sky was hot and charcoal black
And some got out with just
the clothes on their back
Day sleepers had to be shaken awake
No time to figure out what to take
And the saddest thing of all that happened then
Was knowing I might never
see you again

~from the song "Travel Anyway"
by Jim Gilkeson

65.

A Species of Euphoria

Middletown, California, September 12th, 2015
I drive into Middletown from Davis to find people out on the street in front of Hardester's Market, gazing at a worrisome black smoke plume just west of town. Word has it a fire has broken out on Cobb Mountain, just off Bottle Rock Road near—don't laugh!—Jellystone Park, a Flintstones-themed RV park. Four years of drought-dried underbrush fuels wildfires hot enough to create their own miniature weather systems. In no time, this one is totally beyond control. Sap-filled pinecones and acorns explode like Molotov cocktails in every direction as fire races down Cobb Mountain. In one afternoon, the fire covers the eight miles to Harbin and Middletown, consuming everything in its path.

I'm the featured musical entertainment at Mutt & Jess Café in Cobb that evening. After three years as a sideman in two local bands, I'm finally getting into some solo performing, so I've been woodshedding all week to get ready for this. When I hear that Highway 175 is closed, my first thought is, *They can't do that! I'm playing tonight!* I jump in my blue VW Beetle and take off up Highway 175, only to be turned back at Anderson Springs by a state trooper. One-way traffic is streaming down the mountain, not up it. There is no choice but to turn around and face what's coming. What's coming is change, and rapidly. The hot dark orange light throbbing off the bottoms of the thick black

279

clouds just over the ridge can only belong to Harbin Hot Springs. On my way back into town, the end of an era unspools behind my eyes. *Have I really been at Harbin more than fourteen years? Is this how it ends?*

Evacuation

We take out the evacuation list we wrote up during last month's close-call fire and start packing the cars. Computers, personal documents, family photos, music instruments, massage table, Diane's hand-written recipe files, a couple of changes of clothes. By now, there is a solid southbound stream of cars. Fellow Harbinites stop at our little ring of cabins to let the traffic subside. Soon, a sizable gaggle of us is standing by our loaded-down cars, comparing notes. *Did Harbin really burn down? Is this for real? Is Middletown really being evacuated?* A number of people are pretty shook.

We're hanging out, hesitant to get going. The scene turns into our own little hurricane party (only it's a fire), so we go to our cabin and eat, about fifteen of us. Diane sautés the remaining vegetables. I thaw out some chicken from the freezer— there's no tomorrow for that poor chicken if the house goes up in flames. Under the circumstances, I figure it would be poor taste to grill the chicken on the Weber Bar-B-Q, so it goes in the toaster oven. Our neighbor Yav brings turkey soup. There's beer. We eat. People laugh at me when I wash the dishes before we all load up and join the stream of vehicles heading south on Highway 29 into the next chapter of our lives.

Our first night, we share a room with friends Yav and DeAnn at a cheap motel in Rohnert Park near Santa Rosa. Two stars and deserving of both of them. No reaction from the front desk person when we four adults check into a single room. The guys smoking and hanging out on the balcony share greasy grins with each other when they see the four of us, probably imagining the unspeakable acts that would soon be taking place in that room. As soon as our door shuts behind us, out come smart phones and iPads, and we each dive into our respective on-line universes for a good hour. Then we crash, exhausted. Sorry guys!

The long-standing, elaborate evacuation plan for Harbin Hot Springs, which no one ever thought would actually need to be put into action, has worked marvelously, and probably saved lives. We wake the next day to utter cluelessness, but soon the Harbin Facebook grapevine comes alive with harrowing tales of friends pouncing into their cars with just the clothes on their backs, racing the flames to the one road out of the boxed-in valley where Harbin lies. All residents and guests have made it out in one piece. Within days we hear about a handicapped man in nearby Anderson Springs, rescued from his house by a neighbor who holds him in his arms through the entire night in a spring-fed swimming pool as the forest burns all around them. Another man bails out of the Middletown exodus in order to hose down his neighbor's roof and survives by rolling himself up in wet rugs and blankets, then hiding in a ditch while the wildfire rolls over him.

Harbin organizes a picnic for residents in a state park. There, we hear that an evacuation site has been established at the Napa County Fairgrounds in Calistoga. The next day, I take my massage table and join twenty other bodyworkers from nearby towns. In the center of a field crowded with tents and makeshift encampments, we create a little bodywork village made of massage tables under a roof of tarps that shield us from the noonday sun. All of us are thankful to have something useful to do with our hands, which also helps us stay grounded and focused.

Napa County is a good place to be an evacuee. Fairground buildings turn into vast warehouses of donated kitchen wares, over-the-counter drugstore items, and cartons of diapers. Following a daily update from the fire marshal, local restaurants arrive with mass quantities of food for the long lines of fire refugees. Everyone trades war stories. Many people have lost literally everything. And yet, the mood is strangely festive. One of the evenings, a Marin County restaurant serves *paella.*

After ten days of evacuation, holed up in Napa County, Diane and I are safe and sound. We learn that our cabin is still standing, but Harbin and whole neighborhoods in Middletown are gone, the entire area declared a national disaster area. We drive as far as we can in the direction of Harbin Hot Springs, only to be turned back by the National Guard. The burn area of the Valley Fire is bigger than Chicago.

Amazing amounts of resources mobilize. Federal disaster vans, FEMA trailers, and insurance tent offices spring up like mushrooms after a rainstorm. Gigantic trucks haul off contaminated debris as clean-up crews in white Hazmat suits spray water to settle the toxic miasma in the air. By law, burnt-down buildings get taken out entirely, including the foundations, along with three feet of what's under them.

Instead of devastation, I experience a species of euphoria, a hypomanic state that gets me through the initial shock of having the rug of everyday life yanked out from under me. Not tearing around like crazy, just very focused, dealing with one thing at a time, operating from about three feet above the top of my head. In this altered state, events feel as if they are happening to someone else.

The euphoria lasts through the time of the lunar eclipse, a Blood Moon hanging like a swollen, dark orange on the horizon. A couple of weeks in, we get permission to walk the Harbin property, now the landscape of a lost world. We're not there to sift through ashes, so we don't wear Hazmat suits. But masks definitely. We sign a three-page liability waiver, holding Harbin harmless for any mishap or adverse health effects resulting from exposure to the toxic ash of cremated man-made materials, or from stepping on any of the billions of nails and screws that fire didn't vaporize. Old pre-Code hotels like Harbin's are riddled with lead and asbestos, the security guy tells us, so take a cold shower after we leave. Cold so as to not open up our pores and let in the fine residue of ash that will inevitably cling to our skin.

Harbin Temple was once a beautiful, fantastic roundhouse with a spiraling open-beam ceiling. It was the scene of countless gatherings for music, dance, yoga, and memorial services. I stand at the temple's charred remains and wonder at its compact footprint. It's the same with the hotels, the restaurant, movie theater, security office, and, finally, the massage rooms where I worked for nearly fifteen years . . . so much happened in such a small space!

Photos and videos have prepared us somewhat. Still, I watch my mind try, with the numb persistence of a bird trying to fly through a closed window, to superimpose on top of the ashes what stood there less than a month ago. Gradually, I manage to reconcile that memory with the ash and rubble in front of me now.

Wildfire country requires daily visual recalibration. There is something deeply unsettling about a wholesale change in the natural environment. No one knows this landscape anymore after it has shed its clothing.

Wildfire towns require daily social repositioning. *Who's moving away today? What business is closing now?* Harbin is gone, and at least half the people we know from there—friends and co-workers—have left. In time, Harbin will rebuild, but it will surely feature a different cast of people. I think of the residents who have been living full-time on Harbin property and remember the ancient injunction against doing that. I fear that the fire is going to be especially hard on them.

Ten days later, the electric mains are back on. There are no more live power lines whipping around like fire hoses, or dead cables lying in snakes of molten wire on the streets. Going back to our cabin is now an option, but we stay away, except to spend a few hours a day to clean and sort. Middletown is too toxic.

Generous offers arrive. Workspaces to see clients. Short-term places to stay: Manitoba, Hawaii, Lawrence, Kansas, Oregon, and at least two dozen places closer by in Northern California. Unbelievably, a fundraiser for Diane and me is hosted by old friends in Lawrence. Our interim refuge comes courtesy of one of Diane's Harbin clients, who kindly offers us the use of a "little house" near St. Helena. "Little" is relative, of course: Diane and I have been living in a one-and-a-half-person cabin of just under 600 square feet. Now, my blue Beetle is parked in front of a low-lying white stucco house in the middle of a rolling eighty-acre estate in Napa County, owned by a family of vintners. Two grand pianos, protected under their gray felt covers, occupy the far corners of a spotless parquet-floored concert salon. White-trimmed double doors open out to a terraced mini-amphitheater off one end of this "little house." A chilled, very expensive looking bottle of Chardonnay nestles in the fridge's crisper, but we don't dare touch it. The gardeners come on Thursdays.

Epilogue

Fire That Vaporizes The Past

Copenhagen, March 2016

I awaken in a land of bicycles and swans. Copenhagen is a flat, open feeling city with lots of sky and color when the sun is out. Bridges are guarded by naked gods and goddesses. Stallions of green tarnished bronze rise from the depths of the sea. Tourists marvel at the unexpected tininess of the Little Mermaid statue.

I have been flown all the way from San Francisco to Copenhagen to give a two-day workshop on hands-on and energetic skills for the Danish Society for Body Psychotherapy. I stand before a tall red door and steel myself as I ring the bell. The front door latch releases from somewhere in the building, and I make my way up the stairs. The door to Totum Klinikken, the venue for my workshop, stands open, so I let myself in. The place has a clean, friendly atmosphere, all blonde wood and silver gray metal furnishings under a heaven of high ceilings crisscrossed with hip exposed ductwork painted in soft pastels.

The first of the body-centered psychotherapists arrives as I'm setting up the classroom. There's something unsettling about the set of her facial bones, her marzipan-colored skin, and her very blue, almost violet eyes. I'm used to being around beautiful women from my years of living and working on the bodywork staff at Harbin—clothing-optional around the spring-fed pools—visited by people from all over the world. But something about her takes my breath away, like being confronted by an alien species. Beauty shock. She asks where I live in the U.S.

"Northern California."

"Oh . . .!" She is suddenly intense and interested. "Have you ever heard of Harbin Hot Springs?"

"Yes, that's where I lived and worked, until . . ."

The air between us stops.

"I was there!" she cuts in. Her voice is a conspiratorial whisper.

"You were at Harbin?" I ask. It's taking me a moment to absorb the implications. *Does she know?*

"I was there," she says. "I checked out of Harbin on the morning of September 12th. I only heard later about what happened."

Time Winding Down

Mourning is a wavelike phenomenon, one of the beginnings of gratitude. At some point, we're forty days post-Fire. Forty days and forty nights of wandering in a kind of wilderness, the forty days of a quarantine. It's a strange *quaresima,* a time and season of ashes, of death, of time spent in the temple of the god of loss.

Time winds down with autumnal sadness at the crossroads of what is passing out of existence and the hope for what lies ahead. I am visited in meditation by moments of stillness and presence. I don't fear the turning of time. Certain things I have waited for, including my own turn toward age. My longing is that it be graceful and, where needed, graceful when it's not graceful.

The urge to talk of rebuilding, just days, even hours, after the fire comes naturally to people raised on bright, bushy-tailed American New Age optimism, people who believe they manifest everything in their lives. But my soul is in need of something else. Instead of trying to manifest new Harbins, I think back through lines of time to when I was a novice in the Order and

to the terrifying Abbot when I watched him put the Abbey in his
pocket. I decide to do likewise, put Harbin my pocket, so I can
take it with me wherever I go.

Suddenly evacuated, sprung from a daily schedule, and
feeling too displaced to do much else, I have spates of unteth-
ered leisure time. I get busy with my one and only task. I spiral
through inner images of Harbin land, still intact in my memory.
It gives way to the memory of how I got there. In its physical absence, every remembered landmark becomes a point of departure into remembered worlds that I collect back into myself.

In my internal vision, I spiral fifteen years of history at
Harbin back into my heart. I hover above the Gazebo and rise
over Harbin's landscape. Stonefront, Restaurant, Theater, Smok-
ing Deck, Vendor Lawn, Fern, Warm Pool, Hot Pool, Cold
Plunge, Heart Pool, Swimming Pool, La Serena Cafe, Mainside,
Walnut, Azalea, Redwood, Temple, Meadow Building, Village,
Mountain Lodge, North Star, Hilltop House, Fire Circle, Indian
Rock, Watsu Center, Domes.

I spiral over my colleagues on the bodywork staff, over the
massage rooms where my abilities as a healer flowered. Tears
come as I gather up my awkward initiation into Harbin bodywork, and I marvel at this precious entry into a calling.

My spiral continues. *What's becoming of me?* For all my
self-doubt, something has come together here that has never ex-
isted before. Sharp gratitude breaks out in my chest for a life
stretched from flat lands of wheat and cattle to conspiracies with
mystics, healers, and fire, and for becoming . . . *what do you call
it?* My polyglot mind supplies a word that has no English equivalent. What do you call the ones who learn to meet what comes,
and, because they must, find the art of fashioning new meaning
out of the stuff of living in this world? I cover my eyes with my
hands, grateful.

I keep going. My spiral widens out to open American
Space, from beloved Diane's welcoming heart, to high plains and
mountains, to the houses and streets of Lawrence, my years of

love with Ursula, as Bob's student in Denmark. I spiral out and back to Amsterdam, to Germany, to the Order of my spiritual schooling, to my childhood in Wichita, where I was only restless and couldn't wait to launch into my long adventure in the dark forest. To my brother Bruce with gratitude for the childhood we shared, to my parents Hunter and Frances and their lines back to Irish immigrants and clans of Welsh bonesetters, all the way back to Adam and Eve. All my Lost Worlds. All of these I spiral into the pocket of my heart.

I spiral over all that has been and over all that is yet longed for.

AFTERWORD
THREE WORLDS IN A TEACUP

*"You, who saw it all, or who saw flashes and
fragments, take from us some example, try and get
yourselves together, clean up your act, find your
community, pick up on some kind of redemption
of your own consciousness, become mindful of
your own friends, your own work, your own
proper meditation, your own art, your own
beauty, go out and make it for your own Eternity."*
~Allen Ginsberg

It seems important to say here that no one ever appointed me the
keeper of an "official version" of any of the scenes described in
these pages. Attempts to get any of them to fit into a tidy narrative fail. To this day, for example, there are skirmishes in certain
circles about what exactly the Order was, and who its legacy belongs to. Having no dog in those fights, neither clinging to the
good old days of the Order and all its ways, nor joining with the
Order-bashers of the world, I have stuck to my own Order stories and experiences. I offer them with love for who we were,
and who we tried to be, especially to those who came through
the Order with their sense of humor still intact.

Books exist about each of these lost worlds. If you want
rigorously researched background on the Holy Order of MANS,
the semi-monastic order of spiritual mavericks in which I spent

a decade of my life, I highly recommend—in spite of the way certain former members spit on the ground when the book gets mentioned—*The Odyssey of a New Religion* by Phillip Charles Lucas, from which I learned things about the Order that I never knew while I was a member. I know of no more definitive account of the Order.

The Robert Moore Foundation in Denmark has done wonderful work in keeping alive the memory and teaching of Bob Moore who, along with my former wife, was my entry point into the world of energy healing, which has been my professional world for more than thirty years. Just recently, a package arrived from Denmark, a new book about Bob Moore, *Ripples in the Water,* edited by Annette Ikast. My own recollections of my time as a newcomer to energy healing in Bob's circle of students in 1983 are offered with love and respect to the Northern European healer scene that once surrounded this unique and wonderful man.

There will be all kinds of attempts to fit pre-Fire Harbin into a neat little teacup, but, like all these lost worlds, it's too elusive. Harbin is only partly a place on a map or an external landscape. The old Harbin is a memory, an invisible city in the mind and heart. Harbin, if it's anywhere, is inside the people who know it. At the rebuilt Harbin, you can soak in the pools, toggle between the hot and cold plunges, look through the steam at some of the same old stone statues and metal sculptures, and tell yourself for a moment that it is the same place. But the sweetly funky Dionysian outlaw appeal of pre-Fire Harbin is only an echo. The call of the wild is now overlaid with building code mandates of Lake County. Shangri-La now worries about lawsuits. There were always waivers to be signed by guests, in case they get bonked on the head by a pinecone, but now new buildings very correctly require ADA compliance, and green-and-white signs in bathrooms and massage rooms warn about the evils of human trafficking.

For Harbin's history, you can't beat Ellen Klages' book, *Harbin Hot Springs*. Like many experimental communities nestled in the Great Outback of America, Harbin had its share of eccentrics, life-artists, and also some lovely beings whose path led them to crash and burn. In my case, Harbin was where I got my wings in healing work and lived in a pocket culture of love and creativity, a paradoxical dancer perched on one of the many edges of the American experiment.

Each of these scenes has had some kind of afterlife, thanks to dedicated people who have carried on in the name of what once was and what they hope will be. And more power to them.

Acknowledgments

There is nothing like attempting to write a memoir to make me aware of the village of people in my life, especially the women who have been my agents of change at every turn. My gratitude to them is endless.

Writing is hard work, and I have had help. Thanks to old friend Denise Low of Mammoth Publications for invaluable in-depth help in paring down an unwieldy manuscript into one that works. Thanks also to the rotating cast of the ad hoc "Cover Committee," Aimee Eldridge, Bonnie Veblen, Hal Bennett, Paul Hotvedt, and Denise Low, whose collective visual design I.Q. far exceeds mine.

Much appreciation to Mary Kamiński for taking the time to provide insights and feedback about the Order. Thanks to Martha Koen for a sympathetic read of a late draft; her path through the Order coincided with mine at many junctures.

Thanks to my brother, Bruce Gilkeson, for being the first to say, to my great relief, "I have different recollections, but this is *your* memoir." Special thanks to Ursula Gilkeson, Dr. Ulrike Gallmeier, Laurie Ward, Anni Moore, Paula Kellogg, Pia Fallentin, and to several others who, under assumed names, have generously given me the green light to write about them. Like my brother, they all have their own take on our time together, and

I want to thank them for their great generosity of spirit in allowing me mine.

Much appreciation to the good people at Dobrá Tea in Ashland, Oregon, for their curated playlists of kora music in the background and their Dragonwell Green Tea, which became my writing elixir for the first drafts.

Deep gratitude to my life partner, Diane Tegtmeier, for her support, for reading the numerous versions of this book, and for keeping me honest at times when it would have been easier not to be.

And finally, as novelist Nick Harkaway so aptly put it, ". . . a book is not finished until it is read." In this spirit, sincere thanks to you, the reader, for helping me complete *Three Lost Worlds*.

All factual errors are mine, as are all instances where I have fiddled with time-lines for narrative purposes.

In Memoriam

The too, too many Harbin dead since the
Valley Fire, September, 2015

Naoto Sekiguchi
Gabe Real
DJ
Lea "Legs" Jetter
Sunheart
Scot
Harold Dull
Maria
Ed
Kurti
Shale
Jim Conlin
Liv
Hanna
Jed
Chris Mazeros
Elaine Marie
Steve Carter

"Nothing erases the past. There is repentance, there is atonement, and there is forgiveness. That is all, but that is enough."

~Ted Chiang

Author Bio

JIM GILKESON is a craniosacral therapist and teacher of energy healing in California and Oregon. He is the author of two books on energy healing, *A Pilgrim in Your Body: Energy Healing and Spiritual Process* and *Energy Healing: A Pathway to Inner Growth*. In his twenties and early thirties, Gilkeson was a member of an esoteric spiritual order. After leaving the order, he learned energy healing in Europe, where he lived for eleven years. He was a member of the healing staff at Harbin Hot Springs in Northern California from 2001 until that retreat community was destroyed in the Valley Fire of 2015. As a musician, Gilkeson has released two post-Valley Fire albums with The Sitka Rose Band. Originally from the Midwest, he lives with his partner, Diane Tegtmeier, in Ashland, Oregon.

Photo Credits

Unless otherwise noted, all photos in *Three Lost Worlds* are from the author's personal collection.

Cover and author photos by Diane Tegtmeier. Used with permission.

Photo (p. 126) of Order members by John Andersen. Used with permission.

Graphic (p. 177) by Beth Budesheim. Used with permission. (For more by Beth Budesheim, visit her website at www.bethbudesheim.com.)

Photo (p. 181) of Bob Moore courtesy of Moore Healing Association. Used with permission.

Photo (p. 222) of *Energy Healing* by Wendy Cosbie. Used with permission.

Photo (p. 238) of Harbin pool ceremony courtesy of harbin.org. Used with permission.

Photo (p. 255) of Watsu session by Shane Powers. Used with permission.

Photo (p. 260) of Harbin community members courtesy of harbin.org. Used with permission.

Photo (p. 263) of Harbin Domes courtesy of harbin.org. Used with permission.

Also from MAMMOTH PUBLICATIONS

Conjuro, poems (English, Spanish, Nahuatl) ($18)
by Xánath Caraza

Now It Is Snowing Inside a Psalm, prose ($12)
by Diane Glancy

Landed: Poems ($12)
by Caryn Mirriam Goldberg, 3rd Kansas Poet Laureate

\Vi-ze-bel \ Teks-chers\ (Visible Textures), fine arts ed. ($10)
by DaMaris B. Hill

Bitter Tears, poetry chapbook ($12)
by Denise Lajimodiere

Haskell Institute: 19th C. Stories of Survival, prose ($20)
by Theresa Milk

Dark Sister: Poems ($15)
by Linda Rodriguez

Whose Water, poetry chapbook ($10)
by Kim Shuck

White-Skin Deer: Hoopa Stories, prose ($12)
by Elizabeth Schultz

Maggie's Story: Teachings of a Cherokee Healer, prose ($14)
by Pamela Dawes Tambornino

Fat Cats, Powwows: Poems, 2nd ed. ($12)
by E. Donald Two-Rivers

Dioramas: Poems ($15)
by Missouri Poet Laureate, Maryfrances Wagner

Langston Hughes in Lawrence: Photos & Biography ($15)
by Tom Weso & Laureate Denise Low, 2nd Kansas Poet

Book details at: http://mammothpublications.net
Checks payable to:
Mammoth Publications
610 Alta Vista Dr.
Healdsburg CA 95448
$3 shipping & handling; additional books @ $1.00.
25% discount for 3 books or more.
PayPal account: mammothpubs@gmail.com

9 781939 301628